The Importance of Happiness

The Importance of Happiness

Noël Coward
and the Actors' Orphanage

Elliot James

Matador
9 Priory Business Park,
Wistow Road, Kibworth Beauchamp,
Leicestershire. LE8 0RX
Tel: 0116 279 2299
Email: books@troubador.co.uk
Web: www.troubador.co.uk/matador
Twitter: @matadorbooks

ISBN 978 1800460 416

British Library Cataloguing in Publication Data.
A catalogue record for this book is available from the British Library.

Printed and bound in Great Britain by 4edge Limited
Typeset in 10.5pt Adobe Garamond Pro by Troubador Publishing Ltd, Leicester, UK

Matador is an imprint of Troubador Publishing Ltd

For all the children of the Actors' Orphanage
&
Seth and Ezra

Home is a name, a word, it is a strong one; stronger than any magician ever spoke, or spirit ever answered to, in the strongest conjuration.

Charles Dickens
Martin Chuzzlewit
1844

CORA: I know they get a lot of publicity out of it but even so I shouldn't think from their point of view it was worth all the effort.
MAY: It is always possible, my dear Cora, that just one or two of them might do it from sheer kindness of heart.

Noël Coward
Waiting in the Wings
1960

Contents

Introduction

I have been bitterly hurt inside by the English fusillade of abuse.

– Noël Coward's Diaries, 31 December 1956

Writing in Blue Harbour, his house by the Caribbean Sea on the island of Jamaica, Noël Coward was reflecting on what had been, even by his standards, an eventful year. Despite aggressive front-page attacks in the press for his departure from England, and alongside the necessary upheaval on the domestic front, there had been two American television specials. *Blithe Spirit* and *This Happy Breed* also coincided with two new plays opening in London's West End: *South Sea Bubble* and *Nude with Violin*. He also felt lately that he was having 'a little private menopause'.

It had been a whole year since Noël had decided with certainty to become a 'tax exile'. After all, only eight weeks had been spent in England during 1955 and yet tens of thousands (equivalent to hundreds of thousands today) had been paid in high, post-war income tax. These days, too, Noël did most of his writing in Jamaica and most of his performing in the United States. Then there was the simple fact that, despite forty-four years as a dominant force in *The Theatre*, he was, after the War,

THE IMPORTANCE OF HAPPINESS

less successful. Considered deeply out of fashion by many critics and with no great savings and few assets, something had to be done. He'd never, despite being the highest-paid playwright of the 1930s, been good with money.

Noël was the first high-profile celebrity tax exile and he paid a price. Today, of course, it's considered quite normal, and for an iconic but ageing celebrity to *not* have a tax haven is now perhaps the exception. The torrent of abuse by the British press at the time, however, was relentless. Though tired of the constant drubbings over the years, Noël had long said that if he really cared what his critics thought then he would have shot himself in the twenties, though that remark was in relation to the critics' reviews of his plays.

This was different, for it was as if he, the writer of such celebrations of Britishness as *Cavalcade* and *In Which We Serve*, and the performer of endless troop concerts during the War, was having his patriotism called into question. Even his friends had mixed views on the matter. Laurence Olivier was quite put out. Noël justified to himself that he had always paid his tax in the past, would now be a legal citizen of Bermuda and spend even more time residing in Jamaica; two British colonies. And as Winston Churchill allegedly said, "It's every Englishman's inalienable right to live wherever he chooses."

In truth, Noël, sitting on his veranda with his cigarettes and cocktails, calmed by the tropical heat, and looking at that view of the Spanish Main (that often carried on like an 'impressionist exhibition'), was slightly melancholic about England these days. The War had changed so much. The new era of social equality and the rise of harder-edged working-class culture saw much of his own *oeuvre* start to go against the grain. On a slightly egocentric front, he was miffed too that honours, primarily a knighthood, had long been withheld from him, yet bestowed upon all of his contemporaries. He knew that his public were still fond of him, of course, and, after all, he could legally spend three months a year in England, where he would simply have to suffer the extreme hardship of staying at the Savoy. He would also save a small fortune and not have to work himself into the grave. As he told everyone who'd listen these days, his old age was "due to start next Tuesday."

Prerequisites for the 'exile' were that his London home in Gerald Road, Belgravia and Goldenhurst, his Kent estate near Dymchurch, had had to be sold... and also he had had to relinquish his long-time presidency of the charity known as the Actors' Orphanage. The houses he sold with some sadness and regret, but the resignation from the orphanage... he gave with relief. But relief only because of the time and effort it took and had taken for so many years. It had, however, been a kind of personal salvation.

Who ultimately cared what the press were saying when you had seen the smiles of the children in a home that you'd helped to create? Who really cared that a musical had flopped when you'd just raised £10,000 at a fundraiser for an orphanage? Well, okay, you'd still care to a *fair degree*, but perhaps the concern could be more qualified. And who, in the end, cared that you were a tax exile when you'd done so much for so many for so long?

The experience of being president had given much personal satisfaction, purpose and genuine self-worth ever since he had vowed, as a young man, to turn the troubled orphanage around and improve the lives of the children. This had now long since been achieved. In that at least he could take pride and comfort.

It had, however, had its challenges.

*

It was the April of 1934 when Noël Coward became the president of the Actors' Orphanage, and he remained in the position for twenty-two years. How did Noël come to be the president in the first place? Why did he initially want to? And what exactly was the Actors' Orphanage? This is one of the few areas of his famed existence that has never been significantly written of, let alone analysed, in any way. It is, in fact, the last great, untold story regarding Noël Coward.

Noël Coward was a wildly successful writer, actor, director, composer and cabaret act. Forty-seven years since his death in Jamaica, Noël stands the test of time now largely due to the classic films *In Which We Serve* and *Brief Encounter*, along with consistent revivals of some of his light comedy plays. *Hay Fever, Private Lives, Blithe Spirit, Present Laughter* and *Relative Values* are never out of production somewhere in the world. Plays that can seem light as a soufflé but have profound depths below the glitter of the surface. Much like the man himself.

His full body of work is extraordinary: musicals, hundreds of lyrically sophisticated songs, poetry, short stories, a novel, autobiographies, paintings and dozens of further plays, many of which are worthy of rediscovery. Worthy of *discovery* is Noël's work with the Actors' Orphanage. He took his presidency seriously and far beyond the façade, self-promotion and shallowness of show business made a difference to many young lives.

Of the various books published about Noël over the decades, the Actors' Orphanage is often referenced merely in passing but never covered in any detail. Noël himself makes several sporadic mentions of the children, fundraisers and committee meetings in his autobiographies, letters and diaries. And sometimes his plays reference the orphanage in various covert ways, such as the committee of actors in *Waiting in the Wings* discussing an actors' retirement home, or the committee of actors in *Star Chamber* discussing a home for destitute actresses.

The Actors' Orphanage, to be clear, was a convergence of two disparate worlds: the world of the stars of stage and screen, and the world of the orphaned children. It was an institution, a charity that took in the children of actors and actresses that had fallen on hard times. Some of these actors and actresses were famous, some slightly famous, and many simply jobbing actors that couldn't afford to raise their children in this pre-welfare state era. A few, it must be said, simply didn't want children to get in the way of their careers. Some too had illegitimate children that they wanted and needed to keep secret. And sometimes a parent or parents had become ill or died.

As a charity, the orphanage prided itself on never turning away a worthy case. There was full-time domestic staff and teaching staff, a committee and executive committee made up of highly successful and very famous actors. The children themselves were usually aged between six and sixteen, many spending all of these years at the orphanage.

Noël could have easily been a figurehead of the orphanage as *all* the presidents before him had been, but he only agreed on acceptance of the presidency if he could actually have power, take charge and make a difference. This is unashamedly an inspirational story of doing good for its own sake. Noël also inspired the orphanage committee, of largely very good friends, to share his passion and concern. He brought out the best in them, as they all strived to give the children a decent and special childhood despite their circumstances.

Noël's attitude to the orphanage would change over time in that in the 1930s he worked exceptionally hard to improve the terribly austere and abusive conditions of the orphanage. In the 1940s, he worked against the odds to sustain the improved institution through a world war, and by the 1950s he was growing tired but refused to resign until all was solvent and secure.

His life seemed to become intertwined with the orphanage in all kinds of surprising ways... once you start linking the dots.

We shall see how his efforts for the children led indirectly to the blocking of his knighthood in 1942. We shall also see how his highly successful 1950s cabaret career was born out of the orphanage fundraisers. How lifelong friendships were formed and lives changed forever.

A cynic might say that Noël and his celebrity committee did it all for personal gain. For Noël, this meant being seen as the ultimate good egg, the belle of the ball at the glamorous fundraisers, ploughing the charity fields all the way to a knighthood. However, if this was his true motivation he must have been insane.

Over twenty-two years, Noël would, as we shall see, grapple with ceaseless issues and concerns over the welfare of hundreds upon hundreds of children. He didn't make the beds, cook the meals, teach the classes or spend more than a few visits a year *on site* at the orphanage, but he certainly knew exactly what was happening and what needed to happen in the ongoing life of the charity.

It really wasn't an easy institution to take responsibility for: a constant influx of abandoned children, staff issues, discipline, constant fundraising, evacuation during the War (with Noël desperate to make up for his lack of contribution to the Great War), building maintenance, endless committee meetings and, as Noël always maintained was most important, the children's happiness. Noël not only attended most of the committee meetings, hosted and performed at every fundraiser and cajoled endless friends and colleagues to contribute, but on regular occasions he would deal directly with orphanage staff members himself and, on occasion, the children too. One troubled boy even ended up as a godson.

There is a reason that Noël barely mentioned his presidency in his diaries and autobiographies, let alone anywhere else. That is because he decidedly did not want to be seen as 'in it for himself'. Indeed, he had *inherited* the presidency... and its problems. It must be stated too that his long-time secretary, representative and friend, Lorn Loraine, known affectionately as Lornie, worked ceaselessly and absurdly hard on the administration of all of Noël's plans and decisions for the orphanage.

In all of his endeavours, Noël's social charms aided him greatly. Although he appeared stately and mixed often with aristocracy, he was ultimately *showbiz* and actually from fairly humble, lower-middle class beginnings. This paradox meant that Noël had a knack for crossing the social divides, appealing to everybody and communicating favourably with anybody, whether it was encouraging wealthy sponsors, discussing the need for new wallpaper in the bedrooms or taking a look at the current meal plan. Indeed, he never truly belonged to any one set of people. Noël had time for and friendships with royalty, prime ministers, stars, the everyday working actors of the theatre, the general public *and* the orphans.

Arguably the most important relationship of Noël's life stemmed from his humble beginnings and was that with his mother, Violet Coward. He knew that she was ultimately responsible for much of his success. Her love and ambition for the precocious child that he was, without ever being constraining or smothering, fuelled his talent and ambition. Children with no mother available to them, let alone a mother such as his, often broke his heart and awoke his sympathies.

All of the surviving orphans that I have spoken with had the same air of warm nostalgia when I mentioned Noël. Susannah Slater, who arrived at the orphanage aged seven in 1946, recalled that: "He was wonderful. He really did turn that place around and we're all very grateful to him."

This is not just the typical response of the orphans but also the only response.

Noël had found a way to satisfy a deep need to make a difference and a contribution beyond his extreme fame, phenomenon and show-business success. Through the story of the orphanage, we get to the heart of the man. Beyond the flippant, waspish, playboy image of cocktails and caviar was a kind, decent, hard-working and engaged man who shone the way for genuine celebrity philanthropy.

I will continue to call the children *orphans*, despite most of them having at least one parent alive at the time of their admission, as the institution itself was called an orphanage. And, after all, to all intents and purposes, they were 'orphaned' for a time by their parents or parent, although a fair few were literal orphans too.

An indisputable help in writing this book was Judy Staber's account of the post-war years as a child of the orphanage in her book *Silverlands*. Also there are written accounts left by Granville Bantock, Hugo Bergström and Dan Taylor of their years at the orphanage before and during the War. I have also conducted highly enlightening interviews with many of the surviving orphans, mostly now aged in their seventies upwards and dotted around the world. And I have discovered reams of long-archived documents in the University of Birmingham, the V&A archives and elsewhere.

To protect the privacy of the children, I have written of several episodes indirectly, thus preserving the exact identities of those involved. However, where information has been shared with me openly, I have felt freer to be more specific. Some of the archived documents are still under data protection laws, but one can give a sense of the events unfolding and still produce a full, rounded and rich history of the orphanage.

This book tells the story of a bygone age but one well worth remembering. It is often said that through the past we can see our present more clearly. Indeed, what mattered then is the same as what matters now. Home. Love. Family. A decent cup of tea. And if some of the names mentioned in these pages mean little to you (perhaps you're a millennial; perhaps you are, through no fault of your own, quite ignorant), fear not, there's a marvellous *Who's Who* provided towards the back of the book. So you really can leave Google alone for a while and journey back with me now to a long-ago age.

This book is, as well as a tribute to Noël and an untold story from his life, a snapshot into early twentieth-century England and America. Ultimately, though, it is the story of the Actors' Orphanage itself. A unique, now almost forgotten, institution that was home to over 3,000 orphaned and abandoned children of theatricals, spanning across some fifty-three years from 1906 to when the gates finally closed at Silverlands in January 1959. From homes in Croydon, South London, to Langley in Berkshire, to Chertsey in Surrey, to The Bronx in New York and Knightsbridge in central London, we shall see how the orphanage had many ups and downs but ultimately improved greatly. And never more so than under the auspices of Sir Noël Coward.

*

Brian Terriss was a child of Silverlands in the 1940s and early 1950s, and also a very talented artist. He was one of many surviving children that attended an Actors' Orphanage reunion in Chertsey in the year 2000: the only reunion of its scale and kind ever to occur. It was a heightened occasion, these former orphans having been, for the most part, out of touch for a great many years. Here Brian presented Noël's eventual replacement as president, the late Richard Attenborough, with a beautiful painting he'd made of the main house at Silverlands. As Brian shook a grateful Lord Attenborough's hand, he said to him simply, "It was our home."

ONE

A New President

1934

I am the darned president of the show, you know – a position
thrust upon me after Gerald du Maurier died.

– Noël Coward, *Times of Ceylon*, 3 June 1935

The great actor-manager Sir Gerald du Maurier had died in the April of 1934, and Noël Coward became the president of the Actors' Orphanage quickly and equally speedily asserted authority and change. It's clear from committee meeting minutes and transcripts that the orphanage's affairs had been badly handled for some time. Noël donated £500 up front (about £30,000 today), that would eventually build a new dormitory, and with his loyal secretary, Lorn Loraine, inspected the entire premises at Langley Hall in Berkshire. They chatted to the staff and children, had some photographs taken, and Noël played the beaten-up old piano, singing several songs to the children, all the while trying to get the measure of the place.

Everyone was very friendly and obviously on best behaviour – the children and the staff – although the headmaster did seem to have celebrated Noël's arrival by having had a slight tipple or two. Yet Mr Austin was certainly in charge, having been with the orphanage since 1907 and headmaster since 1915. The children seemed okay but could obviously do with more space, privacy and a little less austerity in their lives. The new dorm building would be a start.

Noël had been attending the main fundraiser for the charity, the annual Theatrical Garden Party, where he hosted events and signed autographs, since the late 1920s. He was soon on the committee too, this being a premiere charity in theatrical circles. Though still young (born in December 1899, he was always as old as the century in which he lived), he was unquestionably the most famous committee member. A phenomenon since his shocking play *The Vortex* had opened in the November of 1924 at the Everyman Theatre, Hampstead, he had achieved unparalleled, incomparable theatrical success. He had now been reigning for a decade and was also a confident, natural leader *and* popular. This popularity would inevitably lead to jealousies in some quarters but these things would be risen above. He was an easy choice to fill the boots left by Sir Gerald. He was the theatre world's bright light.

As he was more conscientious and hands-on in the role than Sir Gerald, it does seem that he both inherited the presidency *and* felt a genuine sense of responsibility and compassion. He would need to do more than simply show his face at the garden parties... but why? Sir Gerald and his predecessors were not bad men, despite Sir Gerald having been the West End's original Captain Hook.

It's true that Noël continued to be acutely aware that he had his mother to thank for much of his early success and thus, to quite some degree, everything that followed. They had an unbreakable bond and she was the driving force and close confidante that made him work on his craft, while honestly telling him if he wasn't good enough. This led to an occasionally fraught relationship but also to a deep trust. She was, to be sure, a strong and forthright woman, who *demanded* that her son do well. Noël wanted always to, indeed was eager to, please his mother.

Noël had had to, as a young boy, perform songs to a professionally entertaining degree. If he was to play the piano, he was to play it the best he possibly could. If he was to dance, he was to dance well, and without a single misstep. If he was to act, it must be a pitch-perfect performance. No chance for a laugh lost. No moment for poignancy thrown away. Indeed, Noël was grateful that she pushed him to excel, for it bred confidence. Violet Coward made her talented son feel driven, secure and loved. The orphanage children all too obviously lacked such a parent.

Thus, Noël ever had a place in his heart for such deprived children and knew all too well that his own childhood was, though financially a struggle, a blessed one. His formative years were spent acting in *Peter Pan*, touring in plays such as *Hannele* and learning from his mentor and master, the actor-manager Sir Charles Hawtrey. Lest we romanticise Noël's childhood completely, he did attend schools for brief spells and hate every second of it, avoid sports like the plague and have long periods out of acting work. He could also annoy quite a few people with his confidence and extreme precocity.

Now aged thirty-four, Noël was still precocious and very much in his heyday. He was already known as *The Master*, although this was originally a joke that gradually became a very real term of respect. Lornie, who had known Noël since their early twenties in the early 1920s, would, tongue-in-cheek, say such things as "More tea for *The Master*?" or "Don't disturb *The Master*."

Noël's own humour was not only evident to the public in his plays but also in his interviews with the press and in his cultivated public persona. Early stories to enter the public realm and be repeated ever after include the time that he entered a white tie and tails party in a completely normal suit and said: "Please, I don't want anyone to apologise for overdressing!"

Except that this is most likely a fabrication, a variation of the truth. In a newspaper interview with the *Daily Dispatch* in 1920, selling Noël as a soon-to-be-famous star of the theatre, he tells the story of *himself* being the only person in white tie and tails and *everyone else* as being in regular suits or: "Only 'dressed' in the sense that they were covered."

His opening line to the hostess thus being: "Dear Sappho, why ever didn't you let me know! How uncomfortable you must all be feeling!" Which actually seems funnier and is a lesson to tread carefully when quoting *The Master*. As Noël often said himself, half the quotes attributed to him he never uttered, but he didn't mind taking credit for the good ones.

Noël Coward was his own great invention; a successful boy-actor, he had needed to create his own work in order to become a star. Playing Ralph in Francis Beaumont's Jacobean play *The Knight of the Burning Pestle*, in 1919, one critic observed that Noël: 'Played with a stubborn Mayfair distinction. Demonstrating a total lack of understanding of the play.'

Well, his own early plays, *I'll Leave It to You* (an inheritance comedy), *The Young Idea* (zealous children trying to reunite their parents) and the popular, sophisticated revue *London Calling* (featuring songs and sketches mostly written by Noël and provided for the impresario André Charlot), allowed him to play Mayfair distinction to the hilt and to great effect.

Noël's confidence in who he was came from early days. His persona was born out of the Edwardian era and the aristocracy-led English theatre. Notions of class distinction and manners were firmly rooted; the British Empire still thrived and he was determined to go through life 'first or third class but never in second', although I think we can surmise his first choice really. His supreme confidence instilled by his mother and bolstered by his status as a boy-actor of the West End stage gave him an enviable assuredness very early on. He was ten when he secured his first stage role, his clipped, upper-class accent coming from a combination of loudly and clearly enunciating for his quite deaf mother, pleasing her snobbery, and from fitting into the theatre world of the time. Of course, behind the scenes he had his moments of insecurity just like anybody else and would suffer at least three nervous breakdowns during his long career.

By 1934 and with several major successes, one after another, after another, and dominant in the English theatre, he was more than capable of taking charge of a somewhat lackadaisical orphanage committee. On the committee for a while already, and active and vocal in how things should be run, Noël would recall, decades later in memoir form, how a famous actor gave an impassioned speech at a meeting in defence of a former administrator's dismissal. Noël had backed the dismissal but the person in question had apparently: "Devoted thirty years to the good of the children and this was a disgrace."

Noël replied that the person in question had been paid very well *and* unfortunately handled all the funds a "trifle whimsically". He asked the man's defendant if he even knew where the orphanage was or if he'd ever visited. He conceded that he didn't and that he hadn't. Next, Noël's lawyer produced documents clearly showing how the finances had been mismanaged for years and how the administration had been so lax that many people around the table might be liable to criminal prosecution. The result of this bravura performance was that he was 'feverishly' elected president for an initial five years.

This is how the events were recalled by Noël in his sadly unfinished third volume of autobiography, *Past Conditional*, circa 1965. We might assume that Noël crafted the retelling for dramatic entertainment, except that documents from the time seem to completely validate this account. The only concession made for the memoir is a compression of time; it would take well over a year for Noël to discover the true extent of mismanagement and abuse occurring at Langley Hall, call an emergency meeting at his London house, and affect real change.

Kittie's Dream

The Actors' Orphanage Fund, 'for children made destitute by the profession', had been born, like Noël, in the 1890s. In 1896, in fact, by one Kittie Carson, a retired actress and wife of Charles Lionel Carson, the editor of *The Stage* newspaper. The fund donated money to send children to various orphanages; all the while saving money in the hope that one day they could build their own. This idea was not entirely original; in 1858, the most successful actor-manager of his time, Charles Kean, had proposed a retirement home for elderly actors (a predecessor to Denville Hall in Northwood). The Royal Dramatic College opened its doors in 1865 at a large purpose-built building in Woking and with Prince Albert as its patron. Financially impossible to run, it would close its doors in 1877, but for a while all was well, and in 1864, Kean, William Makepeace Thackeray and Charles Dickens were also proposing a boarding school for the poorer children of actors and actresses. The Shakespeare School would, according to Dickens, "rival Eton!" Members of the public would apparently subscribe and make it a success. They didn't and it wasn't.

At a public meeting at the Adelphi Theatre on the 11th of May 1864, Charles Dickens did however make an impassioned (and rather verbose) speech in which he was clear on why such a school was needed:

"I present the player to you exceptionally in this wise, that he follows a peculiar and precarious vocation, a vocation very rarely affording the means of accumulating money; that vocation must, from the nature of things, have in it many undistinguished men and women to one distinguished one; that it is not a vocation the exerciser of which can profit by the labour of others, but in which he must earn every loaf of bread in his own person, with the aid of his own face, his own limbs, his own voice, his own memory, and his own life and spirits, and these failing, he fails. Surely this is reason enough to render him some little help in opening for his children their paths in life."

The Shakespeare School, however, makes no mention of illegitimate children, which would have been a step too far. And the audience is assured that the children themselves would be diverted and dissuaded from pursuing unstable and vulgar theatrical careers themselves. The Shakespeare School was never to be.

However, Barnado's was founded in 1866, with its first orphanage for the poor and destitute children of London's East End. Impoverished actors' children, however, were still likely to be dragged on tour with their mothers to strange towns. That's if they had a mother.

Twenty-five years later, in 1891, Kittie Carson founded the Theatrical Ladies Guild, which provided clothing to out-of-work actresses for their children. The committee meetings included mass sewing bees, where ladies in heavy Victorian dress sat on wooden chairs and sewed feverishly. Actresses on the whole really did not lead glamorous lives. They were all too often either out of work or indeed touring the country in repertory theatre, living in dusty, run-down digs and scraping by.

Kittie now tackled that perennial problem in the theatrical profession of unaffordable, perhaps illegitimate and sometimes just unwanted children. The Actors' Benevolent Fund was already overstretched and not in a position to help children as well as the adults of the profession. Even if the child was wanted, it was often the case that a jobbing actress simply couldn't cope with a child. This too, we must remember, was a time of considerable social stigma regarding a child born illicitly and out of wedlock. Single parents were often shunned not only by society, but also by their own families. Some mothers kept their babies and *did* take them on the road to repertory theatres, making them up beds in the drawers of the various dingy digs up and down the country. Trying to stop them bawling in the dusty dressing rooms of ancient theatres was hardly ideal or easy.

In the coming decades, the reasons for actors leaving their children at the orphanage, some never even visiting or taking them on holiday breaks, would be numerous. Believe it or not, actors did, on occasion, have affairs… as in *quite often,* especially on (what goes on tour stays on tour) tours. A pregnant actress often meant trouble. Even pregnancy in wedlock could mean unbearable financial burden. Jobbing actresses couldn't afford to stop touring. Often, too, a once-successful actress would all too easily fall on hard times within the fickle world of the theatre. Unemployment was always around the corner. Other reasons for the *need* for the Actors' Orphanage were parental illness, separation, divorce or death. And just sometimes… a mother might simply put being an actress and her career above raising a child.

The word 'orphanage' would sound bad to some, and parents sometimes said that their child was simply away at 'boarding school'. Indeed, up until the late 1930s, classes were, for the most part, held on site at the orphanage, before the children were to start attending local schools instead.

There was, however, always a sheen of glamour to Kittie's enterprise, run from her home in 48, then 90 Great Russell Street, Bloomsbury, and then 16 York Street, Covent Garden. With the 1896 launch of the Actors' Orphanage Fund, Sir Henry Irving promised to be an *honorary* president. He was *the* leading actor of the day. He had received his knighthood in 1895, the first actor to do so, and his final acceptance into the higher echelons of society. For now, the fund simply had to raise the money for a property to house the orphanage. It would take time. Meanwhile, many children were paid for to attend pre-existing orphanages or to be fostered.

In 1899, Sir Henry held the first Annual Actors' Cricket Match, a forebear to all future regular fundraisers, such as the Theatrical Garden Parties, charity matinees and events at the London Palladium. In 1901, Sir Henry also acquired the patronage of the newly crowned Queen Alexandra, wife of Edward VII, as well as the Princess of Wales and the Princess Royal.

Early supporters included George Bernard Shaw and Ellen Terry. The fund's chairwoman, Mrs Cecil Raleigh, would write some 250 novels as Effie Adelaide Rowlands and later (after a divorce and remarriage) as Madame Albanesi. Some of these novels were clearly based on her experiences of the fund, such as *The Charity Girl* in 1900. Her sixpenny novels, *The Kingdom of a Heart* and *Her Heart's Longing*, were also very popular at the time. In 1902, Sir Henry asked theatre owners across Britain to donate one matinee's takings per year to the Actors' Benevolent Fund *and* the Actors' Orphanage Fund. This many duly did, and by 1903, the fund was supporting what was to become its average number of children for decades to come, approximately sixty to seventy children per year.

Sir Henry died in 1905, aged sixty-seven, after, rather unfortunately, falling ill while playing Becket in Bradford. He had hailed from a working-class background in Somerset and against all the odds conquered the theatre world. He was the leading Shakespearean actor of his age. Despite inspiring his business manager, Bram Stoker, to write *Dracula*... Sir Henry was essentially a good man. Perhaps he was just so successful that he was sometimes perceived as intimidating and frightening... and perhaps, at times, he was just a bit of a diva. Sir Henry had not attended committee meetings due to his workload and ill health in these last years; however, he had given the organisation prestige, royal patronage and raised vital funds.

Later in 1905, Cyril Maude would take over as president of the orphanage, also a famed actor-manager of the era. AGMs were now held at the Theatre Royal, Haymarket, where Maude was co-owner, and committee meetings would take place in the green room. In June 1906, Maude inaugurated the first Theatrical Garden Party fundraiser in Regent's Park and it was an astounding success. This event would occur one Tuesday in June for the next forty-five years. A variation on the royal garden party, tents would be erected, carousels planted and stalls set up. Stars would host various traditional fairground games, such as throwing hoops or fishing for a prize. Theatrical make-up demonstrations would take place, along with acrobatic displays, dances and various performances. Tea and sandwiches would be served by a famous actress of the day, and Regent's Park was awash with a sea of, predominately female on a Tuesday afternoon, hats. Everyone paid an entrance fee and strained happily to catch a glimpse of their favourite star, maybe even be able to actually *converse* with them! Selling autographs and conversing at these early fundraisers were the likes of Ellen Terry, Gerald du Maurier, Irene Vanbrugh and Pauline Chase. In these pre-cinema and television days, *theatre* stars were the stars of the day and almost mythical in the minds of the public. These garden parties were truly exciting and magical events.

The Actors' Orphanage always drew random charitable acts, too, sometimes from very unlikely places. In 1911, an anonymous lady donated Barton Cliff Cottage in New Milton to the orphanage; however, it needed expensive new sea defences so was sold. This proved fortuitous as within twenty years the property was no more, having virtually slipped into the sea.

Finally, in late 1906, and thanks to the huge success of that first garden party, the fund leased a property: 32 and 34 Moreland Road in Croydon, South London. A building that is now long gone but was then their very own orphanage at last. It had a house for girls and a house for boys, and a very tall wall between the gardens so that the genders would *never* cross. Segregation, even between siblings, existed, though children would throw notes over the wall from time to time. A Mr Ansell was made manager and the children were initially educated at local county council schools. They even went on occasional theatre or music hall trips. The actor-parents signed an agreement with the orphanage, granting the committee sole care of the child and a fifteen-day notice period if they ever wanted to remove them from the orphanage. If so, they would need due cause and would never be permitted to make any complaint or claim against the committee. Such a *get out of jail* legal document today would, of course, simply not exist or be possible. Kittie Carson, now well past retirement age, stepped down from the committee, but stayed in touch with several of the children, her dream finally realised.

*

Fairly soon in its history, 1911, there occurred something that, sadly, would occasionally be repeated in the coming decades of the orphanage's long life: the perennial problem of staff trouble. It seems that Mr Ansell, the manager, was growing absent-minded of his duties. Complaints were coming in from the locals of Croydon as some of the girls were roaming the streets barefoot and looking very thin and unkempt. Indeed, it seems that conditions at Moreland Road were very austere indeed and somewhat Dickensian. A local public medical officer of health found that there was an outbreak of ringworm and the food was found to be of very poor quality. Most of the children were underweight, several in ill health, and other possible misconduct had occurred.

Mr Ansell never attended any meeting to explain himself and was given until the end of the year to vacate the premises. He quickly and quietly disappeared. There was a long period of time taken now to clean house. Thirty-one children in the orphanage's care were sent to stay with relatives for the short term, and the nineteen with no relatives stayed with a Miss Newley in Leighton Buzzard, which sounds a houseful.

A complete overhaul of the organisation was urgently needed. A new all-female (one can only speculate as to why) committee was formed and they had a lease on the property for a further three years. Ada Blanche, Cicely Richards, Lilian Braithwaite and others appointed a matron and matron's assistant to take charge. Also hired were a new cook, gardener, odd-job man and two house managers. One of the old masters, however, a Mr Austin, had worked his charms and would stay on at Moreland Road.

The houses were newly wallpapered and some new furniture purchased. Notably, the high wall separating the sexes at all times was now knocked down so that *some* degree of mixing could occur. A new playground covered the grounds, and other improvements included fortnightly trips to the local cinema, film being the exciting new entertainment of the day. A new gramophone was also installed for music to be enjoyed, and at Christmas they would see the hugely popular, though now quite elderly, clown *The Whimsical Walker* (Tom Walker) when he performed in Croydon.

1912 would also see them have their first Christmas tree, and the actor-manager Sir Charles Hawtrey arranged for the orphans to attend a charity matinee of *Where the Rainbow Ends*. This was the rival Christmas show to *Peter Pan* and meant a trip to the Garrick Theatre in the West End, with all of the matinee's proceeds going to the orphanage!

The children, now back into a regular routine, many having suffered a degree of malnourishment, disease and possible abuse, now sat back to be swept away by the magic of the theatre. Coincidently, a twelve-year-old Master Noël Coward was appearing in this production in the small role of William. During the Christmases of 1913 and '14 he also played Slightly in *Peter Pan* and in 1915 returned to *Where the Rainbow Ends* in the slightly bigger role of The Slacker. It's possible that the orphans saw these shows too, unaware that on stage was the future saviour of the orphanage when they were to fall on dark times again. Young Master Noël would certainly have been aware of the attendance of the orphans and of the existence of the Actors' Orphanage. And of how the show's producer and Noël's great mentor, Sir Charles Hawtrey, had arranged the charity matinee.

Sir Charles was sophisticated, erudite and funny. To the end of Noël's acting and directing days, if he was ever confronted with a problem in rehearsal, he would think of what Sir Charles Hawtrey, what *his Master,* would have done. Sir Charles was the leading comedy actor of his day; a graduate of Eton, he had turned his back on Oxford to pursue the wicked life of the stage. His translation and performance of the German farce *A Private Secretary* had made his name and fortune, and he originated roles for Somerset Maugham and Oscar Wilde. He would manage eighteen theatres across his career and produce around one hundred plays. For Noël, he was a godsend, providing not only guidance and example, but also much of his employment during these very early years.

As for *Where the Rainbow Ends*, it was written by Clifford Mills and John Ramsey, with a beautiful score by Roger Quilter. It was an adventure story in four acts, where four children with a pet lion cub and a magic carpet go to Rainbow Land to search for their missing parents. Helped by Saint George, they encounter a dragon, a white witch and numerous talking animals. It sounds like a mad drug trip but it was extremely popular. The score was so successful that it had been played at the 1912 Proms.

As for Noël, the irony was that this future epitome of sophistication and elegance was cast as a commoner, William, the pageboy (servant). Offstage, his diction was meticulous; onstage, his opening line was: "Let me go! You're 'urting me!"

For forty-nine years, from 1911 to 1960, *Where the Rainbow Ends* was a fixture of the London Christmas season. Billed as 'A Play with Music for Children', it had premiered at the Savoy Theatre and the then eleven-year-old Master Noël Coward had appeared in that very first production too. The lead child actor of the day, Philip Tonge, played Crispian, while Noël's new best friend, Esme Wynne, was Rosamund and Hermione Gingold played Betty. (Over the coming years, everyone from Gertrude Lawrence to Jack Hawkins would appear.)

As for the story, Clifford Mills and John Ramsey came up with a new take on St George and the dragon. Rosamund and Crispian have lost their parents after their plane goes missing. Now evil Uncle Joseph (who just happens to be a lawyer) and Aunt Matilda reign over them. There will be no more private school, no opportunities or books, but a life of servitude. The nasty little pageboy, William, will now have preference in the house too.

At the beginning, William kicks Crispian and Rosamund's pet lion cub, imaginatively called *Cubs*. Now Crispian is pulling William onto the stage by his ear. The rather ghastly William will remain stagnant in character throughout the first act, with lines such as: "Oo do you think you are! Cook says you ain't got a penny to your name." And: "Bloomin' little toffs – I don't think. Dependants! Yah!" (*He pokes his tongue out*) "Boo!"

Act One ends with Crispian, Rosamund, Cubs and two friends, Jim and Betty, rescuing a magic book, summoning up the spirit of St George, a genie to boot, and getting on a magic carpet... as you do. It will take them to *where the rainbow ends*, that magical land where all lost parents reside. William, meanwhile, has been hiding and sees the whole thing. Aunt Matilda and Uncle Joseph will be told and follow in hot pursuit. William laughs as the curtain descends.

After Act One, William is never seen again. The show's choreographer, one Italia Conti, asked Noël to come on later as one of the hyenas, but Mother wasn't keen. Better to stick with the prestige of just the speaking part than reappear in a leotard, crawling about on all fours and being undignified with three other children.

So, after Act One, young Noël could retire to a dressing room and dream of larger roles in his future, while onstage, the children journey to a magical wood where, under the flag of St George, they are safe from the evil Dragon King. Inevitably, Betty is lured into the deep woods by some dancing fairies and the others must go and look for her.

In Act Three, Jim and Crispian come across a young boy called *The Slacker*, the role that Noël would play during the 1915-16 season. The play was still at the Garrick Theatre, and although the larger role of Crispian or Jim would have been preferable, *The Slacker* was a nice, showy little part.

Described as tall and thin, with 'a slightly decadent air', it was a good fit for young Master Noël. The character also has a 'tired, blasé air', is followed by a green 'protective' light and is dressed in a green doublet and hose. There is also a dragon's tail dragging on the floor, a basket of fish over one shoulder and heavy yellow make-up for an emaciated look. Plus some glittery green eyeshadow for good measure.

The character of *The Slacker* had gone looking for his lost sister but now, seemingly drugged, stays quite happily here in the woods, half man, half dragon. He greets Crispian and Jim with a: "Hello chaps, you look like you've been in the wars a bit. Going to where the rainbow ends are you?"

He then throws himself on the floor because he's so bored, tired and blasé. He tries to get the boys to eat some dragon fruit and it transpires that he is indeed poisoned and would be eaten by creatures in the forest if it weren't for the Dragon King's protective green light.

Jim and Crispian are appalled to find that it is in exchange for his parents' unopened letters that the Dragon King has cast the green light around *The Slacker*.

"Come with us," pleads Jim, but *The Slacker* has his protection, plenty of fish from the lake and no ambition to leave. He has happily given up.

"Come with you – to fight – to work – perhaps to starve – never!" When asked what will become of him in the end, he points to *The Slitherslime*, a hideous bald worm-like creature crawling along upstage. Crispian and Jim were considering eating the dragon fruit but not now. Jim argues that it's better to try and find where the rainbow ends and fail than not to try at all... *The Slacker's* green light suddenly goes out...

"Stop! Stop! It cannot burn because you have called up the influence of an idea. Leave me! Leave me! I shall be eaten by the beasts!" As he refuses to go with them, his light comes back.

"I'm saved! I'm saved!" he yells and gives a hysterical laugh upon exiting the stage. Noël would reflect that a hysterical laugh on an exit never fails to get a round of applause. In this he was right. *The Slacker* proved to be a funny, scary and rewarding little part.

As the play goes on, the evil uncle and aunt are eaten, him by a hyena, her by a bear. Then the children are captured and taken to the Dragon King's castle.

"You children stand guilty to the charge of daring to place yourselves under the protection of an ideal – one St George," says the Dragon King. They are to be imminently thrown to their deaths. Luckily (in a very pro-Empire moment), they manage to replace the Dragon King's flag with that of St George, which makes the man himself appear, fight and slay the Dragon King.

The sun comes out and a rainbow appears. The 'Rainbow Children' enter, barefoot, brightly attired and chipper, singing, '*We'll find lost loved ones*'. The curtain falls and now rises on a sunlit shore where the children continue to sing and dance. A boat docks and Crispian and Rosamund's parents appear. They cannot see their children and are about to leave when they hear singing in the distance. It's Crispian and Rosamund singing *Rock-a-Bye-Slumber,* which the mother used to sing to them when they were very little.

Crispian and Rosamund enter and run to their parents for an emotional hug. (Their friends Jim and Betty are given a very English handshake each.) In an epilogue, we see St George sailing everyone home, and then he stands centre stage for a closing speech. He tells the audience to not be like *The Slacker* and give in. To face the dragon and be like St George! "Youth of all Nations, pledge yourselves to fight, For Peace, for Justice, Freedom and the Right!"

Then St George sings *God Save the King* and audiences would have stood to join in. It was a very pro-British, pro-

Empire play and, indeed, the Empire still flourished. The play would survive the Great War, but later on, after World War Two and with the sharp decline of Empire and the handing back of the colonies, *Where the Rainbow Ends* would begin, finally, to fall out of fashion.

It must have been a rather bittersweet play for the sixty-something children of the Actors' Orphanage to see, starting with those from Croydon in 1912. Lost parents were not only found but also loving and emotional. More profound still may have been a performance in 1915 given for hundreds of children whose fathers had recently been killed in the Great War. One hopes that these experiences were more cathartic than traumatic.

It's also ironic that the great patriot, Noël Coward, went on to play *The Slacker*. It's also quite possible that Noël, witnessing his great mentor, Sir Charles Hawtrey, putting on that first charity matinee during the Christmas of 1912, with all profits going to the Actors' Orphanage, partly inspired Noël to take charge of the charity himself eighteen years later. Generations of Actors' Orphanage children would see *Where the Rainbow Ends* most Christmases, right through to the 1950s. In 1911, the *Birmingham Daily Post* had said:

> *It is a safe prophesy that this beautiful little fantasy will prove to be among the greatest attractions of the London Christmas season…*

And for half a century it was.

*

Alongside charity matinees, the Theatrical Garden Party had become an institution and was still a sell-out success each June.

So popular, in fact, that in 1913 it was moved from Regent's Park to Olympia, with Cyril Maude and his famous friends still selling their autographs and engaging with the public to raise the majority of the funds for the coming year. Around this time too there was an influx of babies and toddlers being brought to the orphanage, and the funds policy of not being 'justified in refusing admission to any eligible case' resulted in the need for two under-nurses; morality in the acting profession, one imagines, often discussed.

The children now ranged in age from practically zero to about seventeen. The actual prospects for them once of age were simple. Girls would most likely become nurses, possibly teachers, and boys would go into manual labour. Social mobility was practically non-existent; it would take two world wars to even begin to change that deep-rooted situation. 1914 saw the start of the first, of course: the Great War, also known as the so-called war to end all wars...

The committee was now run by Marie Tempest, Granville Barker, Lilian Braithwaite and Gerald du Maurier. Cyril Maude, with immaculate timing, found a much better, as well as permanent, home for the orphanage: Langley Hall, Langley Place, Langley, Buckinghamshire (now Berkshire). A country house from 1628, it was much bigger and *belonged* to the Trust. The outer wall dated from 1665, and a little wooden door led into the grounds, with its gardens, rose beds and a central sundial. It had originally been the home of Sir Richard Hubert, the groom porter to King Charles II. By the 1900s, the building had long been a school. The artist John Nash had attended. Nash was soon to become an established and famous painter, depicting, in stark realism, the horrors of the Great War.

By purchasing in March 1914, the major recession of the looming war was neatly avoided. A large staff turnover now occurred; the matron Miss Eady left due to alleged ill health, although there had allegedly been some impropriety with a Mr Pond, the assistant master. The popular Daisy Craft, known 'affectionately' as *Crazy Daft*, was promoted to matron, and a Mr Baumeister introduced reports and prefects, comparing the benefits as to those of Eton and Harrow, ever the models for the perfect childhood and education within class-bound England.

1914 also saw Cyril Maude's resignation, aged just fifty-two. Cyril would now tour the world acting, eventually move into films and live to the ripe age of eighty-nine, finally dying in 1951. Gerald du Maurier became the new president; he was forty-one and at the height of his fame, revered as the original Captain Hook for JM Barrie's *Peter Pan* at the Duke of York's Theatre in 1904. A Harrow graduate, he had also premiered roles in Barrie's *Admiral Crichton* and *Dear Brutus*. (Meanwhile, of course, a now teenage Noël Coward was currently playing Slightly for the second time in the now-annual revival of *Peter Pan* at the very same theatre.) Gerald knew JM Barrie well and was the uncle of the Llewelyn Davies children that had inspired the characters of Peter, Michael, John and Wendy in *Peter Pan*. His career would go from strength to strength, the latest example in the ever-continuing tradition of *naturalistic acting*. It's said that Gerald wasn't given to being melodramatic on stage but was more truthful somehow to the audiences.

This had also been said in centuries past of Edmund Kean, David Garrick and Richard Burbage, naturalism apparently needing a reinvention every few decades, with, one assumes, the changes in social mores. In time, incidentally, Gerald's daughter, Daphne du Maurier, would be a regular volunteer to teach English classes at the orphanage. She was a writer on the verge of success, although with a complicated relationship with her famous father.

The orphanage finally made the actual physical move to Langley Hall in 1915. Langley is not far from Iver Village in the Colne Valley, near Slough, Windsor and Eton. Visiting Sundays (the third Sunday of every month), for those that had any visitors, would provide ample villages for the child and parent or relative to explore. Once in a rare while, an orphanage child would see an Eton boy in their top hat and suit, just from a neighbouring village but in many respects light years away. Yet we must remember that the Actors' Orphanage wasn't a Dickensian workhouse or indeed like any other orphanage or school; it was unique. Not Eton, nor as ideal as a loving home and regular schooling, but somehow distinct and even special.

There were four large classrooms at Langley, one for the six to eleven-year-old boys and one for the twelve to sixteen-year-old boys. And the same for the girls. Four huge dorm rooms existed too, also with the same divisions. There was little privacy. The babies would arrive and be cared for by a staff member, in a sort of nursery set-up, before they were old enough to join in with the rest.

Football pitches and a cricket field for the boys and netball and tennis courts for the girls filled the grounds, along with the vegetable garden, which was now vitally necessary through the rationing of the War. Insurance was taken out against bomb damage, and clothes and supplies had to be stretched to the hilt. Notably, all classes now took place *on site,* and the orphanage essentially became a *kind* of boarding school.

The Theatrical Garden Parties would continue at the Botanical Gardens of Regent's Park, but funds were largely dependent during these difficult war years on penny collections. This was a voluntary 1p in every pound donation from working actors and actresses. Gerald du Maurier donated £300 annually and also hay was sold from the front of Langley Hall. That money was then used to make postcards of the orphanage, which were sold at theatre stage doors and box offices, also helping to keep everything going. It wasn't easy but then little was during the years of 1914-18.

The Theatrical Garden Party of the 28th of July 1915 was covered by *The Sketch Magazine* and is here called, the *Actors' Orphanage Fête*. Apparently, 'The whole thing went with a whirl'. Many wounded soldiers were invited to attend, some with sticks in hand or bandaged limbs. Officers too were on hand and helping out. A garden party must have been quite the light relief. Marie Lohr was selling flowers at the *Temple of Flora*. Irene Vanbrugh was selling chocolates. Winifred Barnes ran the ever-popular autograph sales. George Grossmith headed up the fun at a mini *Egyptian Village*. There were the usual croquet matches, *Le Palais du Dance* and fair games. And the children themselves were on hand, helping out and having fun. How odd it must have been to think, '*This is all for us!*'

If we had been there on that summer's day in 1915, we might have seen Nelson Keys starring as Henry VIII in the 'Grand Giggles' tent in a play called *Henry, Him of Eight, or, How Wild and Woolly Wolsey Huffed King Hal*. Or next door, Gerald du Maurier and the Hartley Manners (Noël's future inspiration for the theatrical family in *Hay Fever)* in another play, called *The Passing of Fanny and Joseph*. What this was about is lost to the mysteries of time.

Somewhat astonishingly, nineteen years' worth of orphanage records, from 1915 to 1934, are very largely missing. By all accounts, Langley Hall itself was, away from the glamour of the garden parties, ultimately a tough and sometimes unpleasant institution during these years, especially latterly; the committee and the by-now-knighted Sir Gerald operating on the periphery and lending their names to the orphanage but doing nothing outside of the annual fundraisers. They were rarely, if ever, *on site*.

Mr Austin, who had arrived in 1907 and by 1915 was the master of Langley Hall, ran a place of hard discipline, strict regimes, segregation and cold baths… but still with the occasional theatre trip and a staging of their own popular pantomime each Christmas. Little is known of the 1920s at all, except that there was a certain increasing reign of terror by Mr Austin. However, from a business standpoint all was solvent and seemed to be working. So no questions were asked and no one outside of Langley knew the reality of what occurred within its walls.

The 1920s is also when the Bijou Theatre was installed, a ray of light in a somewhat grim building at a somewhat grim time. Throughout the year, the Bijou would be adapted, as the raked seating could be removed and the space could be used equally as a gym or an assembly hall… but at Christmas, it was a sophisticated miniature theatre. The Bijou had a nice stage, proper lighting and a safety curtain with a painting of Windsor Castle adorning it. Also there was a dressing room, plenty of scenery *and* an orchestra pit. The pantomime programmes would also reassure patrons that they could smoke during the interval in the *classroom* above the theatre.

The 1920s saw productions such as *The Magic Lamp: Or Aladdin-Up-To-Date* in 1921 and *Scroll of Happiness: An Eastern Vacancy* in 1925. The annual pantomime soon became a local event and was always pictured in the local press. Audiences seemed to genuinely enjoy it. Sometimes, Mr Austin's wife, Mrs Angela Austin, would act in the show and certainly helped to organise it. She also organised events such as *The Will-O'-The-Wisp Children's Ball* of the 11th of January 1927. This was a fancy dress competition held at the City of London School by Victoria Embankment. The new star of *Peter Pan,* Jean Forbes-Robertson, handed out the prizes.

It was the pantomimes, however, that really took off. Indeed, some of the profits from ticket sales went to the local Windsor and Iver hospitals. *The Magic Lamp* took no money at all for the orphanage and donated, seemingly, all profits to the King Edward the VII Hospital in Windsor and to the new Langley War Memorial. But how could they afford to? How were they so cash-rich after the War? Something didn't add up. The popularity and fun of these shows perhaps, too, masked the truth of life at Langley.

Murky financial details aside, the children seemed to live in fear of corporal punishment. Schools and orphanages of this era were, by today's standards and expectations, harsh and even brutal. Corporal punishment, after all, would remain in common use until the 1960s and '70s, only actually being officially outlawed in 1986 in the UK. Somewhere, though, certain things had started to go quite seriously awry at Langley Hall.

*

Meanwhile, a certain Noël Coward was becoming a theatrical phenomenon. In 1924, *The Vortex*, the play he wrote, co-produced, co-directed and starred in, had made him famous. It was an incredibly edgy, dangerous-feeling drama from a young man slightly known for light comedy. In it, Florence Lancaster is having an adulterous affair with a much younger man, while her son Nicky (Noël) struggles with his mother's antics, an apathy for his girlfriend, Bunty, and a cocaine addiction. Its themes of sex and drugs among the upper classes garnered attention all right. In 1924, no one even called another person 'darling' unless they were having a love affair with them. It was truly daring and shocking.

The press called it a 'dustbin of a play', and publicity went through the roof, the run sold out and played in the West End for over a year. By 1925, Noël had four productions running simultaneously in the West End: *The Vortex, Fallen Angels* (two women drunkenly prepare to meet a mutual ex-lover), *On with the Dance* (a new revue) and *Hay Fever* (an eccentric family wreak havoc upon their house guests). Only Somerset Maugham before and Alan Ayckbourn after would ever achieve the same feat. By 1926, he had conquered Broadway too. If anyone was a symbolic and influential *Bright Young Thing* in the 1920s, it was Noël. Alexander Woollcott labelled him, 'Destiny's Tot'. One night, after the premiere of *Hay Fever*, Noël roamed the streets of London, kicking over flowerpots in a sense of jubilation; he was abruptly arrested and spent a night in jail. This mattered little, though, for never again was Noël to worry in any serious way about money or real struggle.

Noël had what every great star needs: an image and a brand. He was dubbed 'The Playboy of the *West-End* World'. The adornments and affectations of the character of Nicky Lancaster in *The Vortex* fixed his image in the public mind. Silk dressing gowns, cigarette holders, cocktails and witticisms in a staccato upper-class accent all combined to create the image of *Noël Coward*. In truth, he was a hard-working polymath, just as likely to enjoy time at his desk as at a party, although he *was* a social animal too. A confirmed workaholic, he would soon suffer a couple of flops and a nervous breakdown, but nothing that the odd trip to Hawaii, or indeed around the world, couldn't fix.

By the early 1930s, he was at his zenith, with a string of further hits, including *Easy Virtue* (a drawing-room comedy with a modern twist), *This Year of Grace* (his most successful revue), *Bitter Sweet* (a nostalgic musical love story which ran for two years), *Private Lives* (the classic comedy of love and war), and *Cavalcade* (a British historical epic). They had cemented him as the most successful living playwright in the world. He'd had hit songs to boot with *A Room With a View, Poor Little Rich Girl, I'll See You Again* and *Mad Dogs and Englishmen* to name just some. Not to mention the Academy Award-winning film adaptation of

Cavalcade in 1933. He was still just thirty-three years old.

The play of *Cavalcade* had premiered at the Theatre Royal, Drury Lane in 1931 and was a patriotic epic through England's history from 1899 to 1930 via one family, the Marryotts, and via too the Boer War, the death of Queen Victoria, the sinking of the Titanic and the Great War and its aftermath. King George V attended the premiere, and when everyone stood for the national anthem at the end of the play, tears were shed. The production had a cast of hundreds, a complex set with a revolving stage and a budget of £33,000. The opening also happened to coincide with a national surge in patriotism owing to a recent general election. At the premiere's curtain speech, Noël said, "It's still a pretty exciting thing to be English."

Noël knew that he had achieved so much so quickly and indeed felt that if success was his only goal in life then he might as well jump off a cliff now, for he'd done it. What else was there? What now? He went travelling again, always hoping to return with a 'Strindbergian soul', although he often claimed that no matter how far his body roamed, his mind never went very far. He wrote a novel about a man called Julian Kane, so bored by life that he commits suicide. Noël decided that it was so dull that the readers would commit suicide long before Julian Kane ever did. He abandoned the project. The 1930s saw little failure and much more success, with *Design for Living* (the complications of a love triangle) and his nine 'playlets' in the *Tonight at 8:30* cycle, which would satisfy audiences for months on end in London and then New York. Through starring opposite Gertrude Lawrence in *Private Lives* and *Tonight at 8:30*, Noël was now cemented in the public mind as witty, charming, flamboyant and... heterosexual.

Private Lives, perhaps more than any of his plays, captures the Coward image and philosophy. On the surface, the play is about shallow people not doing very much; underneath, it is a profound study of passionate love and how two people are torn between living together and living apart. One moment Elyot is confessing his love to Amanda, the next he's threatening to cut her head off with a meat axe. More than that, it's a struggle between social convention and bohemian, liberal freedom: a fine line that Noël, as a homosexual, walked all his life.

Noël was, after entering the theatre at age ten, finally the star he was always going to be. With a house in Gerald Road, Belgravia, an estate in the Kent countryside, called Goldenhurst, an apartment in New York, a Rolls-Royce, a plentiful supply of expensive suits and numerous travelling adventures, Noël had long escaped the slight poverty of his youth. He'd escaped the drab suburbia and the tense search for his next theatrical employment. Most importantly, his *deepest* ambition, to liberate his ageing mother from the drudgeries of running a boarding house, was now fully realised.

DESTINY'S TOT

Violet Coward gave birth to Noël in 1899 when she was already thirty-six years old. His father, Arthur, was a struggling piano salesman, and their lives were insecure, moving often, from London suburb to suburb, and often taking in lodgers. There would be a brother, Eric, born in 1904, and before that there had been Russell, born in 1892, but he had died in 1898, aged six. Hence Noël, born the following year on December 16th, was an absolute godsend to Violet, not to mention fiercely loved and protected. Hence too his name, as it was so close to Christmas.

There had once been grandeur in the Coward family on his mother's side, the Vietchs. Indeed, ancestors included naval officers and an ambassador in Madeira. This was long ago, however, and Noël was not to have the traditional, clichéd, elite English upbringing. This made his success in the theatre world fairly unique and himself latterly thankful, writing:

Had my formative years passed in more assured circumstances, I might easily have slipped into precociousness; as it was I merely had to slip out of precociousness and bring home the bacon!

Also:

If Mother had been able to send me to private school, Eton and Oxford or Cambridge, it would probably have set me back years.

It's interesting that Noël says 'Mother' and not 'Father'; another indication of their strong, indestructible bond and how Arthur Coward was a quiet, unassuming fellow in the background. The desire to free his *mother* from the drudgery of suburban life and hard graft was his primary driving force. She was a rather high-status lady trapped in an increasingly low-status life.

When he was a boy, he and his mother attended many musical comedies of the day, such as *The Dairy Maids* or *The Quaker Girl*, often to see his absolute favourite performer, Gertie Millar. Of course, later on Noël would know Gertie, for later on Noël would know everybody. They also attended pantomimes in Croydon, although this was long before the Actors' Orphanage children were performing their own at the Bijou Theatre. Indeed, there were no pantomimes at the Moreland Road address.

Noël's boyhood was, of course, unlike the orphans', but also it was unlike anybody else's, either. Moving from Teddington to Sutton to Battersea to Clapham and to Pimlico, his early years were full of circumstance. Violet guided his precocious gifts for acting, singing, playing piano, dancing, writing and composing, channelling his great energy and instilling him with confidence.

From 1911, Noël appeared in a succession of West End shows and UK tours, such as *The Goldfish, The Great Name, Where the Rainbow Ends, Hannele, Peter Pan* and *Charley's Aunt*. Appearing often at such prestigious venues as the Savoy, the Duke of York's Theatre, the Garrick and the Palladium; tiny one-line roles gradually increasing in size, until he was a juvenile lead.

His lack of any doubt about how vital his mother had been in his success is partly why he committed himself to the orphanage for so long and with so much more involvement than his predecessors. It was so plain to him that those children lacked the very thing that enabled him to be a success: an ever-present, loving and supportive parent. A parent that would *never* give you up. It *did* break his heart to think of it. His relationship with his mother was the defining relationship of his life. Noël would write to her every Sunday, her whole life long, from wherever he was in the world. She would live in his various homes and be introduced to all his friends, until her death, aged ninety-one, in 1954.

For now, though, in the 1910s, having to take in lodgers as a means to an end was hard on Violet but often exciting for young Noël. He saw it as a reason to dress up for dinner and then he would have an audience for his songs on the piano afterwards. Contemporaries, such as Micheál Mac Liammóir, would recall how Noël, as a quite young boy, spoke in his assured, clipped manner even then. And how he had strength of will and character and ambition even then too. He got to know all the right people and wrote more and more of his own material. His energies and ambitions were indefatigable. Once an actor, he needed to *write* the plays, then *direct* them too; his work ethic and, what he considered to be his real secret, an ability to concentrate, always standing him in good stead from very early doors.

*

By 1934, Noël was ripe for greater fulfilment and a more rounded life. Success, make no mistake, had been a lot of hard work and graft but in another sense it had come easy. This was the man that wrote *Hay Fever* in four days and said: "I believe my colleague Will took six on *Macbeth*."

Luckily, Noël had a close-knit group around him, including his fiercely loyal secretary, Lornie; his manager and lover, the American Jack Wilson; the actress Joyce Carey; and his set and costume designer and long-time confidante, Gladys Calthrop, all of whom, apart from Jack, had known Noël before his extreme success. His enviable career and his fame and fortune satisfied up to a point and for a time but… after every success he would always turn to Gladys or Lornie and say, "What now?"

We should also note that Noël's younger brother, Eric, had died aged just twenty-seven in January 1933. They were never close and Eric was somewhat overshadowed by his famous brother… yet it was, of course, a true shock. Noël had him tended to at Goldenhurst, his home near the Romney Marsh, during his last weeks. He never revealed to him that he was going to die and told him that he just needed rest… then when he did die, Noël had to tell their parents. This can only have heightened Noël's intense relationship and bond with his mother *even more*.

Also, by the time Noël took over the presidency of the orphanage, his manager and lover, Jack, was suffering from heavy alcohol consumption and the long road to separation, and Jack's eventual marriage to a woman, was in motion. All of this life experience can only mature a person and perhaps contributed also to the care with which Noël was to take on his responsibilities at the orphanage. By 1934, he was no longer a *Bright Young Thing*, and rather more of an experienced, mature, thoughtful and sophisticated adult.

Noël often mused on his success and its effects. His fame was so all-encompassing. There was, from time to time, a questioning impact on his soul. Everyone knew him, wanted a piece of him, and expected him to be witty and charming and interesting at all times, as well as in a thoroughly nice mood with them. If he wasn't, then they'd remember it forever and tell everyone they ever met. He'd have to travel to very far-flung shores to be treated *normally*.

One, probably apocryphal, story about Noël to enter the public realm was the time he tried to send a telegram by phone from New York. For a laugh, he wanted to sign himself off as the mayor, Fiorello La Guardia.

"Are you really Mayor La Guardia?"

"No."

"Then you can't sign it 'Fiorello La Guardia'. What is your real name?"

"Noël Coward."

"Are you really Noël Coward?"

"Yes."

"Then you may sign it 'Fiorello La Guardia."

Money and prestige aside, fame was and always would be a double-edged sword. Fame couldn't be turned off. It must be worth more than being mobbed on the street and asked the same questions over and over again. Which is why so many privileged with it, especially of the extreme kind that Noël had, eventually want to find a way to put it, somehow, to some real good. It's almost as a way to save their sense of self and self-worth. Noël was no different.

Did he remember his great mentor, Sir Charles Hawtrey, organising that charity matinee for something called the Actors' Orphanage in 1912? Is that a part of why he accepted a committee position? Sir Charles had died in 1923 but his memory never left Noël. The presidency of the orphanage had indeed been thrust upon him rather. He knew it was because he was a big star, but his relative youth for the position may have also humbled him to take it seriously. He *would* be more involved than Sir Gerald du Maurier had been... although Noël was in awe of Sir Gerald, another great actor-manager of his youth, and, lest we forget, Captain Hook! Yet when *The Vortex* had opened in 1924 to its sensation of scandal and success, Sir Gerald had publically called it: "Dustbin drama."

Noël had responded in print:

> *Sir Gerald... having enthusiastically showered the English stage with second-rate drama for many years, now rises up with incredible violence and has a nice slap all round at the earnest and perspiring dramatists.*

They must have come to some form of acquaintance and even friendship over the coming decade, however, as Noël did join the orphanage committee and attended the garden party fundraisers while Sir Gerald was still in the pink.

Now, suddenly president, that first year or two gradually saw Noël embrace the role as his way to give back. He could use his extreme fame for something more than getting a table in a restaurant or massaging his ego. Sure, he would enjoy the prestige of the role but here he really could make a difference and prove *to himself* that he was more than the superficial star that he was sometimes accused of being by the press. The work for the orphanage rounded out and enriched his life. It was a much-needed tonic for, and healthy diversion from, the ego-driven world of show business. It gave perspective. It was also perhaps an answer to that question... 'What now?'

*

It's also highly probable that Noël had noticed some discrepancy and sensed trouble at the orphanage, thus feeling a genuine sense of responsibility. Langley Hall was overtly strict and limiting for the children, yet a description in an early 1930s brochure paints a *slightly* over-egged and unlikely idyll:

> *Langley Hall, standing amidst the cherry-blossom of a charming Buckinghamshire Village, is an old-world building of a style that links us with the England of that faithful lover of the drama, Samuel Pepys, and of our first great actress, Sweet Nell of Drury Lane, it is a picture of sunlight upon warm red roofs that undulate in picturesque abandon, of walls veiled in lavender, wisteria and russet creeper. Beyond lie the orchard, the kitchen gardens, and the velvet, rose-ringed lawn.*

The brochure also promotes the virtues of the headmaster, Mr Austin; his wife and all of the staff. Mrs Austin had, however, died and is lovingly remembered now as 'Madame Darling'. The classrooms are sunlit, the floors polished, the pantomimes magical; 'Old Scholars' (graduates) return for beloved reunions and the school motto is:

> *We are not born for ourselves alone.*

This is all marvellous and, somewhat, true but far from paints the reality of life at Langley. The main house was quite close to a main road, and it wasn't the most spacious of environments for sixty to seventy children. We also see in the brochure that the Actors' Orphanage is now called a 'Boarding School' with the official title of 'Langley Hall (the Actors' Orphanage)'. Note the brackets. And seventy children attend between the ages of four and seventeen. No mention is made, of course, of the very stark discipline, austerity and regime.

A few older children were designated prefects, and *Old*

Scholars would indeed return as they pleased, even staying over. They behaved as if they owned the place, enforcing many rules on the younger children. Some legitimate, as well as a few rules of their own devising. Rules such as beds must be made every morning, no leaving the grounds without permission, no speaking after lights out, and no talking back seemed reasonable and expected. But unofficial law such as the enforced initiation ceremonies, the handing over of sweets, pocket money and submitting to all of the demands of the old scholars... seemed less reasonable and rather intimidating.

The food was better than in 1911 and they were not malnourished, but it was very basic, although there was enough. Everyone had one night of the week that they detested, of course, usually the boiled fish on a Friday with Matron forcing all to finish the whole meal, no matter what. Some of the staff, however, did induce outright and extreme fear.

Outside of classes they had few toys or books to enjoy and there were many chores and duties: cleaning, washing-up, gardening and endless church services. Some children of the time included Paul Bantock and his younger brother, Granville Bantock, who arrived in 1930 following the death of their father, Leedham Bantock, who had been the general manager of the Lyceum Theatre in the West End. His brother, the boys' uncle, was the famous composer also called Granville Bantock. He, on occasion, would visit and had even offered to look after the children, but their mother couldn't allow him to do that. Paul and Granville's mother had a house but no income anymore and so had to take in lodgers. The boys had to go to the orphanage in order for them all to simply survive.

She would often see them on Visiting Sundays, when the children expecting visitors, would wait in the courtyard after lunch. Eventually, the small wooden door in the ancient wall would open and in would troop a parent, often with a bit of food, maybe a bit of pocket money. Two other boys of the same era, Carol and Hugo Bergström, often had visits from their father. He would take them down to the Thames bankside and barbecue some food. Paul and Granville, however, would go to a local restaurant with their mother for tea and sardines on toast, loving her all-too-brief company very much.

The very small children, such as the four-year-old Granville, would stay in the girls' dorm until they were six and old enough to join the boys. Then gender roles must be clearly defined. For example, boys could *not* play tennis or learn to sew in darning sessions. Granville recalled the food at Langley, as everyone did, as rather disheartening: thin porridge, boiled cod and thinned-out jam. He also recalled the dull trudge to Langley Parish Church for Sunday services.

His many memories also include how the dining hall had boys sit at one end of the room and girls at the other, with no mixing allowed. They would have a halfpenny per week for sweets from the village shop and on Sunday evenings they listened to the Henry Hall Orchestra on the wireless. When they were allowed out, they liked to play by the banks of the Grand Union Canal and in the meadows, but from time to time all the children were gated and not allowed out at all. Often this was due to an outbreak of disease in the village or simply within the orphanage, such as chicken pox or measles. The temporary loss of the weekly visit to the sweet shop was particularly galling.

Other children of this era included two girls who'd arrived soon after Paul and Granville, called Maggie and Jenny. In 1933, a Douglas Foster arrived, allegedly the illegitimate child of an American movie star, although Douglas wouldn't know this himself for many years to come. It was in 1935 that a six-year-old Hugo Bergström arrived with his older brother Carol. He remembered the prefect, Yettey, making him tea and giving him the uniform of grey shorts, grey socks, grey shirt, *black* shoes and a black and white tie; colour obviously something of a luxury. Hugo and Carol's parents were opera singers at Sadler's Wells, but their mother had died and their father had had to go on tour. 1936 saw the arrival of Jerry Hicks, his actor-father having died. Also in the 1930s, the first of *six* Hallywell siblings would arrive. The last would arrive at the orphanage in the 1950s.

The children of this era all absolutely idolised the famous attendee of the orphanage from 1912 to 1922, Frank Lawton. Lawton had broken the unwritten law of not pursuing a show business career and was now, against considerable odds, a film star. He would make a huge hit as the grown-up David in 1935's *David Copperfield,* directed by George Cukor and starring W.C. Fields and Maureen O'Sullivan. Lawton also played the young lead of Joe Marryot in the film of *Cavalcade.* (This was when Noël was just a committee member and attendee of the garden parties, but perhaps it's possible that he had had a hand in getting Lawton a casting.)

Lawton would captain the actors' cricket team at the annual charity match and was ever-popular. The children saw him as a beacon of glamorous hope for those that started life at the orphanage. Indeed, he had first shown a glimpse of his future by playing Robin Hood in the Bijou Theatre pantomime of 1921-22.

Another highlight in the calendar was Sports Day; all would be divided into two teams: the House of Austin (the head) or the House of Nettleford (a committee member), and the long-term sports master, Mr Bomber Howells, would oversee the day's events; sport and competition, as with every school or orphanage in the land, actively encouraged.

There were of course cliques and gangs. A Lenny Mann was a dominant boy, overseeing the building of a boys' den and, also, rabbit hutches. All of which was quite harmless fun. Of course, there were bound to be the usual childhood larks, such as getting into airgun and catapult warfare with the local children of Langley. On occasion, sweets would be stolen. On one unfortunate occasion, Matron was doused with water from a fire bucket.

Matron, incidentally, was the person responsible for scrubbing the younger children with a bristly brush while they sat in a cold bath. Luckily, baths were only once a week. A usual day's routine saw a huge gong struck to wake them all up, have a quick splash of water, dress, get to breakfast and get to class. One time, Hugo got to class early to hide under a desk so as to catch a look at the teacher's knickers. He was caught, of course, but reported that they, "Were white!" He then received the ruler across his hand.

Childhood initiations were compulsory for the younger children joining the older children, once they turned twelve. At this time it was *de rigour* to have the new boy do push-ups in a cold bath, and occasionally their head would be held under the water. There was also an initiation called 'The Rising Sun'; this was where a boy was held down on a table while the others beat his bare bottom until it was scarlet red, although this was small fry and standard boyhood fare compared with the regularity with which some of the masters wielded the cane. And therein was the problem. There was corporal punishment, normal for the era, and then there was sheer abuse.

It was to take time before Noël, Lorn and the committee would realise the full extent of the underlying issues at Langley Hall…

TWO

Langley Hall

1934-1938

---

*I have since often observed, how incongruous and irrational the
common temper of mankind is.*

– *Robinson Crusoe*, by Daniel Dafoe, 1719

During Noël's first months as president, he would, despite
a ludicrously busy schedule, visit Langley Hall on a semi-
regular basis, making the children's happiness and well-being his
priority. He made Langley fully co-educational, cold baths were
ended, food was improved, smart uniforms were introduced,
rooms were decorated, the tennis court was resurfaced and the
boys' dorm was given more windows and single beds to replace
the bunks. It was truly a new era for the orphanage.

Noël often brought famous friends such as Mary Pickford,
Jack Hawkins, Rex Harrison, Mary Ellis, Evelyn Laye, Diana
Wynyard or Ivor Novello to visit the children. The luxury
item of Mars Bars were handed out, and Noël sang and
played the piano. Regular visits were soon to be conducted,
at Noël's insistence, by various and equally famous (though

not necessarily to the younger children) committee members. Predominantly Edith Evans, Sybil Thorndike, Jill Esmond and, of course, Lorn would become familiar faces to the children too. Also on the committee now were Laurence Olivier and Adrianne Allen (both from the original production of *Private Lives*), Jack Buchanan, Raymond Massey and that successful old scholar Frank Lawton.

The committee meetings over the years, Noël hated, describing them variously as 'stormy', 'long', 'complicated', 'boring'. But also as 'constructive' or, at best, 'fairly useful'. He sometimes used these committee meetings as inspiration in his writing. One thinks of the squabbling, egocentric and easily distracted actors trying to hold a meeting in *Star Chamber*, the almost unused play from his *Tonight at 8:30* cycle of ten plays from 1935. In the play, Xenia James is the president of the Garrick Haven, a home for destitute actresses, founded in 1902. Funds are annually raised at the Garrick Haven Fund Fayre, consisting of roundabouts, tea tents, lucky dips, hula hulas and cabarets. Sound familiar?

Xenia gives her inaugural speech:

"How proud I am to have been elected the President of this wonderful charity. We have all known what it is to be poor and needy and a day may come when we may all know poverty again – therefore – I beg you all – together with me, put your shoulders to the wheel and give. Give, give all you can – Garrick Haven must be flourishing long after we are dust and ashes, long after our names are but echoes from a forgotten tune – it is only a small thing really – but for us of the Theatre it is a part of our life's blood."

This speech is obviously satirical but with, as ever with Noël, an underlying truth. *Star Chamber* was tried out for a single matinee (temporarily replacing the Victorian comedy *Family Album*) at the Phoenix Theatre on the 21st of March 1936. Gertrude Lawrence played Xenia and Noël the supporting role of committee member and comedy actor Johnny Bolton. It's been said that the play wasn't good enough or was too esoteric to use. I'd argue that Noël felt it, ultimately, too close to the bone. A mockery of flighty actors and actresses was a fairly safe bet, but a potential mockery of the fine work that they were actually now doing for the Actors' Orphanage seemed somehow cruel and unforgiving.

Then there's the safer premise of the unseen committee of actors that run *The Wings*, a retirement home for elderly actresses, in 1960's *Waiting in the Wings*. Safely retired from the Actors' Orphanage presidency by then, Noël seems to put his own philosophy down about handling committee meetings via Miss Archie, the manager of *The Wings*, as she says to a colleague:

"Listen, old girl – a committee's something you've got to stand up to, and, what's more, they're grateful to you for it in the long run. They don't know what they're talking about half the time anyhow. You know what actors and actresses are like on a committee? Always getting over enthusiastic over inessentials and going off at tangents."

In Past Conditional, Noël wrote: 'As president of the Actors' Orphanage I incurred much criticism for cutting them (meetings) down to a minimum' and how the meetings were 'baleful opportunities for these egos to puff themselves up and waste their own time and everybody else's', as well as 'Members present welcome a chance to show off, which their wives deny them at home.' At least the meetings gave him some material.

It's interesting that *Star Chamber*, written early in his

presidency, sees the humour and room for mockery in the meetings. It's also written shortly before Noël had any notion of the real and serious underlying issues at Langley, while *Waiting in the Wings*, written after his retirement, and more of a straight drama, has more of an honest appreciation of what those meetings were and needed. Noël of course knew actors inside out, and a strong director (or president) was certainly what was required, especially in light of what Noël had inherited from Sir Gerald: a committee almost completely ignorant of actual life at the orphanage.

The deep-rooted problems that existed took time, not only to resolve, but to *fully* come to light. A report is finally published in 1936, called: *Irregularities and Illegalities During the Secretarship of Mr A.J. Austin*. In the report, it's revealed that the elderly headmaster, Mr Austin, is often drunk, ignores all rules, greatly overuses corporal punishment and expects other staff members to do the same. On one occasion, he had tied a boy's wrists to his legs at night because he *thought* that he might be masturbating. In short, he was systematically persecuting many of the children and even firing staff members that did not share his passion for excessive corporal punishment. The report reads: 'Mr Austin is undoubtedly unbalanced, with a tendency to ego-mania.' Sadly, there had been seven years of complaints against him, but the pre-Coward committee were far less involved, less aware, and thus nothing had changed.

Patrick Anslow Austin had arrived at the orphanage during its second year of existence, 1907, at Croydon, aged forty-four. He was now seventy-three and not in the best of health. However, he was long used to figurehead presidents, such as Cyril Maude and to a greater extent, Sir Gerald du Maurier. They had allowed him absolute power, and he was decidedly *not* used to a president who asked questions, let alone one who was consistently showing up, making changes, asking to see paperwork and conversing with the children! He certainly hadn't expected Sir Gerald, twelve years his junior, to die first, either.

1934 and the early months of 1935 saw little information given to Noël, even though he had asked senior staff members for *the full picture of the place*. Perhaps they thought that with the change in presidency, life at the orphanage would automatically improve. It didn't. As 1935 progressed, staff members, particularly a Mr Mowforth, began, gradually, like a trickle *eventually* becoming a torrent, to tell the truth of what was really going on. Drunkeness, beatings, a culture of fear and no say or clue in how the orphanage was run outside of Austin's authority. By December 1935, it was established that Lorn (though not a celebrity but firmly on the committee) would speak for Noël during his long, periodic absences abroad, especially throughout his long Broadway runs. It was at this time too that it was decided that Mr Austin's position *must* be reviewed, that better and official account-keeping was needed and that the Board of Education should be allowed regular visits.

An emergency, yet informal, meeting was held at Noël's London home, 17 Gerald Road in Belgravia, in the January of 1936. In attendance with Noël and Lorn were Laurence Olivier, Lilian Braithwaite, Dame May Whitty, Ben Webster, Jill Esmond, Mr Marriott (Noël's lawyer) and André Charlot. Together they tried to unravel the problem of how best to deal with the issues at Langley, and they really did boil down to one person. Austin. Although he was good at collecting money and very keen on Langley Hall in regards to its cleanliness and scholastic efficiency, these would be the only good things that they could possibly say. There had been seven long years of complaints against the man, and it was perfectly possible, indeed likely, that his reign of terror had been going on long before that.

Austin, even if sincere in his own mind, was seemingly an extreme egotist, a petty tyrant, undoubtedly unbalanced and a bully strongly inclined to cruelty. Yet he was also a sentimental and enthusiastic personality, which worked to gain him some affection and loyalty from some of the children, particularly the older boys that he favoured, such as the prefects and old scholars. Such loyalty he could then manipulate. There had, however, undeniably been a systematic persecution of individual children over long periods. A boy might, for example, have a nervous twitch and Mr Austin would slap his face or even hit him with his stick, to try and beat it out of him. He had, also, an obsession with the so-called sin of self-abuse. Even caning younger boys over mere suspicion, and long before puberty would make this a realistic possibility. Hands had indeed been strapped to legs at night before another staff member intervened to put a stop to it. A boy or two had even been removed, living back with whatever relatives that they may have had.

Even the more conventional and legitimate (for the time) canings were incredibly frequent and always on bare skin, often leaving scars. If a staff member ever took a shine to any child in particular, Austin would then, allegedly, persecute that child. If a staff member ever challenged Austin, they would, allegedly, be dismissed. Indeed, Austin would fire good people and hire bad people, who worked *his way*. On another occasion, a Miss King had to stop him hitting a boy without any discernible provocation whatsoever, and somehow retained her job.

Austin had also given his good friend, the sports master, Bomber Howells, a significant pay rise, despite having an alleged drink problem. Austin himself was often drunk so perhaps encouraged Howells to join him, thus the loyalty between them. Indeed, Austin would, apparently slightly worse for wear, enter classrooms uninvited and disrupt all proceedings. And the old scholars were very loyal as they were allowed to come and wander around freely, anytime, and even sleep at Langley as suited them.

All of these allegations were discussed at Noël's house, the primary sources being the Langley staff. Laurence Olivier chipped in that he'd heard from Frank Lawton, while they were on a recent film set together, that, although *he* had been in Austin's good graces as a boy, Austin was a terrible sadist to other boys as far back as the 1910s. Apparently he would drink, beat a bare-bottomed boy with sometimes thirty strokes of the cane, and without provocation, and then cry. Noël already knew that Austin drank – it was obvious on meeting him for the first time in 1934 – but had no idea of the abuse and bullying.

It became starkly apparent that Mr Austin was something of a Mr Squeers, the brutish dictatorial head of Dotheboys Hall in Charles Dickens' *Nicholas Nickleby*. Serialised for a novel in 1838 and 1839, Dickens had purposefully sought to expose such institutions and masters. In Dotheboys Hall, unwanted children are taken in, starved and beaten. In his research, Dickens had discovered the real-life Bowes Academy in Yorkshire, where its master, a Mr Shaw, had been prosecuted in 1823 after one child went blind and another had died. Indeed, they died at an average of one a year.

Langley Hall wasn't *quite* as horrific as that, for this was twentieth-century London and some semblance of decency had to prevail... and yet...

In the preface to *Nicholas Nickleby*, Dickens wrote of the masters he had come across in Yorkshire:

> *Traders in the avarice, indifference, or imbecility of parents, and the helplessness of children; ignorant, sordid, brutal men, to whom few considerate persons would have entrusted the board and lodging of a horse or a dog; they*

formed the worthy cornerstone of a structure, which, for
absurdity and a magnificent high minded laissez-aller
neglect, has rarely been exceeded in the world.

Austin did care about scholastic achievement and money, but
he could certainly be called a brutal man. Years later, Hugo
Bergström, a child with the charity from 1935 to 1946, would
recall that Austin would walk around as if *looking* for a child to
beat.

It must be said that there were *also* complaints against the
teacher Mr Mowforth. Yet Mr Mowforth and Miss King were
the ones now most heartily welcoming any form of regular
inspection by the committee. Also at this time it transpired that,
shockingly, only half the children were from hard-up theatrical
backgrounds and the other half were merely paying boarders!
Of course the money rolled in! The boarders had no theatrical
connections whatsoever. There were twenty-nine orphans to
thirty-three boarders. Indeed, it seems that after 1927, Sir Gerald
took autocratic leadership of the committee. Paying boarders
were simply accepted and the institution was then referred to as
Langley Hall rather than the *Actors' Orphanage*. There were no
official documents and the committee had had no say or even
awareness of the change. They might attend the garden party
or annual cricket match, be in a play that donated a matinee's
earnings to the orphanage… but they never visited Langley, let
alone knew of any *paying* boarders. Indeed, visits may have been
actively discouraged.

Lilian Braithwaite, on the committee since 1911 and feeling
a little defensive and guilty as she sat sipping tea in Noël's studio,
revealed that she *had* sometimes asked to see papers and balance
sheets over the years but that Sir Gerald simply got vexed and
would tell everyone to leave everything to Austin. She said that
Gerald and Austin got on terribly well and there did seem to be

plenty of money, so from a business standpoint all seemed to be working extremely well.

There's a speech by Lotta in *Waiting in the Wings* that might sum up what Braithwaite was feeling in this moment. Lotta had been on the committee of *The Wings* retirement home for elderly actresses of limited means, long before she became a resident there herself. Miss Archie, not realising this, laments the inadequacy of past committees and Lotta replies:

> *"I remember at the time being horribly aware of my own inadequacy. I was often away on tour and obliged to miss several meetings in a row, then I'd come back and be asked to give my opinion on problems I knew nothing about. I wish now that I had taken a little more trouble. I'm sure we all tried to visualise it all from the point of view of the inmates themselves, but I'm not sure that we succeeded."*

Noël was rather miffed as fifteen months before he had heartily welcomed the presidency, but was only now discovering the horrible truths of the organisation that had landed upon his shoulders. He had had that first 'look-see' in 1934 and had asked the teacher then, Mr Mowforth, to tell him the full picture of the place... but only slowly had Mowforth become explicit. Now, finally, he seemed to be providing *never-ending* revelations.

It must have been a long and frustrating meeting at Noël's house, with at least a few of the persons present feeling some sense of genuine guilt. They would also struggle to try and figure out how to best move forward and fix the multifarious problems identified. They at the very least had to get back to replacing every paying boarder with a worthy case from a theatrical background... while also staying financially afloat, as well as figuring out how exactly to deal with Austin, who surprisingly still had some friends and supporters on the committee. They also had to try and figure out how good or bad Mowforth was, as well as how to wrestle back administration and control of the orphanage. Sir Gerald had left nothing behind but Austin and a dictatorship. And if Austin was a dictator then Sir Gerald had been a totally benign bystander.

Austin was seventy-three and in poor health, but they could hardly just wait for him to die, although some actually suggested this as a legitimate way forward. Noël must have wondered at what had been landed on him. Despite performing nine plays in repertory, eight shows a week of *Tonight at 8:30* at the Phoenix Theatre, his constant commitment to his writing, and an ever-hectic social life, Noël did not now ignore the pressing issues of the orphanage. Finally, so he thought, armed with all the facts and a lawyer, he would take action. Then another bombshell dropped. Noël had never been officially made president. There really was *no* paperwork whatsoever, just chaos. It wasn't a question of poor administration; it was a question of *no* administration.

Everyone *thought* that Noël was the president and *felt* him in their hearts to be the president and *saw* his name on the stationery as the president... but he wasn't. No one was. And it had been this way for some twenty-one months. From a legal point of view, nothing had been official for years. The boarders, since at least 1927 or '28, had paid thirty guineas a year, and some of these were just day pupils. Only Austin and possibly Gerald knew the details. There were no accounts or records but plenty of money. No wonder the name was changed, unofficially, from the Actors' Orphanage to Langley Hall. Austin must have thought a mere name change would magically make his changes perfectly acceptable.

Noël and Lorn must have exchanged a few glances of shock as this, now rather long, informal meeting progressed. No doubt the maid had refreshed the tea and refilled the biscuit tray. They pressed on and tried to establish what exactly had occurred between Sir Gerald's death and the present moment where Noël wasn't technically the president at all.

It seems that immediately after Sir Gerald's death, André Charlot *had* asked for a committee meeting at the Vaudeville Theatre on the Strand in an attempt to make sure all was above board, but only Austin and one old scholar called Stratton had shown up. André told Austin that he didn't want the meeting to go ahead and one week later another meeting was held, this time at André's office. This time, Cyril Maude, Lady Hardwicke and Leslie Henson were also in attendance, along with Austin and Stratton. Hardly a full committee meeting, and little was achieved, except that it was *said* that Noël Coward should be the new president.

It was obviously now up to Noël to succeed where André had failed and to fix the entire organisation. If Austin had banked on Noël being the traditional *laissez-faire* president, he was *quite* mistaken. One thing seemed likely; Austin was unlikely to go quietly. The orphanage had been his personal kingdom and entire life for the past twenty-seven years.

Past committees were somewhat accountable here, for complaints had been ignored for quite some time. Yet if the former president had been a mere figurehead, then they were only following suit. Indeed, Sir Henry Irving and Cyril Maude had also been figureheads. Austin had free rein and absolute power. By the 1930s, there were no meetings, no AGMs, no interviews, no records and no legality. We can be certain that all paperwork was either hidden, missing or, more likely, non-existent. There was a most incompetent, indeed pointless, secretary, a huge mishandling of money and with it, completely inadequate account keeping. Indeed, there had been a good deal of *out-of-court* business.

The orphanage's doctor, a Doctor Woods, obviously found it all such a headache, that he persisted with the notion that they should just wait for nature to take its course and for old Pat Austin to die. Noël, no doubt despairing at the human race, wasn't having any of it and instructed his lawyer, Mr Marriott, there and then to take action. Everything in the entire organisation *had* to be straightened out.

Mr Marriott took charge and would now conduct an official investigation. He would interview the entire staff, including Mr Austin, who was informed that he must be in a fit state of health for their meeting… as in sober.

*

A second meeting was to be held at Gerald Road, this time with Noël, Lorn and Mr Marriott taking tea with Mr Mowforth, Ms King and Doctor Woods. It ended up as an afternoon of Mr Mowforth going into graphic detail of life at Langley, and being backed up by Ms King. Most of the knowledge was now known but there were a few new details. In fact, there seemed to be no end to the revelations, and we can't be sure if they were all true or possible exaggerations. Mr Mowforth would have been fighting for his job and reputation, after the criticism that *he* had received.

It was, however, noted that Mr Howells had a dog-like devotion to Austin. How a qualified matron was removed and replaced by a Mrs Lane, someone far inferior but far less challenging to Austin. Illnesses were apparently ignored and brushed over. The boy, Roy Williams, had developed scarlet fever after being *forced* to perform in the pantomime. Austin was allegedly often prying into the drawers of other staff members and inducing such fear in some that he had only to look at them for them to scurry away like rabbits. Austin openly boasted of this power. The children were encouraged to believe that everything they had to be thankful for was because of Mr

Austin alone and that they must write letters to thank him. They were brainwashed to feel indebted to him for everything in their lives, which might partly explain why some of them thought that they should support and defend him now.

Events progressed quickly. A special meeting was called on the 22nd of February 1936 at the Vaudeville Theatre, for Noël to inform the entire executive committee of everything. Some opposed Noël chairing the meeting himself, so Ivor Novello chaired. It would seem some were feeling rather guilt-stricken and caught out over the recent allegations, proven illegalities and irregularities. They certainly didn't want any of the blame thrown their way. A degree of tension must have filled the air as the committee filed into the auditorium.

Pat Austin had excused himself from the proceedings due to ill health, no doubt to the relief of everybody. Prepare to run to the *Who's Who* now; Adrianne Allen, Jack Buchanan, Robert Douglas, Jill Esmond, Jean Forbes-Robertson, Nicholas Hannen, Lady Hardwicke, Leslie Henson, Jack Hulbert, Dorothy Hyson, Frank Lawton, Raymond Massey, Clifford Mollison, Owen Nares, Laurence Olivier, Stanley Stratton and Arthur Wontner all sat and listened as Noël stood on the stage and listed *every single issue* that had arisen at the orphanage and what exactly was going to be done about it.

He read out the full report on the irregularities from his lawyer, Mr Marriott. The many and various complaints against Austin were also read out, and the (fewer) complaints against Mr Mowforth too. The events of the emergency meeting at Noël's home on Gerald Road, the previous month, were spoken of. And that there had also been a second meeting there, this time with Mr Mowforth, Miss King, Mr Marriott and Dr Woods all present. Everything was now, finally, out in the open.

In conclusion, *everything* was summarised. It could be confidently and undeniably stated that Mr Austin was exercising supreme control over the orphanage through autocratic methods and a bullying style towards the children and staff. It could also be concluded that cruelty to some children had been committed through his overuse, often unprovoked, of corporal punishment. Paying boarders had been taken in for years, old scholars could return and roam free, no annual general meetings had been held for years, no financial reports existed, indeed, no paperwork at all. Money was simply withdrawn by Austin without the knowledge, let alone approval, of committee members. Then there was the issue of his ongoing and excessive drinking.

Noël had also recently had the local fire chief inspect the premises, and his report back stated that despite everything Mr Austin had said for years, some of Langley was a definite death trap. The top floor of the dormitory had one exit with no door, barred windows and wooden walls and a wooden staircase. The Slough Fire Brigade strongly recommended an external fire exit, more extinguishers, regular fire drills and, in the main doorway, an asbestos curtain. All of which was immediately fitted.

Noël concluded his statement on that cold, wet afternoon in February at the Vaudeville Theatre on the Strand, knowing that the executive committee had *surely*, by now, to agree with his proposed changes and with the 'resignation' of Austin. Yes he was ill anyway, but that in no way meant, as Dr Woods and some others hoped, that he would die any time soon. Despite these firm conclusions, some members of the committee *still* tried to defend Austin, which is quite baffling. Was it their feeling of guilt by association perhaps? The guilt of these events having occurred on 'their watch'? The fact that they had stood by for years, smiling at the fundraisers, oblivious to a reign of terror? As for Mr Austin, he was now accusing Noël of slander but could hardly defend himself in any seriousness.

Noël was only *now* officially made president and signed a five-year contract, which gives great insight into his dedication.

Despite the horrendous mismanagement, defensive committee members, and despite his highly demanding career, Noël was on board and in charge.

So it was that in 1936 the charitable purpose of the organisation was reinitialised and the fee-paying boarders that had started attending (it turned out, as far back as 1919!) were no longer accepted. Only the most destitute children of the theatrical profession would be. Old scholars would now need written permission if they wanted to visit. Official paperwork was once again headed, *The Actors' Orphanage, Langley Hall*, as opposed to, *Langley Hall (The Actors' Orphanage)*. The new head office of the fund was now based at 8 Adam Street in the West End. Also, a new trust fund was set up at Lloyd's Bank and a new secretary would document *everything*. New rules and regulations would also be drawn up by the legal team... and Mr Austin's resignation would be accepted.

Also, at least one committee member would *have to* visit the orphanage *every single month*. The committee would now be fully expected to have more of an actual presence. To commit, as it were, to their duties. Noël had stirred the members of the committee into taking an active interest in what was, after all, their principal charity. Anyone still supporting Austin was in the minority and out on a limb rather. It's quite possible that Austin had dirt on some members and was blackmailing them. It certainly wouldn't be out of character.

Noël continued to visit Langley when he could, and when he couldn't, Lorn would be there, speaking with the children, and asking them about everything from school to family to what they wanted to do when they grew up. The children loved Mrs Loraine, the posh-sounding lady with the kind face and immaculate dresses. *All* of her findings were reported straight back to Noël; she was always the ultimate *conduit*.

Mr Mowforth continued to cling to his position, the Austin issue now almost an obsession. When Mowforth had arrived at Langley in 1929, Austin's own sister was leaving and, allegedly, warned Mowforth of her brother. Austin himself, allegedly, told Mowforth to "prepare for a short existence here." Apparently the old scholars of Frank Lawton and his two brothers were always around too, to do Austin's bidding and run things, which created tension and negativity among the children. The Lawton brothers, however, would have been in their twenties by then, and Frank on the verge of his film career… but whatever the truth, there was undoubtedly a most toxic atmosphere.

Now the air had apparently been cleared. Mr Austin was leaving. And whatever the Langley Hall staff thought of the committee in the past (as a joke and an unaccountable and thoroughly redundant group of actors, utterly oblivious to life at Langley, one assumes), they had to now realise that the committee were to be active in the life of the orphanage.

It was March 1936 when Mr Mowforth was officially made the new head but Mr Austin, however, was not done yet. He invited seven of the older boys into his room, two of them old scholars, still walking in and out of Langley as they pleased. They were persuaded to write long, quite sophisticated letters to Noël, saying how awful Mr Mowforth was and how *wonderful* Mr Austin was. These long letters are too specific to be composed without serious input from Mr Austin himself. *All* the things Austin is accused of are apparently actually committed by Mowforth. He is the one who thrashes them with the cane and creates the culture of fear.

The boys who wrote on Austin's behalf shouldn't be judged too harshly. We should never forget that none of them had had an easy go of it. One of these boys' fathers, for example, was seriously wounded from the War and suffered shell shock, while his mother had committed suicide by poisoning. They had both been in the theatre in younger, happier days. Many of the parents' tales were truly tragic. One father had even died on stage, mid-performance.

One can only imagine the tension as Austin was packing up, after twenty-nine years of living at, working at and running the orphanage as a dictatorship. 1936 was not only the year that Edward VIII abdicated the throne of the British Empire, but it was also the year that Anslow J. Austin lost his kingdom too. To make it all the more bitter, his archenemy, Mowforth, was taking charge. Austin was seventy-three, in ill health and out on his ear. Allegedly, Mr Austin, upon finally leaving the premises, blocked Mr Mowforth in a corridor, proclaimed that several boys had written letters to Noël Coward, and that he too would be gone and in a matter of days.

Two days after Austin left the premises for good, Mr Mowforth's classroom was trashed, with his maps ripped from the walls and scattered all over the floor. Concerned too about the alleged letters that had been sent to Noël, Mowforth and Miss King sent their *curriculum vitaes* to Lorn, as if to prove that they were *nothing* like Austin and that the committee must understand that. It was a disastrous and messy culture that Austin had created.

Noël did indeed receive the letters, but he and the committee easily saw through Austin's games. Noël and Lorn drove out to Langley in the Rolls-Royce and spoke directly to the boys about appropriate behaviour, without mentioning specifically the trashing of the classroom, the letters, or anything else. The supposed writers were demoted from being prefects for six months and the two old boys were forbidden from visiting anymore. Writing letters and trashing a classroom were sad signs of Austin's manipulative skills, showing that he could get the boys to do his bidding, despite his long history of abusive behaviour and, even, his imminent departure. Letters of sincere apology and regret were soon arriving on Lorn's desk at Gerald Road.

On the 17th of June 1936, Noël receives a letter from the solicitors Amery-Parkes & Co. He is told that he had been courageous to take on the issues at hand. That he must have the satisfaction of knowing that he had put an end to an extremely autocratic system of management, detrimental to the charity and the children. He's then offered a £30 (approximately £2,000 today) discount on the rather pricey £255 (£16,500) fee, because it was 'a charity matter'. Solicitors!

Dear reader, Noël Coward really did turn the orphanage around.

*

It was a fresh start. The children's entire schedule was now given an overhaul. The Debating Society, Nature Study (gardening) and Physical Fitness before lessons were all added to the schedule, along with a regular fire drill. Boy and Girl Scout groups were set up. Most wonderfully, the Bijou pantomime was to perform three matinees at the Gaiety Theatre in the West End! There would also be a complete suspension of the prefect system for now as the terror it had invoked under Austin had totally coloured the system. There was also a greater control of the gates, so that the children could no longer come and go as they pleased. Despite that being to the chagrin of some, the overall result was that the children were, by all accounts, much more relaxed, had more to look forward to, and were thus far happier.

By June of 1937, *The Stage* newspaper had published the transcript of the orphanage AGM, held on the stage of the Wyndham's Theatre. It's a fascinating insight; there are formalities and pleasantries and everyone's pleased that the Duke and Duchess of Kent will attend the garden party as usual. The previous event had raised £1,500 more than usual. Clemence Dane read the minutes from the previous AGM on the 28th of September, Sybil Thorndike is elected a vice president and H.M. Tennent are thanked for the use of the theatre. We also discover that the committee are now looking for a new home for the orphanage, suggesting that Langley was somewhat cramped and ill adapted. Also, somewhere more rural would be ideal. The *Robinson Crusoe* matinees at the Gaiety Theatre were wonderful. Thanks are given to Ivor Novello for inviting the children to see *Careless Rapture* at Drury Lane and *Over She Goes* at the Saville Theatre for charity matinees. The Lady Mayoress of London is also thanked for having had all the children to tea at Mansion House.

Despite all of this information, *The Stage* reported that it was a quick, formal meeting, perhaps most importantly concluding that: 'Everything possible has been done to make the children happy and to see to their health.' The income and accounts were in very good order and more money was being spent on staff salaries, food and accommodation. From the transcripts we glean Noël's authority and effect on the proceedings. At one point, in a way that only Noël could get away with, he proposes and, as president, seconds a vote to thank himself for chairing the meeting.

That August, Mr Mowforth resigned, claiming that it was for his own happiness. Perhaps there was too much baggage. And it's true too that he rubbed up the wrong way with new staff members, such as the secretary Peter Jackson. A Reverend Ruegg, 'Old Ruggles', now replaced 'Moggy' Mowforth as headmaster, creating a clean slate for all.

It had taken a good two to three years to fully rectify and improve the orphanage but it had been done. To be fair to Noël, he was juggling this heavy responsibility of reordering a corrupt and abusive administration with a career as hectic as it ever was. 1934 to 1937 had seen Noël star in long London and New York runs of *Tonight at 8:30*; write the play *Point Valaine*; write his best-selling autobiography, *Present Indicative*; set up a new management company, to be run by his partner, Jack, called John C Wilson Management; and star in an American movie called *The Scoundrel*. The film incidentally would be a modest hit in its time but Noël refused the five-year Hollywood studio contracts on offer, always maintaining that he preferred a cup of cocoa to Hollywood. Or:

"I'd rather play a bad matinee in Hull than act in a movie… as a matter of fact, I've never played a good matinee in Hull." In truth, Noël knew in his heart that he was a *man of the theatre*. It's what made him and what he considered home.

How he found the time and will during this hectic period to confront the committee, visit the orphanage several times, hold urgent meetings at his house, conduct interviews, confer with lawyers and affect radical change at the orphanage is a true testament to the man and, not least, to his sheer energy. Noël would, however, succumb to a second nervous breakdown in 1937 (the first having been in 1926). His work schedule was once again becoming too intense. Also, his father, Arthur, had recently died *and* Jack had become suddenly engaged and quickly married to a Russian princess, Natasha Paley, thus ending his romantic relationship with Noël, after eleven years, once and for all.

*

Children at the orphanage during this time, such as Granville Bantock, Roy Williams, Hugo Bergström, Dan Taylor and Yettey Taylor all confirmed that life very much improved. Hugo would recall, "I am sure that the Actors' Orphanage became as good as, if not better than, any other orphanage in the land."

One almost sees Noël as the naval officer, Captain Kinross, from *In Which We Serve*, as he took control of the Actors' Orphanage and instigated all the improvements. Handling the committee, addressing the naughty boys about discipline, listening to concerns, replacing staff members... all with the aim to make, if you will, 'a happy and efficient ship'. By the end of Noël's first few years, only Mr Howells (now mellowed and working hard to redeem himself from his association with Austin), the beloved matron, Matey Irving, and her dog Paddy had survived. Matron was, up until Noël's time, the only staff member that you could really call popular, despite her prescribing the powerful laxatives Senna Pods for every possible and conceivable ailment that a child ever had.

1937 had indeed seen the children venture to Mansion House for tea with the Lord and Lady Mayor of London, organised by Noël. The Lord Mayor also then visited Langley for a prize-giving ceremony. Reported in the local press in an article titled *Lord Mayor and Stage Stars at Langley*, in attendance were the new stalwarts of the committee, Joyce Carey and Lorn Loraine, along with Lilian Braithwaite, Ivor Novello, Adrianne Allen, Jill Esmond and Leslie Henson. The mayor of Windsor also popped by. It was, by all accounts, more like a party than a formal prize-giving day. Noël, the Lord Mayor and Reverend Ruegg all sat at a table on a raised platform in the Assembly Hall and welcomed children up to receive their certificates. The prizes might be for being head boy (Paul Bantock), or head girl (Yettey Rolyat), or for music, gardening, drawing, historical knowledge, dancing or needlework. There was also something called 'The Vicar's Prize', for religious devotion, one assumes.

Next came a series of speeches, starting with Noël, who

thanked the Lord Mayor for having entertained the children *and* the staff *and* committee members with tea at Mansion House. Noël acknowledged that there had been one big change at Langley, the arrival of Reverend Ruegg as headmaster, and listed recent success stories: the formation of Boy and Girl Scout groups, the absolute triumph of the Gaiety Theatre matinees, the cricket match attended by Frank Lawton and Evelyn Laye, the garden party attended by the Duke and Duchess of Kent and the stand at the Ideal Home Exhibition in Olympia.

"Every day for four weeks there was a personal attendee of a theatrical star at the stand," and: "In conclusion, I want to thank very sincerely the committee, who have worked so splendidly with me, and some of whom have been associated with me in this work for the past two years and whose loyal co-operation and untiring efforts I can never forget. The greatest reward will be continued happiness and assured future of the children of Langley Hall."

Next the comedian Leslie Henson, pivotal in acquiring the Gaiety Theatre, said a few words:

"The combination of the Lord Mayor and Noël Coward is quite overwhelming for me." He also informed all that Mr Coward would, in the future, "look after you children," and "I have to rush away, I'm meeting a real-life princess, that's why I'm dressed more beautifully than ever." After asking for a loud cheer for the Lord Mayor, he did indeed rush away, but to a second loud cheer, this time for him.

The afternoon seems to have gone on a bit, as next the soon-to-retire Lord Mayor spoke:

"Get as much general knowledge as you can; keep yourself well informed on current topics and be interested in everything that is going on; if you have any aptitude for any particular branch of knowledge go all out to make yourself expert in it," and, "Cultivate a pleasant personality and learn to be good mixers with other people; in this world as it is today you will find your best asset is initiative, you must not be content with a back seat."

He then thanked everyone present for, "This happy home", and promised to attend the next pantomime. Then Ivor Novello had a turn and thanked the Lord Mayor. Then Lilian Braithwaite stood up and thanked Noël, who, even though he had been in America for many months, kept in constant touch with the committee. Dr Woods decided to chip in: "He has your welfare so much at heart."

Noël, who had already made his speech, felt compelled to get up again:

"It is true that I have the interest of the orphanage at heart, it is not true that it is any trouble whatsoever." Noël reassured everyone that he was back in England for several months now and that they would see a lot more of him.

Next came a series of songs performed by the children and, for those that had lasted the course, tea with the staff.

*

Life was better all around and summertime would see those children with willing and capable parents or parent (or guardian) possibly spend a full seven weeks at home with family. The others would stay at Langley but spend more time playing in the lush meadows by the canal. Paul and Granville spent summers with their mother in Kew Gardens and whiled away summer days in Richmond Deer Park. Of course, when September came and they had to leave their mother all over again, the tears would flow.

Summers also saw professional cricketer George Hurst coach the children and prepare a team for the annual charity cricket match against this year's group of actors from the committee, captained as always by Frank Lawton. Lawton's wife, the actress Evelyn Laye, often played hostess in the marquee, where she would organise the tea. Granville had a crush on her for many years, although one year she was stuck in Birmingham with a sore throat and so Granville had to make do with Sir Cedric Hardwicke's wife, Helena Pickard, aka Lady Hardwicke, as she took up the hosting and tea arrangements.

The match would take place on a Sunday, often in good weather and with any number of stars playing, such as Rex Harrison, Hugh Williams, Roger Livesey and Guy Middleton. Spectators might include Beatrice Lillie, Lilian Braithwaite, Jill Esmond, Italia Conti and Antoinette Collier. Noël would always be on hand to oversee things, though never wearing cricket whites himself and certainly not playing. *The Actors* versed *Langley Hall*, and a good quality match was always had. Even the time when professional cricketer I.A.R. Peebles joined the actors' team, they only won by 108 to 106.

Often local press attended and the *Windsor, Slough & Eton Express* of June 1938 reported an *Exciting End to Annual Match at Langley.* Autograph hunters got what they wanted, the food was better for the children that day and a little money was made. It was indeed a happy and glorious day.

The Theatrical Garden Party was more illustrious than ever too, drawing bigger crowds, back to the original location of Regent's Park, than ever before. This was an era when stars, to many people, seemed to be from another planet, untouchable and mythical. So a chance to see them at close quarters was extraordinary. Noël had said during his interview with the *Times of Ceylon* in 1935, "You can imagine what a tremendous success these parties are."

In 1935, the party had taken place at Queen Mary Gardens, Regent's Park, and Noël, now in a position to do whatever he wanted, set himself up on a small stage in a tent and sang some of his songs. There was an admission fee, accompanying pianist and a sign outside that said simply: 'Noël Coward, An Informal Concert.' It was to be this event that was the beginning of his long road to cabaret success. But more of these occasions later, except to say that in 1937, Paul Bantock, head boy, always popular and a highly capable child of the orphanage, was asked to be Noël's runner for the day, fetching him anything he needed and sticking close by as Noël charmed the crowds, fellow actors and escorted the Duke and Duchess of Kent around the grounds. What rich childhood memories these must have made for.

As for Christmases, better food was negotiated and donated, such as cake, cream, sweets and more fruit. Noël would send each child an envelope containing five shillings (a lot of money to a child in the '30s, equalling approximately £15 today). The children all stayed at the orphanage for Christmas Day, as some had no parents or relatives to take them and they wanted to keep the orphanage *family* together. Pillow fights were allowed on Christmas morning and presents were provided for those that didn't have any, such as a clockwork tank or a rubber ball. Hugo Bergström had been desperate for some toy soldiers one year and when they arrived he burst into tears of joy.

The gymnasium was transformed as usual into the Bijou Theatre and a pantomime (such as *Dick Whittington, Robinson Crusoe* or *Cinderella*) was staged with all the children involved. The new orphanage secretary and former West End professional Peter Jackson produced and directed, giving the productions quite a sheen of professionalism. And fantastically they twice performed (*Robinson Crusoe* in 1937 and *Cinderella* in 1938) three matinees at the Gaiety Theatre on the Strand in the West End. Things really had changed. The Actors' Orphanage was less like a traditional, slightly Dickensian orphanage and more like the unique institution that it was supposed to be.

The Bijou pantomimes had more success than ever in those last years at Langley, even before Peter Jackson got a hold of them. On the 10th of January 1936, the *Windsor Observer* gave a rather glowing review. *Cinderella* had: 'Charming performances' with 'pretty scenes and hilarious fun'. Also: 'To describe all the fun, all the charm, and all the gay music and dainty dancing which is packed into the show would take a page.'

In 1935, *Dick Whittington* had had to close early due to an outbreak of winter illnesses but not this year. *Cinderella* had been 'presented by Anslow J. Austin' (playing out his last weeks), and the Bijou was called 'a perfect miniature of a West End Theatre'. The show included two ballet sequences, *The Snowman* and *The Bric-a-Brac Ballet* arranged by a Miss Phoebe Chaplin. The running time was *three hours* but the journalist assured the readers that this was nothing to fear as there were plenty of buses back to Slough and Windsor.

The cast included Paul Bantock, Yettey Rolyat and a most praised Duncan Rider as Buttons. He was called 'outstanding' and 'something special', noted for his comic timing and a real star as the lovelorn Buttons. 1936 to 1937 would see him, now sixteen, return as Dame Crusoe in *Robinson Crusoe*. A real stalwart, Duncan would go on, thirteen years later, to manage the orphanage's short-lived hostel at 27 Rutland Gate, Knightsbridge.

The 1937-1938 revival of *Cinderella* was, if anything, more raved about. Called 'Lavish Panto' by the *Windsor Observer*, the reviewer writes:

> "*After all, they are amateurs, and you can't expect a West End standard.*" *It is in this tolerant frame of mind that one naturally approaches amateur theatrical performances. But there are exceptions – and probably the annual Christmas pantomime staged by the children of Langley*

Actors' Orphanage may be held as one of the great exceptions which prove the rule. Those who are regular members of their audiences know this very well. They do not go to the Bijou Theatre in any kindly but slightly patronising spirit, but because they know full well that you are in for a night's real entertainment of a standard genuinely nearing the professional.

Although:

Young Duncan Rider has left the orphanage to start a stage career. It will be recalled that he was the outstanding personality last year, and more or less carried much of the show on his youthful shoulders. Cinderella has no outstanding personality like Rider.

Yet the head boy and ever-popular Paul Bantock was Baron Hardup, and Dan Rolyat played an Ugly Sister. Eleven-year-old June Bevis played Cinders and was called an excellent singer and dancer but apparently was 'a bit nonchalant' when the Fairy Godmother worked her magic and turned the pumpkin into a carriage. Indeed, this was the *pièce de résistance* of the whole production! A great puff of smoke appeared and turned one of the six-year-olds, dressed as the pumpkin, into the magnificent gold and glittering carriage. Margaret Gillespie, by the way, was 'adequate' as the Fairy Godmother. The reviewer seems slightly harsh considering the entire cast was comprised of six to sixteen-year-old non-actors.

They are also amazed that the costumes and sets were designed and made in the orphanage, when it had been suspected that they were professionally provided. The miniature stage too is 'confined' but makes the overall experience all the more brilliant. All of this ultimately pointed to the sheer quality of the production. The audiences lapped up the horseplay, interaction, sing-alongs, ballet sequences and love duets.

It's also noted that the matinees at the Gaiety Theatre in the West End would run on January 10th, 11th and 12th. These matinees must have been extraordinarily exciting. No doubt highly nerve-racking for some too, but they were all in it together. It's just a shame it only lasted two seasons. All the children without speaking parts would be fitted into the shows somehow, playing 'the little folk' or crowd scenes. Hugo played an elf. And Granville played one of many 'sailor boys' in the previous year's *Robinson Crusoe*.

Two large coaches drove the children into the West End, and the Gaiety must have buzzed with excitement as Peter Jackson oversaw the 'get in' of the set, costumes and props, the children no doubt exploring the dressing rooms, with butterflies in more than a few stomachs. As for the performance itself, a West End stage must have seemed vast… especially to a six-year-old, and utterly thrilling. The Gaiety Theatre sadly closed in 1939, when the elderly building was condemned. The shell of it still exists on the Strand today… but inside? Offices.

The pantomime, along with the Annual Actors' Cricket Match, the Theatrical Garden Party and coach trips to West End shows, was one of the absolute highlights of the year for the children, as well as a favourite event in the Christmas calendar for the local communities. It was the only real loss that the Actors' Orphanage suffered when they finally found that better, bigger and more rural property when they moved a few miles south to Chertsey in 1938.

*

Langley Hall, the former home of Sir Richard Hubert, former school of John Nash and now, former home of the Actors'

Orphanage, was to be used as a group headquarters for RAF Bomber Command throughout the War. Then it became the Roads Research Laboratory from 1945 to 1960, where modern road safety was developed. There would be a period of dereliction in the 1970s and '80s, including a fire. In 1988, the building became a sixth form college, forming part of East Berkshire College in 1992, and since 2011, it has been the Langley Hall Primary Academy for four to eleven-year-olds. Children's voices are once again filling the rooms, a century on from the arrival of the Actors' Orphanage. Some original wall dating back to 1665 still exists and now a plaque reads:

The Actors' Orphanage 1915-1938

THREE

Silverlands

1938-1940

This blessed land, this earth, this realm, this England.
　　　　　　　　　- Richard II, by William Shakespeare, 1597

Twenty-eight miles south of Langley, and eighteen miles south-west of central London, was the much grander property of Silverlands, in Chertsey, Surrey. This move was part of a continued effort to improve the lives of the children and make the orphanage a very special place. Langley had long been insufficient; there were only four large bedrooms for all of the children, so privacy was non-existent. There was also only one bathroom for thirty girls and one bathroom for thirty boys. The hot water was severely limited, making hot or even just warm baths difficult. They were close to a main road (although it was mainly used by horses and carriages, and only the occasional motor car). The grounds were not vast and, perhaps too, it was deemed preferable to escape the ghosts of the past.

The two coaches of children drove out of Langley and passed through Windsor and Egham. They would have seen their new town of Chertsey before heading just south and driving along the Holloway Road. On the left was a hospital and further along on the right were large iron gates. Fear, excitement and expectation filled young hearts.

They entered through the gates and drove up the long, winding, quarter-mile drive towards the house itself. There was an ancient cottage on the right, to be a home to the gardener and his wife. There were vast fields and greenery all around. In the distance, there was a hut that would be used for the Boy Scouts. Further still were the dense woodlands, where many a game of *Cowboys and Indians* were soon to be played out.

Then they came to the house itself and... it was a mansion. Amidst the rural setting it was a spellbinding vision of splendour. No doubt to the staff as well. At the very far side of the property you could see the old horse stables, soon to home two ponies. In the summer preparation, a football pitch had been constructed, as well as a cricket pitch. Bicycles had been purchased and many provisions made for this glorious new home. The loss of the Bijou Theatre was a small price to pay for this wonderful mansion amidst the English countryside.

The children, including Dan Taylor and his sister Yettey, hadn't known what to expect, and Dan was even a little miffed that they had had to leave their home at Langley at all. The second that they saw the house, however, amidst thirty-six acres of fields and woodland, any doubters quickly changed their tune. The only emotions were joy and excitement. The children couldn't believe their luck as they stepped off the coaches and ascended the six steps to the front door and entered the grand hall.

The building itself was Neo-Georgian in design with beautiful wood-panelled walls, parquet floors, a large chandelier and columns dating back to 1845. There were twenty-seven rooms, with high ceilings and tall sash windows. Off the grand hall, to the left, was the huge ballroom. This was now to be their assembly room. It had Rococo mouldings, a grand piano and much retained grandeur. It led through to the dining room and then to a morning room at the back of the property (which would home the wireless) and to a loggia leading to the rear grounds. The right side of the ground floor consisted of a library, a large 'rec room' (already full of games and puzzles), and with a huge skylight. Then there was the warmest room in the property: the headmaster's office. There was also a pantry with a service lift to the kitchens below.

The cellars were vast. A few of the children were worried about ghosts until someone said, "Why would a ghost want to hang around sixty-something screaming kids?" There was an extension on the right side of the building which saw several rooms, that would be used as classrooms, surround a central courtyard. In one corner, stone steps led up to an open-air lookout area. This some of the boys quickly colonised as *their* space.

The first floor had been divided into a boys' and girls' wing, with Matron living on the girls' wing and the housemaster on the boys' wing. The smaller second floor housed the rest of the staff and the headmaster's suites. The entire property was full of hiding places and secret passageways, wondrous to a child. There was no trauma in the move from Langley to Silverlands, and much pleasure.

Silverlands had been an estate since 1420 and the current building dated from 1814. A country house built by local brewer Robert Porter, that in around 1820 became the home of Vice-Admiral Sir Henry Hotham. Hotham had commanded the naval blockade of 1812 against Napoleon and also accompanied the fleet that took Napoleon to his exile in St Helena in 1815. He would live until 1833 and rarely be at Silverlands as he was the Commander-in-Chief of the British in the Mediterranean.

He left the estate to a distant relative, the splendidly named F.A. Hanky, who died in 1892. Now Philip Waterlow of the printing firm Waterlow and Sons purchased the property. Waterlow soon became a baronet and was living the high life indeed.

Then between 1907 and 1919 the Liberal politician and industrialist Sir John Brunner resided in and extended the house, adding the wood-panelled grand hall and library. Next the estate was in the hands of the High Sheriff of Surrey, Dermot Berdoe Wilkinson, who, after a break-in and the theft of his wife's jewellery (and much publicity), had decided to sell. They also left behind a mysterious gravestone in the grounds, saying simply, *The Old Man, 1929.* A pet, one would assume... and hope.

A Silverlands brochure was drawn up and used to encourage subscribers at charity fundraisers. In it, it is quite clear who was eligible for admittance to this much improved new wonderland:

> *By destitute children is meant: (a) a fatherless and motherless child. (b) a child of whom one parent is dead or incapacitated, the other living but unable to support it. (c) a child whose father is permanently and entirely unable by reason of mental or physical affliction to contribute to the support of the child, the mother living but unable to support it.*

This gives insight into what pre-welfare state England was like. The brochure continues that a child will be 'educated, clothed, housed and fed under expert supervision and care'. The headmaster oversees the teaching staff, and his wife oversees the domestic staff. Another insight into the times.

Noël soon made his first visit to Silverlands, bringing with him Mary Pickford, who donated the gift of a cine-camera to the orphanage. Noël, as usual, played the piano and handed out chocolate. Committee members were always encouraged to visit, and many of the twenty members certainly did, at least once a month, in accordance with the new regulations. Mainly by now the committee consisted of close friends of Noël's, and thus were people that he trusted implicitly. Indeed, he'd worked with many in the theatre, such as Lilian Braithwaite (*The Vortex*), her daughter, Joyce Carey (*Easy Virtue, Tonight at 8:30*, and many other productions), and Jill Esmond (*Private Lives* on Broadway). Clemence Dane was also a great support (the inspiration for Madame Arcati in *Blithe Spirit*). Close confidantes, one and all. The secretary, Peter Jackson, was to stay very involved too, but the many *vice presidents* were just, it must be said, figureheads rather. People such as Laurence Olivier and Cyril Maude did not visit, although Dame May Whitty was to become increasingly involved during the approaching crisis of the War.

Committee visits aside, Noël also introduced new uniforms, arranged trips for the children to see more West End shows, and to meet the new Lord Mayor. The sense too was that Silverlands was an obviously more enchanting and relaxed home than Langley had ever been, with more freedom to roam. Surrounded by fields and woodland, it was more secluded and far safer. And the older children could acquire permission to walk the one-mile to town on a Saturday afternoon and watch a film at the Chertsey Picture House.

Of course, all the regular rules were still in place and rigidly followed according to the proclamations of the new headmaster, Reverend Brian Ruegg. Bed-making, chores, tending the vegetable garden, washing-up duty, lights out, and so forth. Now, though, there was always a genuine sense that the institution and the committee were something to genuinely feel lucky about, fortunate for and appreciative of, although this would always be coupled, for many, with an understandable sense of abandonment and sadness. No matter what the improvements were, they were still children without parents.

A good many photographs were taken of these early days at Silverlands in 1938 and 1939. Many capture the children and staff in unguarded, informal and unposed moments, and what is notable is how happy and relaxed everyone looks. Dozens of photographs show everything from young girls playing cards by the fire, children gardening, cooking, drawing, performing gymnastics, riding and grooming the ponies, playing with rabbits and tortoises, scampering about in the large outdoor spaces, riding bicycles and even roller-skating in the central courtyard. You get a sense of the sheer fun that they had, all living and playing together, like a family of sixty siblings. One almost thinks of the lost boys in *Peter Pan*.

Noël is in several photographs too, possibly on his first visit to the children after the move. He is chatting to the Reverend in his wood-panelled office, and looking at what the children are studying in the classrooms, with his burning cigarette in hand at all times, the ash threatening to set alight a small child at any moment. There's also the obligatory photo of him playing the piano for the children. He would always joke that he inflicted his singing and playing on people, but the fact is that it was exciting and good fun for them to see their famous president perform.

Noël seems relaxed and happy too. One wonders if some of this came from the younger children having little idea of his achievements. Free of fame's odd affects, for he was still the most successful man working on the English stage, he may have felt pleasantly free of the expectation to *be* 'Noël Coward'. With the children more interested in games than the theatre, he could simply be the benevolent president. It must have been very refreshing.

*

It wasn't always to be complete sweetness and light from now on, of course. Sixty plus children with abandonment issues would always need due care and attention. The truth too was that the committee would always struggle to know exactly what was going on within Silverlands' walls, and there was always bound to be some issue or another. Unfortunately, the first major one was once again with a staff member.

By the March of 1939, Reverend Ruegg was being accused of kissing the older girls. He'd received anonymous threatening letters from, apparently, some of the children, the implication being that he is being watched, that telling the committee won't help him, and that it's no good hiding under the cloak of religion. He'll also get a few punches instead of kisses and meet his 'Waterloo' very soon. It's also suggested that Noël Coward won't have a chance to kick him out as he'll be knocked out.

Such issues are always delicate and guilt and innocence hard to weigh. This was less clear-cut than the previous issues with Austin. Reverend Ruegg took the matter in hand and read out all of the letters to the older form, at which they burst out laughing and offered to help him find those responsible. They found that one of the boys had told his mother that the Reverend kissed all of the girls goodnight, while his wife kissed all of the boys goodnight. The boy's mother found the idea of the Reverend kissing the seventeen and eighteen-year-old girls goodnight extremely dodgy. She then had a few letters forged and wrote her own, signed, letter to Noël, her son, evidently, having no idea that she was doing any of this at all.

Reverend Ruegg was hired due to his implicitly trustworthy and pious nature but, despite the mother's rather underhand behaviour, kissing *all* of the girls goodnight was, at best, naïve and surely somewhat exhausting. Ultimately, it seemed somewhat inappropriate. The Reverend pleaded his innocence and accused the mother of having a drink problem. He then addressed the older children again and suggested that they must now put this matter behind them and not let it ruin their 'family'.

He also asks Noël to remember all he has done in assisting with the improvements of life at the orphanage, adding, rather puritanically, how he had put a stop to all of the *self-abuse* going on with the boys at Langley. Noël may have rolled his eyes and thought that a little excessive, but let it go and simply asked that the Reverend and his wife not kiss the older children goodnight. Also, that if he does go into a female room, he must have another female staff member present and keep the door propped open, for his own protection as much as anybody else's. Reverend Ruegg felt rather put out by all this, but promised that he would *phase out* the kissing, but that it would be difficult. By the December, the Reverend and his wife were gone. He was replaced as headmaster by a Mr Green.

Staff issues, people management, guilt and innocence, egos and sensitive feelings went with the territory. After all, the staff lived at the orphanage twenty-four seven and within a bubble ripe for drama. Periods of smooth running would inevitably run into temporary times of difficulty. Temporary because the committee would never now turn a blind eye.

*

In the May of 1939, Noël had noted in a letter to the New York critic Alexander Woollcott that:

We are going mad at the moment over the Actors' Orphanage because our Theatrical Garden Party is next week and I am spending every night of this week rushing madly through all the West End theatres making impassioned appeals. I am looking astonishingly pretty

*considering everything. You would be the first to admit
this, however bitterly.*

The impassioned appeals were to stars in their dressing rooms to
attend the upcoming Theatrical Garden Party and to contribute
by giving a turn and hosting an event or stall.

Let's take a closer look at the Theatrical Garden Party of the
6th of June 1939. It was to be held at the Ranelagh Club, Barn
Elms Park, Barnes, in South West London. The public gathered
at the gates in droves, many of whom had no intention of going
in but simply wanted to see the stars arriving. At 3pm, the Duke
and Duchess of Kent declared the garden party open and the
fun was to continue well into the evening. Fair games, dances,
gymnastic displays by the children, fashion parades, make-up
tents and auctions were set up to entertain the vaster-than-ever
crowds and encourage the donations. Stars had also put their
names to various recipes in a book called *Our Favourite Dishes*,
many of them never having cooked in their lives… but it sold
rather well. All this was in an effort to make enough money to
keep the orphanage going for another year.

Noël, immaculate in the cut-away coat of his morning suit,
top hat and chamois gloves, walked around, escorted various
stars to various tents, attended to the Duke and Duchess of Kent,
and then signed countless autographs for cash. The orphanage's
head boy, Paul Bantock, stuck close by as Noël's assistant and
runner for the day. As host, Noël was a sensation wherever
he walked, through the mass of jostling crowds. He judged a
fashion parade of Molyneux, Paquin and Schiaparelli dresses
and headed an auction of ladies' hats and underwear. "How
much for these knickers?"

If we were to walk through the grounds in Barnes during
that summer day of 1939, we would see, immediately on our
right, the *All-Sorts-of-Dogs Show*. Hosted by the cast of *Me and*

My Girl, prizes would be given for the 'Dog with the most Bandy Legs', or the 'Dog with the most Soulful Eyes.' Next we'd see *Ivor Novello's Beer Garden,* and you might pay a bit more than you would in a pub, but your host pulling the pints might make you swoon.

Here now is the 'Grand Giggle' tent, home to a play called *The Boat Race Girl.* Here's a place to purchase afternoon tea, and here's strawberries and cream being served by the cast of *The Women,* currently playing at the Lyric Theatre. The Garden Club seems more high-end, with cocktails being served on the club's tea lawn… and Ivy St. Helier is playing the piano!

Buoyed up on food and beverages, and a sit-down, we now see fair games such as *Fishing for Fizz.* It's one shilling for two minutes of fishing and a chance to hook a bottle of champagne on the end of your rod. Ah, here's the *Band of the H.M. Royal Marines.* They're playing extracts from Noël's recent musical play, *Operette.*

Now the crowds are really intense. Clemence Dane is exhaustingly overseeing the autograph signings in the *Celebrity Court* tent. Now there's a *Dress Salon, Lilian Braithwaite's Fruit Gambles* (very refreshing drinks), *Lilli Palmer's Scotch Pegs* and *Rex Harrison's Helter-Skelter.* One can see hordes of people sliding down the helter-skelter and all thinking, 'There's Rex Harrison!' There are many fairground games… *Chuck-a-Penny, Shooting Gallery, Racing Mice*… there's fortune telling, roundabouts… and *Galloping Horses.* This involves a spinning log from which ladies, in their rather heavy summer dresses, are trying and failing not to fall. They are trying to crawl along it towards a prize at the far end. The giggling is infectious.

Stars are yelling into megaphones, balloons are flying, there's a sea of ladies' hats on all sides, bandstands are blaring… and the masses of tents look really rather lovely amidst this backdrop of the lush greens of the summer trees… We're getting tired now…

There's a St John Ambulance, but I think we'll be okay. Let's press on, although the *Dodge Cars* might make us feel sick. We could get a caricature? Visit the casino? Buy chocolates? More alcohol? This is exciting; in the *BBC Auditions* tent they are looking for talent to record a specially commissioned radio play. And this is more calming; a flower stall and a fruit stall. Kenneth Barnes and the students of RADA are in that tent putting on a play, *Racy Rapture...* It's okay, it's about the boat race, nothing to call the Lord Chamberlain about.

Past the makeshift cinema, Italia Conti's *Conti's Corner* is providing children's performances. It's awfully loud. Here are the lavatories, thank goodness. Here's the car park... how much did we spend? Did we see Noël Coward? Did we see any of the orphanage children as they ran about, and even did a turn, or assisted in a tent? Was that actually the Duke of Kent? Did we *really* ask Ivor Novello for a stiff one?

*

Such events gave another dimension to Noël's career, for here he was like theatrical royalty, loving the part, meeting and greeting and heading the event as a kind of *King of the Theatrical Profession*. Once in 1936, Noël had been miffed after King Edward the VIII hadn't visited him in his dressing room after a performance of *Tonight at 8:30,* but *had* spent quite some time with Gertrude Lawrence in her dressing room. Noël had sent a message jokingly saying that although Edward VIII was the King of England, *he* was the King of the Theatre. The King, allegedly, sent word back that Noël could 'go and fuck himself', which Noël took in his stride.

The venue of the garden party changed often over the years, from Regent's Park to the Royal Gardens, Chelsea, to the Ranelagh Club, to Battersea Pleasure Gardens, to the Roehampton Club...

but the entertainments and the excitement changed little. Stars always attended in droves, to name a few more of this era: Tallulah Bankhead, Marie Tempest, Evelyn Laye, Edith Evans, Cedric Hardwicke, Fay Compton, Leslie Henson, Peggy Wood, Sybil Thorndike, Emlyn Williams, Mary Pickford, Laurence Olivier, Vivien Leigh and Alfred Hitchcock. Younger readers might be inclined to quote (and misread) Shakespeare's *Love's Labours Lost* in regard to some of the names mentioned here:

Let fame, that all hunt after in their lives,
Live register'd upon our brazen tombs.

But these people really were the megastars of their time, when stars were still, somehow, untouchable and had, to many, an aura of magic otherworldliness. As for the public, it consisted of many more ladies than men still, but the crowds were always utterly huge. All of this made the Actors' Orphanage familiar to people and, of course, paid for its very survival each year. It was vital. Noël always maintained that the orphanage should be the premiere charity of the theatrical profession and, to many, it was.

It must be said that much of the organisation, planning and paperwork for these hugely popular and glamorous June garden parties fell to Lorn. It was a year-round duty for her. As Noël was seen as a leading theatrical light, escorting royalty, having countless stars doing him a turn, contributing to a worthy cause and the events of the day being recorded each and every year by Pathé News (see some wonderful footage on YouTube)… it was Lorn that tended to the vast administration of the project, year in, year out. There were venue bookings, tents to hire, staffing, equipment bookings, signs needed, publicity to be arranged, security, scheduling nightmares, endless letters to actors… and it all fell to Lorn.

The years when they were rained out, always a distinct possibility during an English summer, Noël would set up shop, sometimes very impromptu, in a tent and charge three shillings for people to enter and hear him sing for thirty minutes at a time. This proved ridiculously popular and would eventually give him the confidence, and at the suggestion of Marlene Dietrich, to perform in cabaret, also using the same faithful pianist, Norman Hackforth. That was a few years off yet, though, for here we are at the end of the 1930s and with war imminent. Yet for the children their lives had greatly improved and, given their life circumstances, they *were* happier these days. Langley was already a distant memory. The younger children knew no difference but the older ones became gradually and increasingly aware that their orphanage was a bit special. How unfair that all the good work of so many had finally paid off... and now another war was looming ever larger on the horizon.

*

On the 3rd of September 1939, at 11:15am, Neville Chamberlain announced on the wireless:

> "This morning the British Ambassador in Berlin handed the German Government a final note stating that, unless we heard from them by 11 o'clock that they were prepared at once to withdraw their troops from Poland, a state of war would exist between us. I have to tell you now that no such undertaking has been received, and that consequently this country is at war with Germany."

Britain was thrown into fear and uncertainty, not to mention a degree of surprise after the Munich Agreement in September of

1938 between Chamberlain, Hitler and Mussolini had promised peace. By the summer of 1939, though, the writing was on the wall; even the older children at Silverlands could tell trouble was coming as the Nazis strode across Europe. Those children with no one to take them in during that summer of 1939 had been given a two-week holiday in rented railway carriage 'cottages' down on the south coast in East Wittering. It was tremendous fun to be altogether at the seaside with no schoolwork, and lazy days playing on the beaches. However, Spitfires would often fly overhead, and it seemed increasingly silly to say that there'd be no war. Yet many felt miffed that there could be after the horrors of 1914 to 1918.

Meanwhile, Noël was deep in rehearsals for two new plays: *Present Laughter* and *This Happy Breed* at the Theatre Royal, Haymarket. He knew war was coming as he had recently travelled to Poland, Russia, Finland, Sweden and Denmark. The official story was that he wanted to gauge for himself what was going on in the world. The truth was that a certain Robert (later Lord) Vansittart had employed Noël as a secret agent! Mad as it sounds, Vansittart was a senior British diplomat and he used businessmen and celebrities as spies, because they always had reason to travel. Who would ever suspect Noël Coward? It's quite utterly absurd.

What Noël reported back was that everyone he met was convinced that war was imminent, unlike the majority of people in the UK, clutching on to the promises of Neville Chamberlain. No, he was not surprised when the War came and not very surprised that the theatres were closed and his rehearsals abandoned indefinitely. He mused to his now out-of-work cast that there was nothing but the destruction of civilisation to worry about.

On the 3rd of September, the Ministry of Information employed Noël and sent him to set up an office in the Place

Vendome in Paris. He was to report back any *findings*. His spymaster was Sir William Stephenson, known as 'Little Bill'. Stephenson also employed David Niven, Cary Grant, Roald Dahl and many other famous people to be rather unlikely spies.

With office staff, a little French and swathed in authority, Noël was to socialise and mingle and report any gossip. It soon transpired that everyone in Paris seemed to be a spy of some sort and on a 'secret' mission. But Noël did his best, reporting on an illegal radio station, but no one took him very seriously. The impression was that the authorities back home were humouring him, with a smirk.

The UK press, meanwhile, were asking what *is* Noël Coward doing in Paris? The Nazis meanwhile put him on Adolf Hitler's black list for extermination, along with the likes of Neville Chamberlain, Winston Churchill, Aldous Huxley, Sigmund Freud, J.B. Priestly, Bertrand Russell, Sybil Thorndike and Rebecca West. It was West who would later remark to Noël, "My dear, the people I should have been seen dead with."

In the March of 1940, after months of tedious and uneventful deskwork in Paris, Noël was sent to tour the United States. Here, he would be in the guise of a British ambassador, but secretly trying to gauge just how isolationist and anti-war America was. The British press tore into Noël again, this time for leaving Europe in its hour of crisis. Questions were asked in the House of Commons! Noël, of course, could not say anything about any of his war work and information-gathering. This proved most frustrating. Noël would finally spill the beans a month before his death in February 1973.

*

We've got the day off 'cos Noël Coward and Mary Pickford are coming: He's going to tell us about the War or something.

– *An Orphan's War*, Hugo Bergström, 2000

At Silverlands, the children now practised air raid drills, the windows were blacked out, and they all adjusted to the rationing that had started on the 8th of January. The Government's *Dig for Victory* campaign was underway, and more potatoes and vegetables would be grown on site. Trips to town were somewhat curtailed too. Paul Bantock was soon to leave to train for the RAF. Carol Bergström would join the Navy. Everything was getting *real*, although England seemed relatively untouched well into 1940, during the so-called 'Phoney War'.

Poland was overrun but there was no fighting in the West... yet. By the 14th of June, however, following Dunkirk, the Nazis were occupying Paris, and shock and fear took hold, the feeling being that if it could happen to Paris, it could happen to London. It was now a distinct possibility. On the day that Paris fell, the people of London looked shaken, ashen, and some were in tears.

The summer of 1940 saw pillboxes for armed guards installed across England and signposts removed from roads. Church bells were silenced and only to be rung now if any Nazis appeared. In May, Winston Churchill had been elected prime minister and was strongly felt to be the right leader for this time of crisis.

Noël very quickly started making plans for the children to be evacuated for the duration. Even with his recent covert work in Paris, America and soon, Australia and New Zealand, his writing of brilliant plays such as *Blithe Spirit*, songs such as *London Pride*, and soon the screenplay for *In Which We Serve*, Noël always found time to take care of people. Whether it was moving his mother and Auntie Vida to a safer location or indeed handling the not easy task of evacuating an entire orphanage.

Evacuated orphanages or schools of the time would often see the children separated and dotted all over the country, but Noël insisted that the fifty-four children under the age of sixteen would stay together. They were, to all intents and purposes, each other's family.

One day, the orphanage funds secretary, Peter Jackson, arrived at Silverlands. The children were gathered into the assembly room and, quite out of the blue, told that Noël Coward and the committee had decided that all those under sixteen years of age were to be evacuated, very soon, to Hollywood, California. Parents and guardians had been written to for consent, and their president was currently busy in Los Angeles making the arrangements. There would also be a farewell dinner at Silverlands for parents and guardians to attend.

The handful of sixteen- and seventeen-year-olds must have exchanged nervous glances, while the younger children must have thought that they'd just been handed a golden ticket. To them it was, quite simply, like a most wonderful dream. Hollywood…

The farewell dinner was indeed held in the assembly room and many committee members were on hand. It was a bittersweet time for all concerned. No one had *any* clue how long the War would last or when they'd see their loved ones again. And the younger teenagers must have had the thought in the back of their minds that if the War lasted as long as the Great War, then their time to serve would come too.

The evacuation couldn't come soon enough, what with the Battle of Britain raging in the skies for months on end. By September 1940, the Blitz was just beginning, with what was to be fifty-seven consecutive nights of the Luftwaffe bombing primarily London but many other cities too. A million homes would be destroyed and 40,000 people killed, of whom 7,736 would be children. This author's grandmother, Joan Dean, lived in Beckton, East London, near the Thames. It was the most bombed part of the country. Aged just seven and eight during the Blitz, my grandmother said that she and her older sister, Eva, never thought anything *really* bad would happen because their parents were with them in the shelter, night in, night out, protecting them (apart from one night when the bombing was so relentless, intense and *close* that the parents laid on top of the children. This occasion *was* frightening).

One wonders how the orphanage children felt, with no such parental presence to quell their nerves. Silverlands was twenty miles outside of London and much safer, but certainly there was still an element of danger and fear. During the air raids, they could certainly hear the bombs and carnage in the distance and see the flames and smoke that dotted the horizon. The children would now move down to the damp and dimly lit cellars for safety.

Dan Taylor recalled vividly the eerie feeling of being woken in the middle of the night by the air-raid siren and the sound of German bombers passing. All the children grabbing their gas masks and heading down three flights of stairs to the cold cellars, deep below Silverlands. When the air raids started to occur every single night, beds were made in the cellars out of the wide shelves, now with blankets and pillows thrown on top. They often didn't even bother going to their rooms now, just attended to their ablutions and headed straight down for the night.

Silverlands was never bombed but Chertsey was hit at times and the threat was ever-present. Everyone knew that bombs were often dropped indiscriminately, sometimes by bombers simply *offloading* any remaining arsenal before returning to Germany. These could hit anywhere at any time.

Noël and the committee had turned the nightmare into a dream. After the children were told that they were to be evacuated to Hollywood, it was announced in the press. The *London Evening Standard* had published an article on the 11th of July. *They're Off to Hollywood* ran the headline, and the accompanying photo of the children running up a hill at Silverlands shows the exhilaration on their faces. They could not believe their luck. It was beyond belief, the stuff of movies. This also meant no rationing! There was utter joy at this magical opportunity. Hollywood seemed as magical as the movies it produced. The sun always shone and glamour abounded.

Behind the scenes, Noël was frantically trying to get things organised and help the staff deal with copious amounts of red tape. He also needed to cajole his wealthiest friends to sponsor a child each! (For there were to be no garden parties now.) And the dreaded committee meetings were long and arduous, as Noël recalled in his second autobiography, *Future Indefinite*: 'By the fact that all of us, being actors and highly articulate, talked at once.'

A *Hollywood* Committee was set up under the aegis of Dame May Whitty, now herself residing in California. There had actually been a long disagreement about whether to go to the *sunshine and oranges* of Hollywood or to New York, where they already had a wonderful offer of accommodation from the Edwin Gould Foundation. In Los Angeles, Noël, before he left to make pro-Britain speeches (and report back findings and reactions to Little Bill) in Australia and New Zealand, had a meeting with the ambassador there to discuss possibilities. In a letter to Lorn on the 6th of September, Noël wrote that the committee were 'up in arms' over his having done this, and that 'The fussing and fuming going on over the orphanage was something terrible'. He reports too that he had 'achieved (the) great distinction of being cut dead by Gladys Cooper'.

Dame May Whitty was being driven mad by disagreeing members as well as those who *agreed* on ideas, but which were then thwarted by the lawyers. Cedric Hardwicke, according to Noël, was one of the 'few sensible ones' and then adds, 'surprisingly'. Noël took action as usual and put his ballsy American lawyer, Fanny Holtzmann, in charge. Her no-nonsense manner cut through the bureaucracy in a flash and in the end it was decided that they would take the much easier option and move to the Edwin Gould Foundation in the Bronx, New York City, and study at local schools there.

One of the biggest headaches was that so many of the children had one parent alive somewhere, or even two. Therefore, permission had been sought, but this was to go to Los Angeles, not New York. This was decided to be a minor quibble and they would not delay the process by asking for permission all over again. And therefore they could not tell the children, either. It was simply hoped that they would be excited to simply be in America!

Noël was now sending his mother and Auntie Vida to live in the Bronx, New York City, for the duration too. Both were in their late seventies and vulnerable. It seems that Noël was treating, quite literally, the children as he was his own relatives. But why America when so many evacuee children were simply sent to more rural parts of Britain? Well, nowhere in England was definitely safe and no one knew for certain that we would win the War. It would be far better for them to go to America. And also many children of the aristocracy had been sent, very early on, to America. Well, as far as Noël was concerned, if it was good enough for them, then it was good enough for the children of Silverlands.

*

Earlier in 1940, a lot of colour film footage was shot on the cine-camera that had been gifted by Mary Pickford. This footage gives us one final look at Silverlands before the War would change

England and the world forever. We see the children eating in the dining hall with staff members. What appears to be a maid clears the tables, but one suspects this was put on for the camera. There was always a rota of children on dining-room duties. Uniforms seem to be grey shirts, shorts and socks for the boys and light blue dresses for the girls. In other clips, the girls seem to be in their own individual and pretty dresses.

The one black child in the orphanage, although unfortunately nicknamed 'Inky', is seen totally integrated into Silverlands life, as we cut to him playing and diving into the local swimming pool. Here too the children play leapfrog with each other. We then see footage of the press on the day they photographed the children running over the hill at the announcement of the imminent evacuation to Hollywood. Another day. Children play barefoot outside, some sunbathe, some stretch and exercise. Some play on gym equipment that has been moved out onto the grass. A few of the boys play with some puppies. We see the cat, Snowy, known as the school mascot.

Surrounded by green fields and trees, Silverlands seems an English idyll. A whole world in which to lose yourself. We cut to a tennis match, then some boys playing cricket. Mr Howells coaches them in his shirtsleeves and tie below the shining sun.

FOUR

Evacuees in America

1940-1945

It's just Bovril – heavily laced with sherry.

– Captain Kinross, *In Which We Serve*, 1942

The older children knew there would be an element of danger crossing the Atlantic Ocean. That summer, a staff member, Mrs Lennon, escorting a different group of children, had tried to cross the Atlantic on a Dutch liner called the SS *Volendam*. No one on that journey ever made it to North America. The *Volendam* was torpedoed a few hundred miles west of Ireland, although Mrs Lennon survived and was escorted back to England and to Silverlands.

The children still saw the evacuation to 'Hollywood' as an incredibly exciting adventure, though tinged, of course, with sorrow and fear at having no idea when they would see Silverlands or any known relatives again. With luggage, gas masks, packed lunches and passports, on the 13th of September, they waved goodbye to the older children staying behind. We can only imagine what was going through *their* minds. Fear?

Patriotism and an eagerness to serve? Jealousy of the younger orphans? Perhaps all of these feelings combined.

Two buses took the under-sixteens to Euston Station in central London, where they just happened to see a German plane being shot down in the distant skies as they boarded the train to Glasgow. They set off during an air raid, so the blinds were down and their long journey was beginning in the dark. Fifty-four children embarking on quite the adventure.

In Glasgow, they bedded down for the night in rented accommodation and got what sleep they could. Undoubtedly, some of those with relatives had thoughts of the loved ones that would soon be left thousands of miles behind. Yettey had left Silverlands already and was now in the WAAF (Women's Auxiliary Air Force). Her brother, Dan, wouldn't now see her for fifteen years.

The next morning, they headed up the Firth of Forth to the massive ocean liner that would, all being well, take them to Canada for the next part of their journey. (The north of the North Atlantic was considered much safer for crossing.) The *Empress of Australia* was a 22,000-ton ship serving the Canadian Atlantic. A German-built liner of 1911, it had been seized during the Great War. The sea voyage to Canada would prove eventful at first. Aboard the *Empress of Australia* and after some delay, due to engine trouble, they had left late. This proved incredibly lucky as the original convoy they were due to join included the *City of Benares,* which was torpedoed and rapidly sunk. Two hundred and fifty-six people died, including seventy-seven evacuee children (fifty-three were private enterprise and twenty-four government sponsored). There was significant press attention and it marked the beginning of the end of sending children across the submarine-infested Atlantic.

All five siblings of one family, the Grimmonds, drowned. Then there's the story of a twenty-one-year-old vicar's son,

Michael Rennie, who was escorting one group of children on the *Benares*. As the ship went down, he dove in and out of a lifeboat and managed to save thirteen of the fifteen children in his charge... but sadly died himself trying to save the fourteenth. Rennie, exhausted, clambered back into the lifeboat, where he collapsed. In the following hours all but two of the children saved died from exposure. A mural of this tragedy can be seen in St Jude-on-the-Hill Church in Hampstead, London, where Rennie's father was the vicar.

The *Empress of Australia* had a protective convoy for a few days and there had been a little gunfire from German U-boats at one point. The alarm sounded and everyone grabbed a lifejacket and headed to the decks... but they fortunately managed to scare the U-boats off and ultimately had a relatively safe passage. The children played on deck, shared cabins, had plenty of food, with no rationing imposed... and the further away from Europe they travelled, the safer they felt. A few inevitably felt seasick. Peter Jackson was with them to oversee the journey. Many befriended other children on board and admired the many Canadian servicemen returning home. Many sick and wounded. Some wild-eyed with shell shock. Or PTSD as we'd call it today.

Meanwhile, some of the parents and guardians were going frantic after hearing that the *City of Benares* had been sunk and so many killed. They just hoped and prayed the *Empress of Australia* would make it. These were not relaxing times. Indeed, the Atlantic was full of U-boats. Very soon, government schemes and even private schemes for Atlantic crossings would become very limited, as they were deemed far too dangerous. The Actors' Orphanage was one of the last of such private schemes and they were certainly on their way. This evacuation had cost the fund £4,000, equivalent to about £50,000 today.

From July to September 1940, the US took in a total of three and a half thousand evacuees, and it was assumed that if Germany won the War, they'd never go back. In those early months, the idea of a swastika on Buckingham Palace was a distinct possibility. And no one had any idea how long the duration of the War would be... Some people questioned how parents could send their children so very far away, but this was somewhat less relevant for the children of Silverlands.

The Children's Overseas Reception Board, CORB, had been set up by the government so that the evacuation was not purely elitist. A total of 30,000 parents had signed up for their children to go to the USA. If the *City of Benares* hadn't been sunk, many more than just three and a half thousand would surely have made the crossing.

One child evacuee was the future Baroness of Crosby, Shirley Williams. She would spend three years in Minnesota. Early on, it was thought that UK evacuee children would also make for a good ploy for American sympathies to the war plight. There was a degree of political motivation *and* they needed to avoid pure and blatant elitism. The first children to arrive, after all, were those of Oxford and Cambridge professors. Yale took in 125 of them. Yet, somewhat ironically, moving from the UK to the US usually resulted in an escape from the strident British class system.

The *Empress of Australia* had additional children to those of the Silverlands group on board, including orphans. Some of the Silverlands children put on a performance of *Sweeney Todd* for the others during this long ocean voyage. Together all the children could play endless games of hide-and-seek. The ship's inside pool was drained and full of covered furniture, providing an excellent hiding place. Peter Jackson must have had quite the challenge, keeping an eye on them all, although they all convened regularly for every meal in the rather plush dining saloon. There must have been time for much reflection and thoughts of the green summer countryside of Silverlands and all that they had left behind... and much fantasising about Hollywood too.

It was only in Canada that the fifty-four, non-CORB scheme, Actors' Orphanage children were told that they were going to New York and not Hollywood after all. One suspects that this didn't dim their excitement *too* much. Still, it must have been confusing and strange. On October 4th, they had docked in Halifax, Nova Scotia, taken a train to Montreal and spent a night in a hostel. Some kind ladies had given each child a small bag containing a toothbrush, soap, comb, candy and a pad and pencil. It was only here, the next morning, after breakfast, that Peter Jackson told them of the change in plans. There were certainly some sighs and groans but before there was time to think, they were on another train, heading south, on the long journey from Montreal and into the United States and into New York. It was October 5th when they arrived. The entire journey from Chertsey had taken three weeks.

Other evacuee children, many now friends, would travel with them to the Gould Institute. But they were only there for a medical examination before being moved to other parts of New York, such as a large house in Tuxedo Park, some hours north. It would seem that accommodation had indeed proved the difficulty in Los Angeles and that the Gould Institute in New York was very accommodating. It was obviously decided to tell everyone after arrival in New York in case, after months of planning and expense, any child or parent changed their mind. Now it was too late for that. The children were still *in* America and this was absolutely thrilling enough to a poor English child.

Visas would be updated annually and only for the duration of the War. The American Embassy, then at the Grosvenor House Hotel in London, had had to see everybody's passport, birth certificate, have two photographs, a letter from the Gould Institute and receive a ten-dollar fee per child. (If only the visa process were so simple today!)

On October 13th 1940, Princesses Elizabeth and Margaret

made their first ever radio broadcast, from Windsor Castle. To hear the fourteen and nine-year-olds' voices was quite thrilling. It was a broadcast to all the child "evacuees around the world", and the future queen said:

> "To think of all the new sights you must be seeing, and the adventures you must be having. But I am sure that you, too, are often thinking of the Old Country. I know you won't forget us; it is just because we are not forgetting you that I want, on behalf of all the children at home, to send you our love and best wishes – to you and to your kind hosts as well."

*

Noël knew all about youthful excitement where the United States was concerned. While appearing in an American comedy in London in 1921, called *Polly with a Past*, Noël had developed an overwhelming urge to visit the great land. So he did. In *Present Indicative,* he wrote:

> *My faith in my own talents remained unwavering, it did not seem unduly optimistic to suppose that the Americans would be perceptive enough to see me immediately in the same light in which I saw myself. In this, I was perfectly right. They didn't.*

Noël had crossed the Atlantic to New York and… nothing happened. Except that he experienced, as an audience member on Broadway, the beginnings of the Jazz Age boom. Broadway theatre had more lights, more glamour, more excitement and more razzle-dazzle. Actors spoke dialogue so quickly, even speaking over each other, even throwing away the more superfluous lines… They acted far less reverentially. All of this technique and style Noël was determined to take back to the London stage, although he was rather forlorn in New York in 1921.

Despite looking gallant at the theatre in his suit, he had only a few pennies in his pocket. He spent more time cowering in a tiny apartment beset by ravenous bed bugs. Feeling poor and lonely, he tramped the New York streets, sat on park benches and contemplated daring robberies. He certainly had plays to tout, but the producers had all left town for the summer. Sat in Battery Park, watching the ships that were heading to England, he 'did a lot of manly fist clenching'.

He did manage to sell a short story version of *I'll Leave It to You* to *Metropolitan* magazine and they had paid $500. He said: "For $500, I'd gladly turn *War and Peace* into a music hall sketch!" Then he sold another story, *The Young Idea*. It was a relief, as he had had to send Mother some money, as one of the lodgers, Mrs Herriot, had, inconsiderately, 'abandoned the drawing room suite in early June in favour of the grave'.

Noël did, as always, make friends. He met young, poor, struggling actors, Alfred Lunt and Lynn Fontanne, and they all made a promise that they would act together one day in a huge hit. Noël also met a strange theatrical family called the Hartley Manners, or the 'Hardly any Manners' as some called them. They had a large house outside the city where the matriarch, Laurette Taylor, covered all the mirrors so that she would not be reminded of the loss of her youth. The family also played charades with intense ferocity and some screaming. They invited lots of guests to the house at weekends, whereupon they would ignore most of them… and so began the formulation of the play *Hay Fever*.

*

Before 1940 was over, Silverlands would become a training facility for nurses as well as a convalescent home for the nearby Saint Peter's Hospital, also requisitioned for the war effort. Two large air raid shelters were fitted in the gardens at the back of the main building, quite ruining the view. Noël's Kent estate, Goldenhurst, was also requisitioned, as an officers' base. He wouldn't get that back until 1951. His London home, Gerald Road, was bombed, and Noël, now back in London, not too painfully moved into the Savoy for quite some time. His diaries record:

Had a few drinks. Pretty bad Blitz, but not as bad as Wednesday. A couple of bombs fell very near during dinner. Wall bulged a bit and door blew in. Orchestra went on playing, no one stopped eating or talking. Blitz continued. Carroll Gibbons played the piano, I sang, so did Judy Campbell and a couple of drunken Scots Canadians. On the whole, a strange and very amusing evening. People's behaviour absolutely magnificent. Much better than gallant. Wish the whole of America could really see and understand it. Thankful to God that I came back. Would not have missed this experience for anything.

In New York, the children would see a lot less of Noël as he was to be extremely busy for the duration. In March 1941, Winston Churchill had put an end to Noël's spy work, for he was getting too much attention in the press. Noël was not only glad to be back in England, but glad too to be using his talents: writing, directing and performing. The play *Blithe Spirit* was a mega hit that would run longer than the War itself. He would soon write, co-direct and star in the heroic naval film *In Which We Serve*, record patriotic songs such as *London Pride, Could You Please Oblige Us with a Bren Gun* and *Don't Let's Be Beastly to the Germans*. In due course, he would tour three of his plays throughout the UK, before eventually performing troop concerts all over the world. Not to mention countless hospital visits to wounded soldiers. The tours would involve endless months of travel, rehearsals, performances, press interviews, patriotic broadcasts, official luncheons, dinners and meetings. He would perform on a variety of platforms, ranging from the vast rooms of Middle Eastern palaces, to atop a few planks of wood, hastily thrown over some mud, in deepest Indo-China.

Noël was to find his feet and many ways that he could contribute to the war effort. At the beginning of the War, at a social occasion, Noël had a private word with Winston Churchill, asking him how he could *best* contribute. Churchill told him to sing *Mad Dogs and Englishmen* to the troops, "while the guns are firing"… Noël thought that, 'if the morale of the Royal Navy was at such a low ebb that the troops were unable to go into action without my singing Mad Dogs and Englishmen to them, we were in trouble at the outset'. Not to mention the fact that singing during gunfire was rather impractical. To Churchill, Noël (hardly, by his own admission, a *great* singer or a *great* piano player) remained a simple singer of ditties. But now, after his covert work, Noël realised that working hard to boost the morale of the country and the troops through his work *was* worthwhile.

While the children were getting settled in the Bronx, Noël did, however, visit Washington DC to see if President Roosevelt had a good use for him. The president asked him to sing *Mad Dogs and Englishmen*. This was getting bizarre. The two world leaders' pathological passion for the song was irksome to Noël. They even had a disagreement about the order of the verses and whether the second was before the third. Noël had to concede that Roosevelt was correct. "Britain can take it", came Churchill's reply.

It's proof enough that Noël was a person of consequence,

that he acquired meetings with the prime minister of Britain and the president of the United States during wartime. Noël needed to find a purpose; his usefulness during the Great War was non-existent and haunted him rather... but at least then he had excuses. In 1918, Noël had been drafted as a soldier at the tail end of war. In his defence too his existence was so tied up with the theatre that he was hardly soldier material. Also, this graduate of ballet classes and Christmas shows was graded B2 as opposed to A1. This was due to a TB scare in 1915 and meant that he was incredibly unlikely to see the front line.

Early in training, he had tripped during morning parade, hit his head on a slat and suffered concussion. Noël played this up to the hilt and spent many months in hospitals in Colchester, then Romford, where at least he could write. Plays, novels and poems all poured forth... none of them very good yet, but often quite funny. Noël's plan of becoming a star and getting his mother out of the kitchen was being delayed. Yet he also knew, despite being a typically solipsistic eighteen-year-old, how reprehensible these thoughts were when millions of young men, with far graver responsibilities, were dying.

In 1939 and 1940, Noël had long been a *star,* and as the so-called great patriot who'd written *Cavalcade,* hiding out in New York or California for the duration was not an option. He was a man of renown and influence. He *could* stay in the US, socialising in New York, but the press would turn on him and, more importantly, he would judge himself. Noël would later write in his war autobiography, *Future Indefinite*, that:

> *Now was the moment of all moments to think clearly and unemotionally. If I bungled this moment, I shall never be comfortable with myself again, and what is more, whatever books or plays I live to write in the future would be tainted by the fact that I'd allowed to*

slip through my fingers, the opportunity to prove my integrity to myself...

*

To make the Silverlands evacuation to America work financially, each child was sponsored by one of Noël's famous friends: Mary Pickford, Lynn Fontanne, David Niven, Douglas Fairbanks, Charlie Chaplin, Cary Grant or Marlene Dietrich, for example, these stars often taking the duty, or 'favour to Noël', quite seriously. Mary Pickford sent a chatty letter and pen to her 'child', Dan Taylor. Somehow, Noël (with Lorn's constant help) had made the time to persuade fifty-four, busy famous people to perform this duty and sponsor the fifty-four children.

The Edwin Gould Foundation on Stillwell Avenue, Pelham, the Bronx, New York, was a charity providing accommodation for needy children. It was ideal and, according to Noël, 'Wonderful to the children and I suspect has spoiled them forever'. They were called 'limeys' a bit, and some of the boys realised that short trousers beckoned the call, "Where's the other half of your pants?" But, make no mistake, life seemed suddenly quite miraculous.

The Institute had a large road out front and a large recreational space up to a railway at the back. There were no orange groves or palm trees, and the buildings were amidst miles of New York suburban houses. However, there was also no rationing, blackouts or bombs. The accommodation was divided into six roomy 'cottages'. Bedrooms were large T sections marked A, B or C, with four beds to a room, and each cottage had its own kitchen, always stocked with plenty of food and its own cook! There were large bathrooms with hot showers, a far cry from the shallow, ice-cold baths of yesteryear at Langley. A Mr Griffin was the principal and by all accounts very nice. Doctor Levy looked to all their psychiatric needs and Mrs Whiting was the Director of Social Services. This *was* a new world.

The Institute had a very relaxed atmosphere, a swimming pool and tennis court. The children discovered hot dogs, hamburgers, popcorn, waffles, peanut butter, corn-on-the-cob, donuts, Coca-Cola, Halloween and Thanksgiving. They listened to *The Lone Ranger* on the radio. The boys started to get crew cuts. It was all rather exciting… but the fear for any loved ones still in England never left them. Nor did thoughts of Hitler and his dark plans. In one cine-camera clip we see some of them running across the playground holding a large Union Jack flag aloft. A gift perhaps from the Institute.

They lived among many orphaned and deprived American children here but had their own building so could be a bit cliquey. And culture shock would have been far more immense in 1940 than in today's homogenised world. Cine-film footage shows how smart their clothes are now and how spacious their surrounds. In fact, the committee felt that they were so thoroughly spoilt in New York that the only real problem was that they really might never want to return home.

The younger children had schooling at the Institute and the teenagers boarded the large yellow and white bus each morning to attend the Christopher Columbus High School in the Bronx. Here, their English accents were mocked a little. Some would alter their accents over the coming years, consciously or unconsciously. It would lessen the constant cod impressions of their English accents by their peers, and the endless remarks. On the whole, though, they were accepted.

It was all a little overwhelming at first, yet fascinating. In a school of thousands, the Silverlands children were certainly a minority. There were also thirty-five children to a class and in a large ethnic mix. They had been used to twelve children in a class in rural England. And had only ever known one black person before. They attended *Home Class* and in Assembly pledged allegiance to the American flag, sang *God Bless America* and later that day might have a class in American History. Sometimes, thoughts of the green fields of Silverlands, of England, would enter their heads…

We should also note that it was always hard for the children to explain their situation to the Americans. It wasn't typical or comparable to anything else but they didn't know anything else, either. They hadn't attended a traditional English boarding school. They didn't have money but lived in a mansion amidst vast and beautiful grounds. There was the glamorous celebrity connection. Some were orphans but most had at least one parent somewhere. Only they could understand their unique young lives.

They were in a less picturesque setting for the evacuee years, but the freedom they had in New York was quite utterly liberating. They could roam the city and there was less use of and thus less fear of corporal punishment. Some of the children managed to visit the New York World Fair (one of the most expensive in the world) before it closed, the Union Jack and Spitfire on display at the British Pavilion no doubt catching their eyes. They would find too that they could take trips right into Manhattan, the elevated railway costing a nickel a time. Trips were arranged to see plays (they saw Gertrude Lawrence in *Lady in the Dark* as well as in *Othello,* with Paul Robeson) and music concerts; the likes of Glenn Miller, Tommy Dorsey and Benny Goodman dominating the scene.

On November 5th, a presidential election was held, and anyone British was undoubtedly relieved that Franklin Delano Roosevelt was elected to a third term over the isolationist Republican Wendell Willkie. It meant US involvement in the War had more of a chance.

On November 23rd, each child was taken into a house of

someone from the Christ Church in Pelham Manor and given Thanksgiving dinner. They joined the church themselves, finding it to be a more cheerful service than the one in Chertsey, full of community spirit *and* a large breakfast every Sunday. They also joined the Scouts or Guides for one evening every week, forming British troops within both organisations but very much belonging to the whole.

Christmas they found was not too dissimilar, though they were discovering that New York winters were painfully cold and equally the summers would prove swelteringly hot. The Gould Institute had a Christmas tree and presents, Dame May Whitty providing gifts for those that didn't have anything. She was still taking responsibility for this American venture, which was just as well as Noël was possibly the busiest he'd ever been in his life.

They visited Central Park, Broadway, the Bronx Zoo, Carnegie Hall, the Empire State Building, the Rockefeller Ice Rink, Times Square and, on one memorable occasion, Charlie Chaplin visited and took them to a screening of *The Great Dictator.* He also made them sing *There'll Always Be an England,* whether they wanted to or not. Another time, they saw Boris Karloff on stage in *Arsenic and Old Lace,* before meeting him backstage afterwards. They also had visits from the likes of Cary Grant and Douglas Fairbanks Jnr. Perhaps a sponsor would visit *their* child from time to time, such as Margaret Webster visiting Granville when she was in town with a play. Meanwhile, his brother, Paul, was in Canada training for the RAF, but hoping to visit his little brother soon.

In the Easter of 1941, a pro-British event was staged in Central Park and the children were invited, along with the local press, to play Easter games. This event was blatantly created to persuade American involvement in the War, as it was now desperately longed for by those back home. And the children were caught up in history at this Central Park event, as unwitting propaganda for their country and cause.

In spring, the swimming pool opened and was a source of great pleasure, especially as the heat intensified, although a mumps outbreak kept a few of the children playing chess in the sanatorium for a while. For the summer holidays, arrangements were overseen by the Gould Institute's super-intendant, Mr Griffin. The children were placed with families from the church but the older ones could work at the foundation's summer camp, Camp Gould East, on Long Island, as junior councillors. Here they could make a little money for future schoolbooks and supplies. These summers included camping by the clear waters of the estuary, fishing, horse riding and beach trips. Footage taken on the orphanage cine-camera shows idyllic images of the children as they play on the grass or dive into the large, cooling lake. Hugo would remember these American summers as the best of his life.

Meanwhile, Germany had invaded Russia, seemingly giving the UK some respite as the Nazis concentrated attentions elsewhere for now. Churchill and Roosevelt seemed close allies, and hope for American involvement in the War was high. Then the Pearl Harbour attack by Japan on December 7th 1941 shocked America to the core. The children were much more surprised by this announcement on the wireless than they had been two years before, when England had declared war on Germany; well, that had been expected for months.

Noël had written a play, *Time Remembered / Salute to the Brave*, which was a propaganda piece to persuade Americans to join the war effort. In it, Leila Heseldyne takes her children to America for safety, but ultimately deems it right that she herself be at her husband's side back in Europe, while the children shall stay in America (much like Noël had evacuated the orphanage children to America but felt he himself should be in England). After Pearl Harbour, the play was quite redundant and quietly disappeared into a drawer.

Now the children were *allies* with the Americans, although compared to the Blitz that they'd lived through in England, nothing much seemed to change in the Bronx, except that disagreement between Americans about whether they should join the War or not had rapidly changed to a pro-war majority. Victory was surely inevitable now; it was just a question of when. Things seemed to get worse initially; as Singapore fell, the War in the Pacific was hard going and the Nazis were making progress into Russia.

Soon Carol Bergström left the Gould Institute to join the British Navy and was stationed in the Atlantic on HMS *Ajax*. And then in the March of 1942, Paul Bantock, now an RAF pilot, was shot down and killed. The popular head boy of Silverlands dead at eighteen. His young brother, Granville, all of fifteen, was sent into a black mood, and friends and staff at the Gould Institute rallied around as best they could. In total, six boys from the orphanage would be killed in the War.

In the August of 1942, and while Noël was performing in *Blithe Spirit,* a comedy about death, Prince George, the charismatic Duke of Kent, died when his RAF plane crashed. He had been Noël's closest royal friend, the patron of the Theatrical Garden Parties, and a sometime weekend guest at Goldenhurst for many years…

This was also the year that Noël's long-time set and costume designer, and very close friend, Gladys Calthrop, lost her only child Hugo, who was also killed… nobody could escape this bloody War.

*

A big event for the children during this same year was the staging of a musical revue, *Gratefully Yours*, for friends and supporters, at Pelham High School. It was billed as 'An Expression of Thanks for American Hospitality', and Peter Jackson, veteran of the Langley Hall pantomimes, was on hand to produce and direct a strong show. Suddenly, and post-Pearl Harbour, they were to perform *Gratefully Yours* for a week, April 7th to 12th 1942, at the Imperial Theatre on West 45th Street! Gertrude Lawrence and Constance Collier (no doubt roped in by Noël) performed the opening act! Some new material was added, with one sketch written by the Broadway team of Howard Lindsey and Russell Crouse. Despite the inevitable fluffs and missed cues, the audience were rapturous, and the proceeds went to the British/American ambulance corps and the theatre wing of the war service. These events must have at least equalled the excitement of those Gaiety Theatre matinees in London a few years earlier.

They next performed the show in May, for a final time, for the deprived children of the Lower East Side at the Henry Street Settlement Theatre on 466 Grand Street, some of the proceeds this time going to the ambulance corps but also to the settlement for the poor children of the Lower East Side in attendance. The tickets were sold to friends and supporters of the settlement and then simply given to the children so that they enjoyed *and* benefited from the show. Charity kids performing for charity kids across the cultural divide.

This final performance was reviewed in the *New York Herald Tribune* under the heading: *50 English Child Actors Win A Royal Delancey Street Salute*, a reference to the local two-fingered whistle. The show is described as an intimate revue in eleven scenes for 500 tenement children, a full house. The actors are aged from eight to sixteen and Constance Collier acts as a 'sort of Greek Chorus'. Songs included: *California Here I Come* (a little ironically for the Actors' Orphans perhaps), *God Save the King* (for UK patriotism) and *My Country 'Tis of Thee* (for US patriotism). There was a satirical sketch about cricket versus baseball that went down a storm, plus the dances, the *Shag* and the *Lindyhop*. Best friends Hugo Bergström and Pete Gifford did a sketch as pearly kings. Special mention went out to Gloria Davis for her rendition of *Chattanooga Choo Choo*, and for Peter Gifford as the shoeshine boy. Here the show is credited as being directed by Mrs William Cahan (Gertrude Lawrence's daughter) and Mrs Dura Chase of the Gould Foundation. They raised $1,000, equivalent to about $15,000 today. And it was another amazing once-in-a-lifetime experience for the children.

*

Meanwhile, at the movie theatres of America and the cinemas of England, the public were soon to see Noël as Captain Kinross aboard the HMS *Torrin*, saying to his crew:

> "I will give you not three weeks, but exactly three days to get this ship ready to sail. None of us will turn in or take our clothes off or sling our hammocks for the next three days and nights until the job is finished. Then we'll send Hitler a telegram saying the Torrin's ready, you can start your war!"

In Which We Serve was a critical and commercial success on a big scale. Noël received much praise for his work and for the British morale boost. Louis Mountbatten, whose ship the *Kelly* and its sinking formed the inspiration for the film, was most impressed and pleased. In America, the film won a special Academy Award, and in the UK, the King asked Noël if he would accept a knighthood.

For some reason, though, Winston Churchill stepped in and in a letter to the King, in regards to Noël's knighthood, wrote:

> I could not advise Your Majesty to proceed with the proposal on the present occasion.

The reason given was that the previous October, Noël had had three court summonses over a minor tax issue. He'd had no idea that his money taken to the US for his covert war work was, in fact, illegal. The law had recently changed and Noël, never one for monetary awareness, hadn't a clue. The press crucified him again and, of course, he couldn't mention what exactly he had been doing in the US for the MOI. The result of the court case was his being cleared on two charges and being fined £200 on the third.

In Which We Serve, by the way, would also introduce us to a fresh young actor called Richard Attenborough, aged just eighteen. Richard was to find in Noël a mentor, and in Richard, Noël was to find a true and loving colleague, and one that would play no small part in the future of the orphanage. For now, though, there was still no end to the War in sight. As the Actors' Orphanage boys had successive birthdays, they feared and braved the future.

*

Some of the children of the time recalled in written accounts or in talking to me their various memories of the New York years. Jimmy Burke, aged nine at the time of his arrival, recalled how they occasionally had to practise air raids with their hands over their heads in the corridors. He too found America more exciting *and* more relaxed. The school was *fully* co-educational, there was *far* less punishment, much better food and the classes were okay; you just had to adjust to history being taught from America's perspective! He, like many, didn't see his mother for the entire five-year duration. Jimmy did, however, spend the New York holidays in Manhattan with two ladies that he absolutely adored: an English teacher and a gardener. It was only years later that he realised they were lesbians.

Dan Taylor worked as a councillor at the Crow Hill Camp in the summer of 1942. It was owned by Mrs Lucinda Ballard, who had also been the costume designer on *Gratefully Yours*. A Broadway veteran, she had some clout and connections. Taking a shine to Dan, she secured him a full scholarship to the private Hill School in Pottstown, Pennsylvania. Dan would be one of a handful to fully integrate into American life and never return to England.

Hugo Bergström loved everything about his American life and quite lost his accent. He did, however, concede that the education was poorer, but how could it not be? They had gone from twelve to a class at Silverlands to thirty-five per class within a school of thousands, although it must be said that Hugo and two friends must have been so excited by their new surrounds that they initially did no schoolwork whatsoever. Berated for very low grades, they snuck out of a window late one night and vowed to hitchhike to Texas. It was just a few minutes before a cop saw them and escorted them back to the Gould Institute.

Granville Bantock had spent a summer on a farm with a nice family in Maryland and he wanted to stay in America too, but when his brother Paul was shot down, their mother, understandably, wanted Granville back in England and with her. Aged sixteen in the October of 1942, he was leaving not just America but the Actors' Orphanage family that he'd known for the past twelve years. As well as a girlfriend, Jane, and an education.

The War still raging, he made the dangerous Atlantic crossing aboard the MV *Thorstrand* and, luckily, made it safely back. One imagines a great mix of emotions in Granville's mind as he boarded that ship alone for the long three-week crossing. Back to an England of bombs, blackouts and rationing. Yet he knew his mother needed him.

Mr Griffin had seen Granville off at the docks and bade

him write on his arrival in England. Many would write to Mr Griffin upon their various arrivals, often to report how unhappy various other parents were that they had not received any letters from their loved ones. The children resettled in England also often expressed to Mr Griffin how they deeply wished to return to America after the War.

*

An AGM was held in London in the middle of 1943 and Noël was there, on a break from his six-month tour of *Blithe Spirit, Present Laughter* and *This Happy Breed* around the British Isles. Not to mention the countless factory concerts and hospital visits (and before he was to embark on his extensive tour of the Middle East). He would give his annual address to the committee and any attendant subscribers. There are excellent reports on all the children in America; the Gould Foundation and Mr Griffin are wonderful. Special mention is also made of Dame May Whitty and the Hollywood and New York sub-committees. Special mentions too go to Gertrude Lawrence and Constance Collier, no doubt for their work on *Gratefully Yours*. Gladys Cooper and Sir Cedric Hardwicke gain a mention too for 'practical and personal help'. It goes on in this pleasant vein as the secretary, Miss Rodda, is thanked, as well as H.M. Tennent for donating a matinee of *Watch on the Rhine*'s profits.

Then we come to the War and its effects. Frank Lawton and Jack O'Halloran are now Army captains. One former boy is now in the Australian Army, one in New Zealand. Duncan Rider is a corporal in the Royal Army Service Corps. Carol Bergström and one other are in the Navy, one in the Royal Marines. One in the RAF. One, Bruce Comet (of French parentage), is fighting with the French forces in the East. And Tony Young recently led a paratroop raid on Bruneval in Northern France.

As for the girls: Yettey Rolyat and Effie Shields were now in the WAAF. Two former girls were in the ATS and two in the WRNS. Two were making munitions. Then there's mention of Norman Bloomfield. He had joined the Army in 1938 and had been missing since the Battle of Crete. Then there was Paul Bantock, of whom Noël said:

"Paul Bantock, who was head boy at Silverlands and one of our best scholars, joined the RAF and was killed in an air accident this spring just after he had come back from his training in Canada." And finally Noël says, "I feel very proud that the Actors' Orphanage is doing its part so well at such a vital time in our history."

In 1943, back in New York, some of the older girls were working for British Information Services and one for the BBC at Rockefeller Plaza in Manhattan. By December, there were only thirty children still left at the Gould Institute and Noël finally managed to visit before 1944 would see him travelling the world to give endless troop concerts and hospital visits to wounded soldiers. On the 15th he had written to Lorn before his visit to the Gould Institute and, contacting friends such as Gertrude Lawrence and seeing shows such as *Oklahoma!* aside, he reported back his irritation at orphanage business. Several girls were simply refusing to go back to England, and his heavy wartime workload left him with little patience for any form of selfishness.

> When I get back from Washington, I am going to talk to the four rebellious girls who seem to be making fair bitches of themselves.

Noël's humour never leaves him, of course:

> We are hoping that Prudence Coop will improve in character on account of the fact that she is beginning to

lean emotionally in the direction of the Catholic Church.
Personally, I feel that this will merely mean that she will be
able to confess having stolen June Bevise's drawers, receive
absolution, and make an immediate pounce for Myra
McKenzie's brooch, but I may be cynical.

The time in New York had also seen Noël butt heads with committee member, Brian Aherne. Brian stated that he didn't know why they evacuated to America in the first place, for his brother's children had stayed in England for the Blitz. To which Noël replied that it was fine of Brian to come to New York himself to represent the family. Brian then suggested that the orphanage fund was vastly rich, to which Noël replied that as far as he could remember, everything that Brian had understood all his life had been invariably inaccurate. 'It was, on the whole, an exciting little meeting.'

On the 30ᵗʰ of December 1943, Noël wrote to Lorn again. He had now been to the Gould Institute, along with Dame May Whitty. The children looked well and cheerful and he admired how well run everything was. Then came the long talk to the four girls wishing to remain in America:

I explained at the outset that feeling for one's country
is something to do with one's roots and not with one's
circumstances.

Two, Sheila and Myra, still refused to go back, while June and Mary remained stubborn but conceded that they would go back. Eventually, Sheila broke down 'under the emotional pressure of my eloquence and said she would definitely return', although her father had told her not to. Meanwhile, it transpired that Myra was in love with an American but then, finally, after a lot of giggling, she too conceded to go back. 'It was all rather touching, really, and

I felt desperately sorry for them.' June expressed her desire to act and Noël promised to help once the War was over. He concludes that they are actually sensible, nice girls... just young.

Noël suggested to Lorn, imploringly, that they provide accommodation for their first few weeks back in London, that the committee must step up in this regard and not just Miss Rodda. And that they must help the girls acquire whatever war jobs they want. He felt that America had spoilt them and that wartime England would now seem terribly lean and austere. Yet he is firm in his belief that they return soon, as austere England will be good for their characters and, besides, they couldn't just magically become American citizens.

Noël also philosophises that 'unwanted' children may lack natural patriotism compared to those with parents and a proper home as a background. Despite being overwhelmed by his conscience, he is still thankful that they evacuated in 1940 and resolves that they shall just have to handle the problem of the children's readjustments to life in England very tenderly.

*

Reports were kept on all of the returning children, many now seventeen or eighteen years of age and needing to go out into the world. The first to return had been Granville and he had been interviewed in London by two committee members, where he expressed a desire to become a veterinarian. They found him a job at the Dispensary for Sick Animals in Ilford, where, after two years, he would qualify for veterinary college. His mother, however, after his brother Paul's death, wanted him close to home. Granville took a job at Teddington Technical College Laboratory.

Others, like Carol Bergström, continued in Naval service. But he would call into the orphanage office periodically, when on leave. Meanwhile, the girls were called up by the Ministry of Labour for War Jobs. Gloria Davis had been up for a job at the BBC but the War was all-consuming. Only Naomi Gillespie failed the medical and was thus free to pursue her dreams of a stage career. She asked, as they always and quite sensibly did, the committee for help. The fact is that the committee did help in any way that they could. Temporary accommodation was found for the returning children, job placements were secured… it's just that the ongoing War was making such placements pointless.

Noël had long philosophised on war and the mixed emotions it induced. He'd published an unproduced anti-war play in 1931 called *Post Mortem*. The premise was simple: what if the men who died in the trenches of the Great War could come back now, and see how little we have done to justify their sacrifice? The lead character, John, a ghost from the War, compares the death of Christ with the sacrifice of the war dead:

> *"In comparison with the War, the crucifixion becomes microscopic in importance. Christ was one man, the War millions."*

In *Cavalcade*, the mother, Jane Maryott, of two sons lost to war, toasts her husband, country… and sons:

> *"First of all, my dear, I drink to you. Loyal and loving as always. Now, then, let's couple the future of England with the past of England. The glories and victories and triumphs that are over, and the sorrows that are over too. Let's drink to our sons who made part of the pattern and to our hearts that died with them. Let's drink to the spirit of gallantry and courage, that made a strange Heaven out of unbelievable Hell, and let's drink to the hope that one day this country of ours, which we love so much, will find dignity and greatness and peace again."*

The War tested everyone's patriotism and Noël saw clearly the island of his birth, with its bad weather, basic food and the complaining nature of the people. Yet he found, like so many did, that he *was* a true patriot, declaring later that he *was England* and England *was him*... whether it liked it or not. Indeed, the war years had, finally, seen his image as a *cocktails and caviar playboy* reinvented rather, as a great patriot.

The War meanwhile raged on, although events were turning the tide. The Battle of Stalingrad, the Dambusters raid, a great increase in the bombing of Germany, the Russians beginning to push the Nazis back, the Americans continuing to push the Japanese back... but still the *end* was not quite in sight.

Silverlands meanwhile was ploughing on as a training facility and residential home for nurses practising at the nearby Botleys Hospital, now renamed Saint Peter's. The gardener, Bert Hazell, and his wife were still living in the cottage down by the main gate. As well as tending the grounds, they had four children to raise *and* were taking in a few babies and toddlers for the Actors' Orphanage, despite having no idea when, perhaps even *if*, it might return.

*

Finally, by the 8th of May 1945 and VE Day, it was all over. The *London Evening Standard* caught up with the remaining children, five years on from the *They're Off to Hollywood* article of 1940. They were still in New York but the voyage home was imminent. This piece said: *27 Young British Blitz 'Exiles' Returning with Revolutionary Ideas.* The other twenty-seven children, having made up the original fifty-four evacuees, obviously having aged out, had already returned to England, like Granville, or found a way to stay in America, like Dan, or had died in service, like Paul. Those returning to Silverlands were allegedly bringing an 'American Outlook to London'.

There is talk of how they have fashionable hairstyles, well-cut clothes and how the *little boys* who left were returning as muscular footballers hoping to join the RAF or Navy. Notably, many had wanted to stay in America; it was now like home, they had friends, were in the midst of their education, had gone through puberty there and knew New York far better than they knew London.

Brenda Lorden was adamant, when interviewed, that she found America more exciting, wanted to marry an American, attend a US college and have a career in fashion design. At which point Ursula Weait thinks that Brenda might be getting a *bit* ahead of herself. In fact, Brenda would go on to reacquaint with Granville a few years later and they would happily marry. One of only two 'orphanage marriages' to occur during its long history.

Ursula, on the other hand, *did* want to get home and longed to see her mother. The *Standard* also asked about the difference between Americans and Londoners, and the answer given is simply that they are more informal in America, and the British, formal. Finally, Carol Lester observed that: "The accent is on youth over here, decidedly. People even seem to *enjoy* seeing a child have a good time."

Hugo Bergström wasn't keen to return to England, either. Now sixteen, approaching seventeen, he had come of age in New York and had had many formative experiences. He was one of the lucky ones that got to know his sponsor a little, in this case Lynn Fontanne. He'd also, after seeing her in *Lady in the Dark*, been taken by Gertrude Lawrence to the 40 Club. He'd met Cary Grant! He loved this town but, along with the others, boarded the HMS *Sheffield* back to England and a certain uncertainty.

Hugo was truly torn between the US and UK. He had an American accent! But ultimately he decided that he needed to see his father again. Crossing the Atlantic, he reflected on his five years in New York. Glamorous stars and school aside, he remembered magical summers, where the Fleming family had made him feel like one of their own: "The holidays I had with them were among the happiest days of my life."

It was all extremely bittersweet. Reverse culture shock was awaiting them and they knew it. Reorientation might be painful. The ocean voyage was every bit as long and thoughtful as the one they had taken in 1940. Several of the returning children would actually, over the next few years, return to live in America. Some would go to Australia or New Zealand, some to Canada. Postwar England must have seemed bleak and hard to come back to. A bankrupt country, rationing continuing until 1953, countless bomb sites and, quite simply, a poorer quality of life.

Some, such as Jimmy Burke, were desperate to do their part despite the end of the War. According to his 1948 orphanage report, Jimmy was asking firmly for permission to join the Navy, but the orphanage wanted him to wait until his eighteenth birthday in 1950. Which demonstrably shows that they cared. Jimmy would have time to grow up and gain responsibility as a prefect at Silverlands first.

Back in 1945, Jimmy was still only thirteen and Silverlands was being fixed up and readied for the return of the twenty-seven total remaining children. They would stay briefly that summer in a hostel at Lennox Gardens, Knightsbridge, readjusting slowly to life back in England.

*

Noël was now back in England too; shattered, melancholic, relieved. His London studio house was long repaired from the bomb blast, but his Kent estate would remain requisitioned by the army until 1951. He rented White Cliffs, a small cottage at the base of the White Cliffs of Dover, with room for Lorn,

Cole Lesley (Noël's assistant since 1935), any guests and his dog Matelot. Falling rocks were always a worry, not to mention high tide, but Noël always loved the sea, his Naval ancestry running deep. His mother and Auntie Vida were placed in the cottage next door, and it proved a good escape from London. It seems somehow fitting too that 'Captain Kinross' should spend the post-war years by the White Cliffs of Dover.

The last years touring troop concerts, including through difficult conditions in Burma and Indo-China, a car accident in India and holding the hand of a soldier as he died in hospital... had all taken a toll. Everything was different now. On VE Day, Noël had joined the crowds outside Buckingham Palace to cheer the King. Amidst the jubilation, he also felt an undertow of deep sadness.

The country was eager to move on, recover and change, but this new world of the end of Empire, proposed social equality, and the breaking down of old barriers and distinctions, was not one Noël could easily adjust to. Also, Noël had only just discovered for certain that Churchill had blocked his knighthood back in 1942. Most assumed that it was due to that minor tax issue (which it was), or perhaps an un-comfortableness regarding Noël's sexuality, which ignores Churchill's sometimes actually rather relaxed attitude to such matters. One famed, possibly apocryphal, story being that of his personal secretary reporting that a Tory MP had been found the night before in St James's Park with a guardsman. Churchill said:

"Last night? Very cold last night?"

"Yes," replied the secretary, "I believe it was the coldest night in thirty years." Churchill paused and said:

"Makes you proud to be British."

FIVE

Return to Silverlands

1945-1950

For not an orphan in the wide world can be so deserted as the child who is an outcast from a living parent's love.

– *Dombey and Son,* by Charles Dickens, 1848

When Hugo stepped ashore at Southampton, he thought: 'Jesus, where do I belong? Where in tarnation do I go from here?' Miss Rodda met the much-diminished group of orphans off the ship and escorted them in the train to the Lennox Gardens Hostel in central London. On the journey, she called Hugo over to sit by her for a moment, whereupon Hugo was told that his father had joined ENSA in the War and been badly wounded by a bomb in France. He was alive but not a well man and in need of a constant steel corset. Hugo stared out of the window for much of that journey, thinking of his father and also unable to believe the amount of bomb damage that he was seeing. And the weather, of course, was grey.

Silverlands was being prepared to resume business as the Actors' Orphanage. The gardens and landscape had been badly abused over the five long years of war and would need some serious attention (and funding). The summer of 1945 was a strange interim period in the life of the orphanage. Miss Rodda kept a close eye on the returners and one day invited Hugo to breakfast at her house in Surbiton. As he ate the toast with no butter, he remembered all of those American breakfasts that he'd left behind. Scrambled eggs, pancakes, bacon, maple syrup... Hugo burst into tears. Miss Rodda put a kind hand on his shoulder.

Hugo was seventeen when they returned to Silverlands that September. He was ageing out but because he was particularly anxious and unsure of his future, the Hazells took him in at the gardener's cottage. To all intents and purposes, he became one of the family, even calling them Ma and Pa. Hugo helped with the grounds but also took a job at a local farm. His American accent remained; he had lived in New York from the age of twelve to seventeen, after all, and his nickname became 'Tex'. In 1946, he was called up by the Army and stationed in Germany... but on leave, he would always return to the Hazells' cottage by the gates of Silverlands.

The returning evacuees, full of Americanisms and having *all* acquired at least transatlantic twangs to their accents (not to mention strikingly different fashions, such as bobby sox), were soon mixing with brand-new arrivals at the orphanage. Those that had aged out often came, like Hugo, to Silverlands to visit and touch base. It was the only home they'd ever known. The Bronx and Chertsey. Some didn't visit... choosing to move on with their lives and to not look back. Parental abandonment inevitably left some deep psychological scars and, despite the committee's best efforts, some wanted to forget their beginnings... at least for a time.

Rationing in Britain would continue for another *seven years*, and the rebuild of bomb sites would take even longer. Winston

Churchill, having led the nation to victory, had been swept out of office in July 1945. Labour's Clement Attlee had won 393 seats to Churchill's 197. Change was in the air as the old class system was weakened and starting to crack around the edges. Working-class culture was in the ascent, and it can't be overstated just how much the War had changed the landscape of British life.

Noël Coward was, in retrospect, to have seen his heyday end in 1945, as the critics and journalists started to relentlessly label him old-fashioned and as a creature of the 1920s and '30s, destined now for the scrapheap. He was to prove them all wrong in the end, and he would eventually write in his diaries that 'The Age of the Common Man has taken over a nation which owes its very existence to uncommon men.' Noël was born during the reign of Queen Victoria, when the British Empire ruled over a fifth of the earth. He had risen through a strict social structure by sheer hard work, a little luck and ironclad determination and had conquered society... and now the whole system was altering. On one hand, the politicians were working towards a fairer society... on the other hand, the Empire was in serious decline. In fact, it was over.

However, for right now, *Brief Encounter* had been adapted for the screen by David Lean from Noël's short play *Still Life*, and it was and is a stunning artistic achievement and one of the finest British films ever made. And the recent films *Blithe Spirit* and *This Happy Breed*, also directed by Lean, had also done rather well. Noël was also busy preparing a new musical to reopen the previously bomb-damaged Theatre Royal, Drury Lane, to be called *Pacific 1860*. It was an escapist, rather pro-Empire show, starring Mary Martin. And as for the orphanage? He was certainly back on duty.

A verbose ex-naval officer, Commander Aggitter, was installed as headmaster, and Noël brought Gertrude Lawrence, her having gotten to know lots of them in New York, to visit the children as they resettled. (She was currently appearing in the London run of *September Tide* by Daphne du Maurier.) The committee by now was well and truly made up of Noël's very good friends: Adrianne Allen, Joyce Carey, Clemence Dane, Lorn Loraine, of course, and Stanley Holloway, to name but a few. Regular committee meetings resumed at 8 Adam Street (near the Savoy) and would often take place on a Friday afternoon. After which, Noël would drive down to his house at White Cliffs (with his new partner, Graham Payn) for the weekend. He would resume visiting the children at Silverlands at least a few times per year and always around Christmas time. And he still ensured that *someone* on the committee visited at least once a month and, more often than not, it was or included Lornie.

All schooling would now take place off site at local schools, as it had done in New York. These primarily included Lyne Primary School and the Stepgates School, which was a little rough and a bus ride away. Uniforms were basic, the usual mix of whites and greys, and the education standard satisfactory. As ever, the orphanage tried to steer the children into suitable careers as best they could, even attempting to facilitate slightly more ambitious careers. One boy was regularly taken to visit the local horse stables as he was passionate about becoming a jockey. One girl was provided a course in shorthand and typewriting so that she might pursue a journalism career. As ever, a career in *show business* was actively discouraged. In 1934, Noël had penned the song *Don't Put Your Daughter on the Stage, Mrs Worthington*, knowing all too well the brutality of the acting profession. He was sure that the orphanage mustn't become a *Mrs Worthington* itself... unless perhaps, just once in a long while, a child really did show eagerness *and* some talent.

Money would once again come primarily from the freshly reinstated Theatrical Garden Parties and then from the subscribers, charity matinees and galas. The orphanage by this time cost an average of at least £10,000 a year to run (about £400,000 today).

Silverlands was soon back into a routine and in full swing. The assembly room was again adorned with a portrait of King George VI, and also one of Princess Elizabeth. A bust of Sir Gerald du Maurier resumed its pride of place in the main hallway, along with the two large glass-fronted bookcases. One locked and containing sweets, the other a selection of large, heavy books. Less for reading and more for naughty children to have to balance on their heads while waiting outside the headmaster's office. (Inside, the office was cosy and wood-panelled, with its own fireplace. You might get a beating but at least it was warm.)

There was a portrait too in the hall of William Terriss playing Romeo, a successful actor of the 1880s and '90s. He had been stabbed to death while entering the Adelphi Theatre's stage door, in 1897, by a disgruntled young actor called Richard Prince. Prince was committed to Broadmoor Criminal Lunatic Asylum, and Sir Henry Irving was critical of the unusually lenient sentence, remarking, "Terriss was an actor, so his murderer will not be executed." Prince wrote to Sir Henry from the asylum saying that he would kill him soon too. Charming. One of the boys, Brian Terriss, believed that the murdered actor in the portrait was his grandfather. The children, after all, often had no idea of who their relatives were and no way of finding out. And, often many years later, would discover all kinds of show-business connections.

Not long after the War, a young boy called Gerry Norman arrived at Silverlands. Gerry would prove popular and end up as head boy. In 1947, his actor-father, Harold Norman, had also been stabbed and killed. This time, it was actually on stage, and accidentally, by the actor playing Macduff to Norman's Macbeth at the Oldham Coliseum. The Theatre, it seems, can be quite deadly. Not to mention *the curse of Macbeth.*

Also, back in the grand hall again was the large brass gong, struck to announce meals and assemblies. (Outside, there was a bell tower to call the hordes in from the gardens and woods.) Under the elaborate main staircase was a cupboard containing a telephone. Chertsey 3368 was the number, and many a child spoke to a relative in that cupboard. Giving updates and making plans to see them soon... or not.

The grand piano was back in the assembly hall, where occasionally a child might manage *Moonlight Sonata*, but more often than not *Chopsticks*. Noël's visits would, of course, see him play and sing some standards of the day, the children joining in in various pitches. There was also the large wooden wireless radio to be enjoyed at set times. The large recreation room was full again of board games, such as checkers, chess and Monopoly, though most preferred to play *Grandmother's Footsteps* or *British Bulldog* instead. It also now had a ping-pong table and a very small stage. There was also the small library, woodwork area and materials for weaving and art. Excitingly, uniforms would not be imposed outside of school, and a certain amount of individuality could now be expressed. There was now to be an enjoyable distinction between school and home.

The view from the loggia at the back of the house, with its marble-floored porch, was spoiled slightly by the two brick air-raid shelters left over from the War. Outside too were the football field, tennis court, cricket pitch, athletics area and general playground. Down by the Hazells' cottage was the vegetable garden and once again, with the help of the children, all of the eggs, potatoes and vegetables would be grown on site. Livestock would include poultry and pigs. The wheat and barley for maintaining them would also be harvested.

Back inside, the bedrooms, all on the first floor, with their high ceilings and sash windows, had six white iron bedsteads to a room. Floral wallpaper adorned all the rooms, and each child had a shared wardrobe and one drawer each. Bath night was still once a week and bathwater was shared so you had to be canny or lucky to get the early slot. But it was warm.

*

In 1946, two sisters had come to the orphanage, Susannah, aged seven, and Judy, aged three. The new heads, the Aggitters, had not only a daughter, Vanessa, but also a black and white terrier, called Judy... much to little Judy's dismay. (This is Judy Staber who wrote the excellent account of her experiences in the book *Silverlands*.) The two new girls had a very successful mother, the actress Joan White, but she was constantly working in the theatre and it ruled her life. When her husband had had to leave suddenly, less money meant a smaller house, no nanny, and a need to embark on long theatrical tours. The girls would have to be sent to Silverlands and that was that.

Joan had a nice home in London still but she had decided to, perhaps needed to, take in lodgers, including the actress Joan Sims. In truth, Joan wasn't very maternal and her career was hectic and terribly important to her. Susannah's very name came from the play *Susannah and the Elders,* which Joan had been starring in at the time of her pregnancy. Susannah and Judy remember *Silverlands* as their home.

Joan and the two girls arrived at Silverlands by a taxi cab from Chertsey Station. Joan said goodbye and left Susannah and Judy at the grand front door with Commander Aggitter. An older child took their luggage to their rooms and they were introduced to Matron and the rest of the staff. At dinner, they would meet sixty plus fellow children, who were to become kind of siblings. It was a daunting experience, but a shared one, for it had happened to Paul and Granville at Langley in 1930, and countless others all the way back to Croydon in 1906.

Children were left over and over again at the gates or by the front doors. Sometimes there were many tears; sometimes emotions could be kept pent up inside. This experience alone was damaging to the psyche of a small child. It wasn't a boarding school. They knew it was called the *Actors' Orphanage*, and they knew, for the most part, if they had a living relative. (Some children thought that they didn't, only to find out years later that their parents were, indeed, alive.)

Norma Gumley would sit on the front steps every Visiting Sunday (the third Sunday of every month), waiting for a mother that would never come. Then, all too often, several years later, they would be plucked from the orphanage just as suddenly as they had arrived, their parent apparently wanting them back and now in a position to support them. No time was given to say goodbye to their childhood friends, no time to think, no time to… get emotional. The intervening years at least had provided some sense of home.

Visiting Sundays still often involved a parent taking their child out for the day, perhaps for a walk through town and to a café. Tea and cake at the Bridge Hotel by the Thames was popular. They might also give their child some money, clothes, gifts… no doubt the sight of these added to the sadness of those with no such visitors and no such gifts and no such adventures in town. Sometimes while these excursions were happening, back at Silverlands on the Sunday afternoons, something called an *adoption parade* would take place. This was for those children with absolutely no living relative. A child would be brought into the main hall dressed in their Sunday best while strangers would say hello and look them up and down. *Some* ended up being adopted, many didn't, especially as they grew older.

For many reasons, some children were only at the orphanage for a short spell, it being almost a stopgap for them. For others, though, it was their entire childhood, from their earliest memories to going out into the big wide world as seventeen-year-old adults.

*

Children, we know, can be cruel. All the Matron Matey Irvings in the world or the most caring committee couldn't stop that. The stigma of 'telling' was ever great between the children, and initiations for new arrivals were par for the course. Some girls in Susannah and Judy's era were rolled up in their thin mattresses and peed on. Many had their heads flushed in a toilet bowl, and some were locked in the 'Den of Death'. This was a successful way for a bully to display their authority over others. One such boy was Ken Collinson (actually Peter but called by his middle name, Ken, because there was already a Peter at the orphanage). Ken was at Silverlands from 1945 (aged eight), before his behaviour saw him, not expelled, but moved to a second orphanage building, Rutland Gate, in 1950 (aged thirteen). Ken assumed himself as a kind of unofficial head boy; gathering a small gang of the older boys around him, he would steal all the sweets from the cupboard or lock new arrivals in the Den of Death. This was a small room underneath the central courtyard. It was dark and dingy and through the grate above could be dropped insects, dirt and phlegm. The message? Ken's in charge, don't mess with him. The fact that he would go on to be a successful film director one day, might not, to some, seem wholly surprising.

Children could sometimes go too far before finally being found out and dealt with. Ken held a certain reign of terror before the staff, and eventually Noël himself would realise that they had to step in. Notably, Ken created, at least once, the Sneak's Chair. A young unpopular boy was deemed a bad egg by all but had also broken the rule and told on someone. He had sneaked and, as such, was destined for the Sneak's Chair. Late one night, long after lights out, the deeply disliked and unfortunate boy was tightly tied to a chair and dangled, face towards the ground, by Ken and his young cronies, over the balustrade of the main hall. Perhaps not surprisingly, the boy peed himself and, equally not surprisingly, he learnt to keep his mouth shut.

Incidences went from the minor to the extreme throughout the orphanage's long history, many of which were commonplace in any such institution of the era. Indeed, far worse went on at several of the prestigious British boarding schools. Much behaviour too that seems rather terrible now was perfectly normal then. For example, many of the boys smoked Woodbine cigarettes from the age of twelve onwards. Burning down the Scout Hut in 1949 would be less acceptable.

All of the children still had certain duties or chores. Cleaning, washing-up, gardening, and so forth. Boys might be assigned to 'Coke Squad' for a time. This involved shovelling the delivered coke (coal, not narcotics, obviously) into wheelbarrows and taking it from the main gate all the way up to the house's central courtyard and tipping it into the great furnace. Any gardening was *sometimes* less of a chore and perhaps more of an enjoyment. All the children had overalls and a pair of Wellingtons, and everybody adored the gardener, Bert Hazell. His cottage had goats and chickens and was where they grew all the vegetables, letting the children help out as they pleased. The Hazells had four children of their own by now and also continued to take in any (and there were a few) babies left at the orphanage for Mrs Hazell to rear, until they were ready for the big house. And they were still providing a home for Hugo when he was on leave.

A bit of the land at the rear of the property, near Lyne Lane, was rented out to a local farmer to keep some of his machinery on and some pigs. These too could be enjoyed by the children. In 1953, Marlene Dietrich would sprain her ankle while hobbling down to the pigsty in extremely high heels.

In mid-twentieth-century England, a good many people still went to church 'religiously', and every Sunday the children walked two by two all the way along Lyne Lane to Trinity Church. At least the Anglicans did; the few Catholics went to another church also nearby. In the left pews at Trinity Church sat the regular churchgoers of the local community and on the right side on the front pews were about twenty mental patients from nearby Saint Peter's Hospital. Behind them sat a good forty of the – possibly rowdy – orphanage children. Talk about community spirit.

Despite the chores, the corporal punishment, the occasional washing-out of mouths with soap, the continued rationing, the bullies, church service every Sunday and the somewhat enforced letter-writing to any relatives that they might have... their president and the committee were always held in high regard. And the sheer splendour of Silverlands appreciated.

*

Incidentally, in 1947, while in America directing a doomed revival of *Tonight at 8:30*, Noël was catching a train to Baltimore with his sometime American lawyer, Fanny Holtzmann. A discovery had allegedly been made. Fanny had done some digging and investigating and discovered that the source of the 1941 Bow Street court case over tax issues and undeclared monies in the US was, according to Noël's diaries, 'a lot of Hollywood and New York British renegades, livid with jealousy about me and resentful that I should ask them to subscribe to the orphans and not subscribe myself.' A bit rich considering his earlier donations, as well as the fact that he had turned the orphanage around and vastly improved, well, everything.

Noël really had had no idea that he was supposed to declare the money at the time, and his business manager (and former partner), Jack Wilson, was not the best. Indeed, he was spiralling into alcoholism, but Noël always *wanted* to see the best in him and thus trusted him.

To recap, Noël was in America in 1941 on covert war work, which he obviously couldn't divulge. Money to fund this work went accidentally and innocently undeclared. The jealous 'Hollywood and New York British renegades' allegedly instigated a court case, which resulted in much negative publicity, stress and sheer frustration for Noël. And of course was the excuse that Churchill had used to block Noël's knighthood in 1942. So we can say that technically Noël's knighthood being delayed by some *twenty-eight years* was, indirectly, because he was, while being a spy and propagandist in America, trying to cajole fellow celebrities to fund the orphanage's evacuation to New York. This was certainly something to *rise above*, but at least he now had a better idea of exactly what had happened.

This is of course if we believe, as Noël clearly did, what Fanny Holtzmann had reported back. She was, after all, a highly respected lawyer. It is also worth noting that if, as some had occasionally insinuated, Noël was only the Actors' Orphanage president because he had wanted a knighthood, he assuredly did not resign from his position or responsibilities after the prospect of a knighthood was all but lost.

As the years went by, it would become increasingly ludicrous that all of Noël's contemporaries and then juniors were knighted but not *The Master* himself. Being a friend of the royals was no help, and as Sir Alec Guinness would say, "We have been like a row of teeth with the front tooth missing."

*

Judy Staber recalled that as very young children they had no idea who 'Noël Coward' was and, "All I knew was that from time to time this nicely dressed, posh-sounding man came to see us. He would come upon us outside, playing hide-and-seek in and around the air-raid shelters and would call out, 'Hello, boys and girls. Having a jolly time, are you?'"

Two other sisters arrived in 1947: Liz Eastham, aged five, and Caroline Eastham, aged four. (Their father was an agent and their mother an actress.) Liz thought that Noël appreciated the innocent affection the children showed him *because* they didn't know that he was so famous and prestigious. He hadn't, after all, been anonymous to the wider world since 1924. Susannah recalled him as, "Debonair, nice-smelling, very tall, with beautiful hands, elegant, suave, immaculately dressed, funny and always very kind."

Many that I've spoken to have some wondrous memories. Susannah, a natural performer and pretty, was often selected for special occasions, such as presenting the Queen (later the Queen Mother) with flowers at a 1949 film premiere. Meanwhile, Liz was taken to stay at Richard Attenborough and Sheila Sims' house, Old Friars, in Richmond, the night before the Queen's Coronation. She was surprised and in awe the next day that *a maid* served breakfast. At the Coronation itself, they sat in the stalls right outside Westminster Abbey.

The Attenboroughs had been on the committee since 1947 and were hands-on and just as involved and conscientious as Noël. When I spoke to their son, Michael Attenborough, he recalled his parents taking him to visit the orphanage in the 1950s and was at first embarrassed, as he was acutely aware of his family's wealth as they pulled up in a Bentley, and feared the hatred and resentment of the children. He was soon assuaged, however, as they were always thrilled to see his mother and father, and thus him too.

Richard, after Noël gave him his first job out of RADA, in *In Which We Serve,* had gone on to serve in an RAF film unit during the War. Returning to acting, the stage play and then film version of *Brighton Rock* had made him a star, and thus he and Sheila were asked to join the committee. (Sheila being a famous actress in her own right already.)

Liz also spent a summer staying in the loft at actress Joyce Carey's house. She remembers Noël visiting and bringing them all strawberries and cream during the Wimbledon season. Her younger sister, Caroline, has memories of Noël and Marlene Dietrich taking her hands and walking her around the gardens at Silverlands. "He was like a daddy, very nice, so sweet to me."

In 1948, Caroline, aged just five, was taken to stay at Noël's London home in Gerald Road, for she was to join him at a premiere the next day and had to practise her curtsy and prepare to meet the Queen. Caroline remembers going over and over the curtsy, and then sitting in a big leather chair with Noël and a lady sat opposite (most likely Lorn), and then being chatted to as she was tucked into bed.

The next day was like a fairy tale; little Caroline had a grand breakfast and was walked by Noël to his posh car and, sat in the back, they drove through crowds of people. There was a red carpet and much excitement. Noël, leaning down, said, "Don't forget your curtsy." Caroline had simply to hand the flowers to the Queen, say, "With love, Your Majesty," and do *the curtsy*. She handed the flowers, spoke her line perfectly, went to curtsy and… fell over. One imagines much more amusement than any crossness. All this time later, Caroline said, "Noël did more for me in that one weekend than my daddy ever did."

Noël was, as always, clear that birthdays and Christmases were to be celebrated and made special. On birthdays, if no relative was forthcoming with a present, the committee would provide one, and for dinner you could chose whatever pudding you wanted. Christmases always included two coaches being booked to take everyone to the pantomime at the Theatre Royal,

Windsor. Often too they would continue to go into the West End and see those perennial Christmas favourites: *Where the Rainbow Ends, Peter Pan* or *Toad of Toad Hall.*

On Christmas Day, all of the children still had to remain at the orphanage; otherwise, some would be left behind while others went off with their families. This way some sadness could be avoided and the orphanage *family* were kept together for the day itself. Boxing Day instead could be spent with a relative. Christmas morning would start with an allowed pillow fight, a better-than-usual breakfast with everyone dressed in their Sunday best. Later, Father Christmas, looking suspiciously like Commander Aggitter (or his 1949 replacement, Mr Savage-Bailey), would descend the grand stairs, past a large tree on the landing, with his sacks of presents. Those with no gifts from relatives would be, as ever, provided for by the orphanage. Also, everyone would always get a postal order for five shillings from the committee and another one, also for five shillings and later for ten shillings, from Noël personally. Next came Christmas dinner, sometimes attended by special visitors such as Mr Savage-Bailey's sister and brother-in-law, the actors Dulcie Gray and Michael Denison. Then the listening on the wireless to the King's speech was absolutely compulsory... and in those days, thrilling.

The other holidays of Easter and summer could still be spent with relatives for those that had them and those that were *wanted* for the holidays. Susannah and Judy were some of the luckier children in a way, as they sometimes joined their mother on tour, staying in the digs and seeing her shows. When she was in London, they could stay at her house, 16 Linhope Street, near Regent's Park. A nice house but always filled with the long-term lodgers, such as Joan Sims. The girls had to sleep on the floor of their mother's room or on the couch in the parlour. The lodgers were always told that the girls were 'home from boarding school.' Linhope Street never did feel like home, though. They would also, on occasion, stay with their elderly grandparents in Didcot, their grandmother reading them stories outside, under the wisteria.

The many children with nowhere to spend the holiday simply stayed at Silverlands for the long summer break, Norma Gumley still hopelessly waiting for her mother to arrive. A two-week holiday was still always provided in August, however, when rooms would be rented in a coastal town such as Bexhill-on-Sea, Selsey Bill or Bournemouth. These were such adventures for the children that Susannah and Judy were always sure to leave Linhope Street and go too. The fun of all staying together but in a different locale to the lovely but overfamiliar Silverlands was giddy-making. Playing on the beaches and in the sea with countless friends on long summer days, with no schoolwork to worry about, was rather special.

Back to the school year, and Monday nights now offered a dance class in the assembly room, which mainly the girls attended but a couple of the boys too. On committee visits, a little show might be put on, with a small chorus line and the odd solo song from one of the more confident children, such as Susannah. Another absolute highlight in the calendar occurred every Saturday. After morning chores, each child received a little pocket money that was almost always used immediately that afternoon when a Mr Lazell, the sweetie man, arrived. He parked his Austin in the courtyard and opened his boot to reveal a grand assortment of Liquorice Allsorts, Jelly Babies, Smarties and other such wonders.

The War was truly over, and Silverlands was back in its routine.

*

The late 1940s were strange career-wise for Noël. His long, largely unbroken, streak of success and theatrical dominance was finally waning. The grand and expensive Drury Lane musical Pacific 1860 had flopped. The critics would attack all of his work from now on as *old-fashioned* and *pre-war*. 1947's play, *Peace in Our Time*, was a departure for Noël. It was a serious study of what might have happened to London had Germany won the War. Perhaps it was too soon, for it also flopped. So too did the American revival of *Tonight at 8:30*. By 1949, Noël was turning back to cinema, starring in a screen adaptation of his short dramatic play *The Astonished Heart*. He starred alongside Celia Johnson and Margaret Leighton; it was hoped by all to equal and repeat the success of *Brief Encounter*... it also flopped.

However, in 1947, Noël had played his trump card and revived and starred in the ever-successful *Present Laughter* at the Theatre Royal, Haymarket. Also, his personal life was full of happiness. Graham Payn had been a boy-actor in Noël's 1932 revue, *Words and Music,* and in 1945, in his late twenties, had worked for Noël again. This time starring in the short-lived revue *Sigh No More.* Noël and Graham became an item, with Graham also acting in *Pacific 1860, Tonight at 8:30* and *The Astonished Heart.* Graham was a talented actor, singer and dancer, but more than that, he was a kind and gentle soul. Not to mention quite devastatingly gorgeous.

Born in South Africa in 1918, his parents divorced and he soon ended up in England with his loving mother. He worked as a boy soprano and in 1931 played at the London Palladium as Curly in, yes, *Peter Pan.* Graham would never become the *star* that Noël wished him to be, but he was a loyal and loving companion until the day Noël died.

In 1948, Noël, inspired by his friend Ian Fleming's writing retreat on the north coast of Jamaica, purchased his own land there. Near the small remote town of Port Maria, Noël built Blue Harbour. It still stands today, with many of the original furnishings and the same stunning view of the warm and soothing Caribbean Sea. Here Noël, Graham, Cole Lesley (Noël's personal assistant and close friend), and many, many friends could relax, far away from the West End or Broadway. Noël would write in the mornings (poetry, war memoirs, short stories, a new musical), relax down by the saltwater pool in the afternoons and entertain his guests in the evenings. Despite the tropical heat, he made sure that he had a piano and plenty of books too.

Meanwhile, Lorn was more likely to be in London keeping the office going. When Noël would return, refreshed, to London, he was no longer the *King of the Theatre* that he had once been, but he was still extremely famous and popular and still *the* person to see at the Theatrical Garden Party, Pathé News still filming featurettes for the cinemas year in, year out.

The Theatrical Garden Party had resumed immediately after the War, with Noël and Lornie again putting long hours into its organisation. Now they would be held primarily at the grounds of the Roehampton Club. Entrance would cost two shillings and six. They were just as popular with the public as ever, although Noël would often, as the years went by, describe them as exhausting, and many times, it being England, it would be cold and damp. Noël would still lead the Duchess of Kent around the grounds (the Duke now sadly several years gone), sing in a tent for an admission fee and host the odd auction. Other charismatic auctioneers over the coming years would include the fresher and characterful faces of Peter Ustinov and Robert Morley. You were now also likely to catch a glimpse of Richard Attenborough, Sheila Sim, Raymond Massey, Moira Lister, Dulcie Gray, Michael Denison, Vic Oliver, the Crazy Gang, Margaret Rutherford, Danny Kaye, John Gielgud, Trevor Howard or Gertrude Lawrence. Many regular pre-war attendees were still around too, such as the Oliviers and Sybil Thorndike.

Every star still had to do 'a turn', such as Tommy Cooper

performing his magic tricks or Cesar Romero dancing with the public. *Our Favourite Dishes* continued to be published, including *Richard Attenborough's Risotto*, a dish he'd never made in his life. Robert Morley was fond of running the *Cats on a Wall* game. Tents were still labelled with such titles as 'Dancing in a Tent' or 'Nips of Tea'. Many of the children were still always there, helping out and even performing. A gymnastics team appeared in one of the tents, providing summersaults and climaxing in a human pyramid with Susannah at the top.

*

Silverlands *was* still an orphanage, of course, and away from the glamorous episodes, life was and had to be a routine of school and discipline. Lights out was at 8pm for the young form, 9pm for the older. Corporal punishment was still a part of life. Commander Aggitter could be intimidating when necessary; a former naval officer, he was very tall with a large paunch. Dressed immaculately in a waistcoat and watch-chain, he would discipline naughty boys with a slipper, cane or belt… depending, one assumes, on the level of misbehaviour. Mrs Aggitter would punish the girls and always with a bamboo switch, often plucked by the naughty, offending girl herself from the gardens, knowing that they were to be whacked with it presently, Mrs Aggitter sending them back if the selected bamboo was too small or dainty.

The routine was the same whether male or female; trousers must be dropped and ankles grabbed. A lighter punishment was the defaulters' table. This is where you sat at meals if you'd been naughty, and all you were given was bread and water: a punishment that went all the way back to the days of Moreland Road in Croydon in the 1900s. Not that the regular meals were *haute cuisine*. Cooking for sixty-odd children day in, day out led to a fair bit of lumpy porridge or even, on occasion, tripe – the offal from the lining of a cow's stomach and often *something* of an acquired taste. Judy and Susannah both recall putting this into their knicker pockets for later disposal, but the unfortunate smell of the tripe remaining about their persons for quite some time.

Meals generally after the War were lacking for the whole of Britain, let alone the orphanage. Breakfasts were cereal in the summer and the lumpy porridge in the winter, although bread and jam was always available. Lunch would be served at school and was also very basic. High tea would be at 5pm back at Silverlands. All hands would be checked for cleanliness on entrance to the dining hall. Each child would stand behind their chair at one of the long green Formica tables. Food would be dished up, grace would be spoken, and then and only then could everyone sit down and eat.

Mondays meant beans on toast; Tuesdays was scrambled eggs on toast. Wednesdays? Sardines on toast. Thursdays saw macaroni and cheese, and Fridays meant boiled fish. Weekends, thankfully, saw roast dinners, using vegetables grown on site. Pudding was more often than not suet pudding. To drink there was always plenty of weak, dribbly tea. Lovely. And two children would be on the long washing-up duty after every meal.

During these years, Matron Matey (Dorothy) Irving was still around, and whatever the injury, the result was often the same: a heap of stinging salt poured onto it. Matey would last until 1950 and then there would be a series of matrons until Miss Rennie arrived in late 1952. A long-term popular staff member wasn't always easy to find in this very particular setting.

Staff members worked essentially twenty-four seven, had adequate but not excessive salaries, lived on site and with naughty children as a constant threat. They must have only really relaxed when the children were at school. Even after lights out, they knew that some naughty child somewhere in the house was trying to sneak about and possibly raid the larder. As they also knew that some child or other would be murder to get out of bed in the morning. No matter what they did, there would always be, from time to time, a child talking back or even cursing. A bit of shoplifting at the local Woolworth's in Chertsey. Even the occasional runaway.

In 1949, the ultimately rather too strict headmaster Commander Aggitter and his wife would be dismissed. Word of bullying and, once again, perhaps too much corporal punishment was reaching Noël and the committee. (Noël must have been almost blasé about having to let people go at this point.) Noël had written in his diary on the 22nd of September 1949:

Stormy Actors' Orphanage meeting when I flew at everyone, myself included, and I think galvanized them into some sort of awareness of their responsibilities.

The Aggitters' replacements, the Savage-Baileys, were unfortunately not savage enough and might as well have been drinking Baileys, so lax were they in *their* approach. Susannah reflected that they were simply 'too kind', and that sixty-odd parentless children needed some kind of discipline. Getting the balance right at the orphanage was never ever easy.

Kittie Carson

Moreland Road, Croydon 1906

*Paul and Granville Bantock,
Langley Hall,
Berkshire circa 1930*

NOEL COWARD

Noël Coward 1930

Noël Coward at Langley Hall 1934

Theatrical Garden Party, Regents Park 1937 (featuring at centre: Paul Bantock, Noël Coward and the Duke and Duchess of Kent)

Cinderella poster 1938

Silverlands, Chertsey 1938

'They're off to Hollywood!' London Evening Standard 1940

Empress of Australia 1940

Noël Coward as Captain Kinross, In Which We Serve, 1942

*Susannah Slater
1946*

*Judy Staber, Susannah Slater, Liz Eastham,
Caroline Baldwin, Silverlands 1948*

*Rutland Gate, Knightsbridge, Christmas 1950, featuring Susannah
Slater, Duncan and Yolande Rider (at head of table), and Peter
Collinson (third from right)*

Mary Martin, Susannah Slater, Noël Coward, Charles Russell,
Cafe de Paris 1952

Noël Coward at Silverlands 1953

Noël Coward, Marlene Dietrich and Jon Morris at Silverlands 1953

Laurence Olivier and Noël Coward. Night of 100 Stars, London Palladium 1954

Richard Attenborough and Noël Coward 1969

Noël Coward's grave, Firefly, Jamaica 2017

SIX

Troubles Anew

1950-1952

There are Bad Times Just Around the Corner
— Noël Coward song for *The Globe Revue*, 1952

In 1950, the Actors' Orphanage Fund purchased 27 Rutland Gate in Knightsbridge. A posh, five-storey London terraced house at a cost of £11,500 (approximately £370,000 today, although today it would actually cost significantly more). The new property was to house the fund's office, host the committee meetings and serve as a central London hostel for graduates of Silverlands. Here, the seventeen and eighteen-year-olds could live while they completed various forms of vocational training. Many of the girls could attend secretarial school, and the boys could take various apprenticeships. Rutland Gate was almost a halfway house between Silverlands and the big wide world.

The young adults would have greater freedom here with London on their doorstep. They were together too as a great support system for each other as they strived to begin their adult lives. After a long day in a strange place at a new job, they could at least return to a few familiar faces. Evenings would be full of chat about how their various apprenticeships and placements were going and who they were meeting. As well as talk of current music, films and who they might be in love with... and of course there would be much reflection and gossip on their years growing up at Silverlands.

It was a graduate of Langley that was made the housemaster and general manager of Rutland Gate. Duncan Rider, star of the Bijou Theatre's pantomimes of the 1930s, and now aged thirty-nine, was put in charge of the building, along with his wife, Yolande. He had survived serving in the War and needed a new role in life. By 1950, he was more than ready for this new challenge and for returning to the charity. It was a bit like a homecoming.

Among the first intake at Rutland Gate were a dozen seventeen and eighteen-year-olds, and a solitary ten-year-old girl... Susannah Slater. Whereas Judy, Liz and Caroline would spend eleven or twelve years at Silverlands, Susannah had been moved out after four. The reasons were complicated. Susannah was rather a handful all right, but she was also very independent, confident, ambitious and talented. Also, her mother had friends on the committee.

Of the move, Susannah recalled, "I was very privileged, we saw more of Noël and the others. Before the committee meetings and visits we'd feel very nervous. Before Noël arrived we'd be cleaning the stairs, polishing the metalwork." And, "Mrs Rider was like a mother to me. She was wonderful." Yolande Rider was French and exotically beautiful. Susannah felt a little bullied and intimidated by some of the older children around her but not too badly, and with Yolande looking out for her she was just fine.

Susannah had indeed been very spirited at Silverlands, often caned and very often on the defaulters' table, with only bread and water for a meal. On one occasion, her mother was called after Susannah had been caught in the bushes with one of the boys, Michael. Joan White, showbiz to the core, merely said, "I was eight when I was caught doing a similar thing."

Susannah wasn't like many of the other Silverlands children: "I could stand on my own two feet but others found it harder." She often called upon a phrase that Noël used but is also attributed to Judy's godfather, Tyrone Guthrie: "Rise above it, no matter what happens, you must rise above it." Of course, she had many of the same issues as the others, often wondering who her father was and where he was. And holding some mixed feelings about her glamorous mother: "Only an actor can make an orphan of you while they're alive."

Yet Susannah had a keen ambition to enter show business herself. Ideally, she wanted to be a dancer, and was actually encouraged by her absent mother. Even Noël, once he knew that she could and wanted to dance, encouraged her to apply to the Royal Ballet with his blessing. She didn't get in, due to a weak ankle, but then Noël suggested musical theatre, and she was accepted at the Arts Educational Drama School in Green Street, off Park Lane. Hence also, her living at Rutland Gate.

During the Christmas of 1950, Susannah went back to visit Silverlands. On the 7th of December, the BBC filmed a feature on the orphanage for a show called *In Town Tonight*. The aspiring ten-year-old actress was brought in to say, "Here's a carrot for Rudolph!" to a shaggy horse with antlers glued to its head, a wagon behind it, and presenter Brian Johnston dressed as Father Christmas. This was also the occasion of the photograph of Noël at the piano with the younger children in party hats and holding balloons, the older children worrying that the little girl on Noël's lap would piss herself.

The orphanage still usually actively discouraged a show-business career almost as a point of policy, as it has never been an easy choice. Over the years, however, talent did prevail, with graduates such as Peter Collinson, the director of *Up the Junction* and *The Italian Job*. And Anthony Ainley, the actor from *Upstairs, Downstairs* and *Doctor Who*. And long before that there was, of course, the film actor and star of *David Copperfield*, Frank Lawton.

In good time, Susannah would work at Frinton Rep, Salisbury Rep, tour the UK in *The Spider's Web* with Margaret Lockwood, act in a television adaptation of *Toad of Toad Hall*, sing with Max Bygraves, sing as an Ovaltiney on the radio and dance in Hanley, Stoke-on-Trent, as a Tiller Girl. She was still, despite very good reports at Rutland Gate and having a close relationship with Mrs Rider, a handful. As a young girl free to roam London, Susannah had a lot of fun. By 1954, and with the closure of Rutland Gate imminent, she would be put on a plane to join her mother and continue her career in Canada. Judy, meanwhile, wouldn't see their mother for another seven years. Now the sister she so looked up to had gone too. Feeling abandoned all over again, Silverlands really was the only home that Judy had.

Noël would stay in touch with Susannah for some years, often by telegram. Noël knew all about childhood ambition himself, of course. It was that 1910 advertisement, calling for child actors, in the *Daily Mirror* that had caught the eye of Noël and his mother and started it all. It said, 'Talented, attractive boy wanted'. They decided that Noël was talented. Attractive? Moot point but they'd better give it a go. He got the job, playing 'Prince Muscle' in *The Goldfish*, a children's play at The Little Theatre. He never looked back.

*

In the early 1950s, Noël was still having difficult years professionally. The musical *Ace of Clubs* had flopped, and his funds were low. Yet his created family were always there. Graham Payn, long established as a member of the intimate circle now, along with Cole Lesley (his personal secretary since 1935), Lornie (now Noël's representative), Joyce Carey (still an actress in many of his productions) and Gladys Calthrop (still his set and costume designer). And the new home, Blue Harbour, Jamaica, was a constant delight, especially through the British winter months. Yet... Noël was feeling the post-war blues.

He felt that he'd wasted the last five years and lost his position as the *King of the Theatre*. *Ace of Clubs* had even been turned down by his long-term producer, Binkie Beaumont. Producers used to fight over his productions. Now a new play, *Home and Colonial,* written for the Oliviers, was also turned down. How had it come to this? How could he be a sensation at twenty-five and struggling at fifty?

Noël *was* offered the lead role in a new Broadway musical called *The King and I*... but he had always created his *own* work. He was so much more than a mere actor for hire. Not to mention the fact that a long Broadway run in a musical with his quite limited singing voice didn't massively appeal. Despite huge pleas from Rodgers and Hammerstein, both longing for him to star as the King of Siam opposite Gertrude Lawrence's Anna, Noël turned it down. He needed time to think, and harboured thoughts of an entire year off. There would be four trips to Blue Harbour in 1950, one, household staff aside, completely alone.

As for the Actors' Orphanage, however, Noël never shirked his responsibilities. Rutland Gate was their new great venture, but the expense of a second building, alongside already dwindling post-war funds, was leading them ever closer to financial crisis. The Theatrical Garden Party was making much less of a profit in these days of rationing and hardship. It was still a heck of a lot of work and now usually made only about £4,000, which was very short of the £10,000 needed annually to run Silverlands, let alone Rutland Gate. Once-solid profits had now drastically dwindled. Out of desperation, the garden party was changed to the *Theatre and Film Carnival* and held over *two* days, instead of the usual one, at the Roehampton Club. It was not a success, largely due to the sponsor, the *Daily Mail*, somehow doing none of the promised publicity. And the paper had made a deal that they would be the *only* sponsor. The carnival ran at a loss of over £1,000. It was as much fun as ever but disastrous for the orphanage. Even in these circumstances Noël did his best. His diary of the 3rd of June, 1950, records:

Second day of the Theatre and Film Balls-up. Worked hard from 2pm until 10pm. Signed thousands of autographs, sang hundreds of songs, handsomely supported by my dear ones.

Noël's impromptu tent cabaret performances were still a huge draw as crowds lined, often in the rain, eager to see him sing his own songs.

In 1951, they returned to the title of the Theatrical Garden Party, this year at the Royal Hospital grounds, Chelsea. A sole publicity deal was decidedly not given to any one newspaper. Noël gave back-to-back thirty-minute concerts all day long and they were an absolute riot, as Noël went through thirty years of material, from 1923's *Parisian Pierrot* to 1951's *Don't Make Fun of the Festival* (a satire of the Festival of Britain, *not* of the garden party). There was a simple placard outside a tent that said: 'NOËL COWARD AT HOME: Admission Three Shillings.' His faithful old pianist and veteran of the wartime troop concerts, Norman Hackforth, suggested that they could take the act into a professional venue, so popular and successful was it proving. Soon, close friend Marlene Dietrich, having a huge success herself with cabaret at the Café de Paris in Leicester Square, suggested that Noël do the same. And so did Beatrice Lillie. After all, he had performed to the troops during the War, and they weren't always the easiest of audiences.

Noël was trepidatious at first; he had frequently described his singing voice as, 'Frankly, non-existent' and as having, 'No tone, little music, lots of meaning'. It was, however, singing his songs in a hopeful bid to make a success of the 1951 garden party that finally gave him the confidence. On the 12th of December, Noël descended those gold-bannistered stairs at the Café de Paris, with Norman ready at the piano, for the first of many times. It was an absolute triumph, and Kenneth Tynan insisted that to see Noël at his best you *had* to see him in cabaret.

Classic songs of his from the 1920s and 1930s were revived amidst highly satirical and wittily urbane new songs. A winning combination. His phrasing, diction, gesture, expression and sheer charm creating a set list of songs that one moment made you nostalgically emotional, the next, highly amused and elevated.

The cabaret at the Café de Paris, evidently born out of the orphanage fundraisers, would now become a fixture on his calendar. An annual one-month residency saw the profits keep his personal finances afloat, and that was with several charity shows given purely in aid of the orphanage. Noël's reinvention as a sophisticated cabaret star was a career reviver too, yet there still wasn't enough money to completely support Silverlands and Rutland Gate.

Enter Charles Russell and Lance Hamilton: a couple that had taken over Noël's American business management. They were also gifted producers, and a new fundraiser idea was devised. A show would be held at the London Palladium, *Night of 100 Stars*, a midnight matinee. That show would include Noël and Marlene singing *Land, Sea and Air* and such stars as Danny Kaye and Errol Flynn. There would be scenes, songs, dances and speeches. In the next few years, there would be at least one of these midnight matinees a year, called everything from *Midnight Cavalcade* to *Stars at Midnight*. They proved a life-saver for the orphanage.

Noël and Lorn would enjoy months of gossipy letters from Russell and Hamilton as they discussed who would be a good turn and who bad. It was Lorn who had the duty of writing to every possible star and trying to schedule them into the event. Many of the multitude had scheduling conflicts, of course. Still, it was somewhat easier to organise than the garden parties had been, for this was one big, contained show.

These wildly successful shows would feature countless tantalising novelty acts over the coming years, such as, on one memorable occasion, the rather middle-aged Laurence Olivier, John Mills and John Gielgud singing *Three Juvenile Delinquents* from *Ace of Clubs*. As well as Kirk Douglas and Burt Lancaster singing *Maybe It's Because I'm a Londoner* in slightly off Cockney accents. You might also have seen something unusual and fun such as David Niven in the foyer as an usher. The shows would also feature a long dance sequence where *everyone* would do a turn and join in. Richard Attenborough, Googie Withers, Dulcie Gray, Margaret Leighton, Jill Esmond, Robert Morley, Edith Evans...

The orphanage's older children were up past their bedtime, in order to sell the programmes, which always stated, 'No child ever refused, if orphaned or not but of theatrical parentage and in need' and that, '£10,000 must be raised every year.' That first show alone was such a huge success, making much more money than the garden parties had for quite some time. In fact, it made the sum of £10,000.

Thus it was that after 1951, there were to be no more garden parties. The last one had run to a cost of over £6,275, making little profit, despite all the proceeds from the entrance fees, programmes, donations, autographs, gift shop sales and auctions. A forty-five-year beloved tradition had ended. There would be no more *Fishing for Fizz*, mini-golf, *Celebrity Courts*, art galleries, *Magic Circles*, *Dance Cabarets*, *Circus Stars*, fortune-tellings, beauty tents, make-up tents, darts, roll-a-pennies, skittles, shooting galleries, *Kokonuts*, treasure hunts, swimwear parades, RADA performances or Noël singing in a tent on a damp Tuesday afternoon. Not to mention *Garden Teas* with Raymond Massey or *Cats on the Wall* with Robert Morley. Pathé News had filmed the garden party every year and they were an institution. The turning point had been the post-war British economy. It was the end of an era. RIP Theatrical Garden Party: 1906-1951.

Although 1951 really was superb for Noël. The Café de Paris shows aside, he'd had his first bona fide hit play since the War. *Relative Values* was classic Coward yet also quite contemporary (although it had a good dig at social equality). There had also been hit songs produced for the *Globe Revue* and, of course, the success of *Night of 100 Stars*.

Although it was a huge headache to produce the midnight matinees, Noël and Lorn had much help now from the young Richard Attenborough. Noël would cajole and encourage every star he knew to contribute, as well as headline the show himself. Lorn would handle all of the administration. Young Richard, meanwhile, would produce and direct the show. This was no small task with so many performers (and egos) involved.

The shows were so successful that the Jewish National Fund offered to fund the whole operation *several* times a year… if they could split the profits. This was tried for a while, but the committee had grave concerns. They would dilute the effect and, after all, one show a year by and for the orphanage was perfectly effective. However, Rutland Gate still needed funding, so they did extend to two shows a year.

Adding to this newfound success, in January 1952, Noël performed a special two-hour cabaret set with Mary Martin at the Café de Paris, the first solely in aid of the orphanage. Many supporters were in attendance, such as the Duchess of Kent, Richard Attenborough, Sheila Sim, JB Priestly, Pat Kirkwood and Gladys Cooper. It all went very well and raised £2,000. Four hundred guests had paid five guineas each and before the cabaret, in the rather camp pink-lit surroundings, had enjoyed smoked salmon, chicken and ice cream. All very decadent.

The press in attendance gave wonderful reviews and used a supposed feud between Noël and Mary Martin as the hook. There was some truth that Noël and Mary hadn't seen eye-to-eye on the flop musical of 1946, *Pacific 1860*. She had refused to wear a hat. But it was more a case that they simply hadn't had much contact since. Mary, whenever quizzed about the supposed 'feud', would quip, "These things always come right in the end, you know – after all, talent is thicker than water."

It was just a few short weeks later that King George VI died, and such frivolity as the Café de Paris show would, at best, have been postponed. At Silverlands, the orphans were solemnly told, "Our king is dead, children." They wore black armbands and an enforced sadness was expected.

Noël performed again with Mary Martin (she was in town this year performing *South Pacific*) in the November of 1952. Susannah was on hand, from Rutland Gate, to present them with a bouquet of flowers. This time, the audience included Laurence Olivier, Vivien Leigh, Edith Evans, Emlyn Williams, the Lunts and Maurice Chevalier. And this time the cabaret went on until 1am and raised £3,000 for the children (about £85,000 today). Financial troubles were certainly on the way to being solved.

One night only shows in aid of the orphanage and Noël's June residency at the Café de Paris would continue until 1954, before the absolute triumph of a 1955 season (and a live album) in Las Vegas saw Noël end his cabaret career on a high. The opening night of the Las Vegas season saw the Hollywood elite in attendance, from Frank Sinatra to Judy Garland to Lauren Bacall. There's no doubt that the Café de Paris shows were a good rehearsal for this great triumph.

It's wonderful to think that, wartime troop concerts aside, it was really the impromptu singing in a rained-on tent, in a desperate bid to make some kind of success for the orphanage funds, that Noël's gloriously successful cabaret career was born. From that wet tent one Tuesday afternoon to the Café de Paris to *Live at Las Vegas* and also to *Together With Music*, a 1955 live CBS television special with Mary Martin. Thirty million Americans saw that performance.

*

Back at Silverlands, another problem to be fixed during this period was, yet again, staff trouble. 1949's replacements for the rather-too-strict Commander and Mrs Aggitter, Mr and Mrs Savage-Bailey were far too *soft*. They were, by all accounts, very nice and kind people but with absolutely no authority. Noël wrote as early as the 20th of October ,1949, in his diary that:

> *He is obviously a kind man but, I fear, on the weak side. The children were in wild spirits and I was cheered to see they were not looking down-trodden and dismal.*

He adds interestingly:

> *I had a talk with Savage-Bailey about sex and told him not to get too fussed because all children had sex curiosity and too much emphasis on its sinfulness would only make it more attractive, and that as long as he kept*

it with-in bounds he could close an eye discreetly every now and then. I am sure this was good advice although perhaps not strictly conventional.

This demonstrates that Noël really thought about all aspects of what was going on at the orphanage. Boys and girls played *Doctors and Nurses* and this was hardly cause for a severe punishment. Also, in this age of no sex education whatsoever, they had to figure things out somewhat, somehow.

Noël himself had taken baths with his best friend as a boy, Esme Wynne. It was all quite innocent, although once he did kiss her on the cheek... there was a dramatic pause before they burst out laughing. He did, however, feel that he had lost his innocence one day when, while walking back from the theatre with the most famous boy actor of the day, Philip Tonge, he was told the facts of life. It was a barrage of pornographic misinformation that made Noël feel sullied and shameful. He ran home to Mother and declared: "Mother! I've lost my innocence!" This time, it was his mother's turn to laugh.

Noël's later healthy, progressive, liberal attitudes in this regard often found their way into his work. Larita, in 1926's *Easy Virtue,* was challenging Victorian convention and repression as being connected to religious hysteria as she says to her severe mother-in-law:

"All your life you've ground down perfectly natural sex impulses, until your mind has become a morass of inhibitions."

And:

"You've placed physical purity too high and mental purity not high enough."

Design for Living in 1933 had seen a love triangle between Otto, Gilda and Leo, searching for a new kind of domestication. *Present Laughter*, written in 1939, sees Garry Essendine, the erudite West End star, say of sex:

> *"To me the whole business is vastly over rated. I enjoy it for what it's worth and fully intend to go on enjoying doing so for as long as anybody's interested and when the time comes and they're not I shall be perfectly content to settle down with an apple and a good book!"*

Yet Noël was a very dignified person, not crossing private behaviour with public behaviour. Emlyn Williams had given a charity performance of his play at the Aldwych Theatre, *Accolade,* for the orphanage in October 1950. It was about a successful man whose knighthood was withheld due to his homosexual past. I shouldn't think that the children actually attended this one. And Noël was less put out about the withheld knighthood theme and more about it being too explicit about homosexuality. He deemed it, 'Expert but vulgar'. He also had to get up and give a speech from the box at the end, 'thanking absolutely everyone'.

The show must *always* go on and Noël was *always* expected to give a speech. There would also be a fundraiser performance of his new period play *Quadrille* in 1952, starring the Lunts. Noël was there and, of course, expected to give a speech at the curtain call. He fulfilled his duty, despite the fact that Gertrude Lawrence had unexpectedly died in New York that very day… and he was heartbroken.

Noël had known Gertie Lawrence since 1913. They had starred together in *London Calling, Private Lives* and *Tonight at 8:30*. She had been starring in *The King and I* in New York and struggling with her voice… but no one knew that she was dying.

Noël loved Gertie as much as he could any woman (possibly excluding his mother). She was an actress who could sometimes overplay, but, when she pitched it right, was pure stage magic. She was bad with money and with men and had a personality that, like Noël's, could charm the world.

In 1913, when they had acted in *Hannele* together in the provinces, they were 'miscast rather as angels'. The splendidly named Baliol Holloway played a schoolmaster who turns into Jesus and then back into the schoolmaster, which involved very quick changes. Backstage, during one performance, Noël and Gertie heard from Baliol an outburst of four-letter words of the most invective kind. Gertie turned to Noël and said: "Sounds to me as though Christ has lost his trousers."

Her death, Noël never really got over: "No one I have ever known, however talented, however gifted, contributed quite what she contributed to my work."

In 1952, after that performance of *Quadrille*, the stars of the show, Alfred Lunt and Lynn Fontanne, looked after Noël and promised to make him a chocolate cake. Incidentally, also in 1952, the children attended a charity matinee of the seemingly eternal *Where the Rainbow Ends,* though its days were soon to be numbered, the overt colonial message increasingly out of fashion. It was during this same run that Noël took his secretary and friend, Cole Lesley, to see the show. Noël bathed in nostalgia, forty years on from when he had performed in it himself... once, in front of the Moreland Road children in that faraway show organised by Sir Charles Hawtrey...

*

Back at Silverlands in 1950, Noël had continued to find the Savage-Baileys too soft, and the situation was escalating. He had written in his diary on the 14th of April:

Long Orphanage meeting. Children behaving very badly, insulting everyone and stealing left and right. Went over their menus and school reports. Interviewed Mr Savage-Bailey, who stubbornly believes that sweet reason, kindliness and long moral explanations is the right way to handle a lot of illiterate young hooligans of very mixed parentage. It is becoming increasingly clear that his theory is not practicable. He is a kind little man, but like so many idealists, he is a cracking fool. The dear children obviously share my opinion and run rings around him.

Mr Savage-Bailey, too kind, offered too little in the way of punishment, and his psychological approach was not going to work here. The Savage-Baileys were let go, finally, in 1951. Unfortunately, what replaced them would leave much to be desired...

So it was that a Miss Berry came in, far too much the antithesis of Mr Savage-Bailey. It must have been a case of a good interview masking the true character of the woman. Physical and emotional damage was, unfortunately, suffered. Not quite so much from her as from the new housemaster she brought in in early 1952, a Mr David Victor Gordon. He would, allegedly, beat the last child back from games, take pocket money away, make the smaller children walk up and down naked after bath-time, wrestle them, punch them and even held Judy's foot to bonfire embers, burning it enough to leave a scar. Judy was still only seven years old, and despite Susannah having left her young sister her teddy bear, it was no compensation as she lived in constant fear of Mr Gordon and Miss Berry. As, unfortunately, did all the children at this time.

Noël visited on the 23rd of January 1952 and was, unfortunately and rarely for him, totally fooled. After reporting to the committee that the children were happy, well, clean and well fed, he wrote: 'I have formed a very favourable opinion of the new resident master, Mr Gordon.' Noël found him enthusiastic, energetic, pleasant and cheerful! He has the 'right kind of authority', and even a 'sympathetic understanding of the children', then adds, in a kind of obliviousness to foreboding, 'Perhaps I should mention that my visit was not unexpected.' If only Noël really had known earlier what a rotter Gordon was to be at Silverlands.

For now, though, Noël was more concerned with how the sitting room and the boys' bedrooms had no lightshades and that the glare couldn't be good for their eyes. 'It also looks unnecessarily cheerless.' Noël also urges the committee to consider a new home in London big enough to house Silverlands and Rutland Gate. It would be an easier place for the committee to visit and keep an eye on things. More schools would be accessible too. One suspects the motivation here was also to reduce the financial cost of maintaining two separate buildings.

Miss Berry was a very large woman with glasses and a strict, severe demeanour. After the softness of the Savage-Baileys, the committee must have thought she'd achieve the necessary discipline that had been so lacking. Her job description was as Super-intendant Matron, and to attend to administration, health, well-being, discipline and supervision. She was to obey the committee and eat in the dining room with the children. Mr Gordon's job description was to supervise sports and games, hobbies and activities and he had 'full responsibility and authority on his own sphere of activity'. Miss Berry, despite her strict and severe demeanour, did not like to give out the punishments herself, so, lamentably, left that to Mr Gordon.

Mr Gordon was thick-necked with a broken nose and short ginger hair. Thankfully, he was only to last a few months in 1952. It was, however, long enough to, allegedly, wreak quite some damage. As housemaster, he slept in the boys' wing and kept them in permanent fear, for he was, according to many of the children, unpredictable. A fitness fanatic, he was allegedly prone to sudden bursts of violence. Some of the children, on occasion, actually tried to run away, such was the fear and tension that he induced.

His behaviour was also simply mean. One morning, all the children packed their breakfast into his car and then walked four miles to Virginia Water for a designated picnic. Meeting Mr Gordon outside the Wheatsheaf pub, he allegedly demanded all of their pocket money in return for their breakfasts... most didn't even have their pocket money with them. Gordon apparently drove off and they, some as young as four, now walked the four miles back, starving and exhausted.

Mr Gordon was soon nicknamed 'Bully Boy Gordon'. At bath-times, he would watch the boys and might suddenly force someone's head under the water or start parading them up and down the hallway completely naked, while laughing. He might wrestle a child to the floor and slap them. All his cruelty, of course, took place when no other staff members were around to witness it.

The girls didn't escape the bullying, either. Judy was not as confident as her older sister, and was always a little in awe of her and missed her. She couldn't stand up for herself like Susannah could. One weekend, Judy was taking a walk in the grounds when she saw a smouldering fire made by some of the boys earlier in the day. Mr Gordon appeared from nowhere and indeed held her foot to the embers, melting part of her shoe and badly burning her. Matron Rennie fixed up her foot but made Judy promise not to tell anyone that Mr Gordon had done this. We can only hope that Matron Rennie was playing down drama for the sake of the children, and then quietly informing the committee of the man's apparent violence.

Another girl, Ann Penn, tried to run away one day but was

caught at Chertsey Station. Another night, four of the boys got up and left together. They simply started walking, out of the grounds, but to where? They soon got lost and eventually turned back to face their punishment.

Then, late one night, Brian Terriss was approached in his bed by Mr Gordon. Earlier that day, Brian had come to the assistance of one of the smaller boys being attacked by Gordon. Brian had forcefully pulled Gordon off the boy and then they had both made a run for it, hiding in a cupboard. Also, in an earlier incident, Brian had been sure to be the last one back from games so that a very young Liz or Judy would not be beaten, simply for being the last back. Mr Gordon would always say, "Last one up to the house gets a hiding!" And apparently he always meant it. In the rec room, he would put the slowest runner over his knee and spank them… it was always a smaller, weaker child.

Now Brian refused some late-night gifts as a form of apology, but really bribery. So Mr Gordon allegedly punched Brian hard as he lay in his bed. Brian, his life becoming a living hell, punched back as hard as *he* could. In that moment, Brian had become a real-life Nicholas Nickleby, the young man who gave the Master a dose of his own medicine. The young man who had defended the poor, defenceless Smike from the brutish one-eyed Master Squeers. After landing the punch, Brian, in just his pyjamas and bare feet, ran. Down the long hallway, down the stairs, through the grand hall and out, out into the cold night and all the way down the hill, to the gardener's cottage. He confided *everything* to Mr and Mrs Hazell. He slept in their cottage that night.

The next day, Noël was informed and Mr Gordon was sacked. His ally Miss Berry soon left too under a cloud of complicity. It was Mr Gordon, though, that the children of 1952 would fear ever bumping into again, for fear of wanting to do what Brian so courageously had done. Punch back.

For now, though, there was huge relief within the walls of

Silverlands. There are very few records from this period and practically nothing concerning Mr Gordon and Miss Berry. The extent and nature of the abuse is for the victims to know, but it may be deduced by the lack of records that Gordon's behaviour was particularly atrocious. A scandal for the Actors' Orphanage, however, would help nothing and no one, least of all the children. Thankfully, at least, this had been a much shorter reign of terror than that of Austin's all those years before.

*

It never rains but it pours. Around this time, one of the local girls' schools, Stepgates, had reports of abuse by a male teacher. The police were called. The children were immediately switched to a nicer (and private) school called Frithwald. It provided a better education, had smarter uniforms, and in clement weather they could walk there, two by two, along the Holloway Road. After the age of thirteen, the children then attended Fullbrook or Halliford School. Incidentally, at parents' evenings at these schools, the orphans rarely had a relative appear, so they would sometimes put on songs and dances for the other children's parents.

At Silverlands, the new housemaster was a Mr Whitehouse, who was unpopular with some and was replaced quickly by a former Olympian called Mr Weedon. He, *thankfully*, proved very popular. It was as if a clean slate was being put into motion once again by Noël and the committee. It's a tragedy that no matter what the committee did, they couldn't be there twenty-four seven to protect the children and monitor the staff.

Thankfully, many staff members over the years were positively adored, such as the new matron, Miss Rennie. She was accused of being too lax and relaxed but perhaps, for now, that would be a welcome relief. Then there was the new general secretary (and temporary headmaster), Patrick Waddington. Miss Rodda had left the position in late 1952 and it seems that Winifred Rodda may have struggled to get back on track after the recent difficulties. Also, she had been there since 1935 and perhaps, simply, she was exhausted.

Mr Waddington was an Oxford and RADA graduate with a large moustache and rather theatrical manner. His dogs, George and Malcolm, were a firm favourite with the children. Patrick was a good and capable, if eccentric, man. He also brought in a succession of beautiful au pair girls from Germany and Denmark to help out and keep an eye on things. They were very popular with some of the boys.

But whether over the years the staff were good, bad or somewhere in the middle, some of the children would always be a problem, of course. The sense of abandonment, whether they had a parent alive or not, would always be profound and hard to fathom. A kindly staff member, or a visit from Marlene Dietrich or even Richard and Sheila Attenborough, was never going to replace a parent. Susannah and Judy remember getting on the bus one day and pretending that the driver was their father. "Ah, there you are!" they'd say.

Most of the inevitable behavioural problems were merely child's play, of course. On one occasion around this time, a female staff member's wig was stolen. Miss 'Wiggy' Williams was one of the shorter-term matrons of the early 1950s, and this incident may have been the reason for that short term. Miss Williams was known for her extreme 6am wake-up calls, pulling off the bed blankets and saying, "Rise and shine, ladies of the *corps de ballet!*" Most of the children not quite knowing what that obscure French reference meant.

One morning, her tightly curled red wig was not in her room, and all the children were told to look for it while Miss Wiggy Williams remained out of sight. It wasn't long before

Liz and Judy saw the strange red hair on the bust of Gerald du Maurier in the main hall. Scared they'd be blamed, they quickly left for school.

A more serious issue would be bullying, and in 1950, Ken (Peter) Collinson had been increasingly guilty of it. Many of the children feared him, as he was causing merry hell, and school expulsion was even on the cards. Noël appeared at Silverlands and took Peter for a walk around the grounds. They sat on a wall and Noël said that nobody knew better than he did himself about being naughty, but surely always being the naughtiest boy in the school must get a bit boring? He told Peter that he was an intelligent boy, so why didn't he try being the best boy for a change? At least for a trial period? Noël also believed in bribery and told Peter that if he tried to be good, he'd give him ten shillings.

Apparently it worked, at least for a while. Noël could certainly relate to some boyhood angst. He had hated school with a passion, once biting a teacher's arm for correcting his grammar. *The Theatre* saved Noël and he left school pretty much for good in 1910, aged ten. Becoming an autodidact, he consumed books: "I read and read, I belonged to the Battersea Park Lavatory... Library, not Lavatory... Freudian slip."

Noël stuck by Peter, he knew that he was troubled and wanted to help. He even became his godfather and helped him get connected when he wanted to get into show business. Noël tried to find the reason for his behaviour, writing in his diary on the 10th of July 1950:

He is being torn to pieces by his divorced parents. He is in an emotional turmoil. I promised that I would look after him and be his friend. I honestly don't think he will transgress again. Actually he practically broke my heart. I may be over-sentimental but a sensitive little boy bereft of all personal affection is to me one of the most pathetic things in the world.

Peter's parents had divorced when he was two and he was then abandoned by his mother. He lived for a time with very elderly grandparents in the East End, who weren't up to caring for a small child. And so he ended up at Silverlands and certainly with some psychological issues, but then who wouldn't?

By late 1950, Peter, still misbehaving, was placed in Rutland Gate. Here at least Susannah would have someone around slightly closer to her in age. He was fourteen to her ten. (And both of them would escape the reign of Gordon and Berry.) In 1952, thanks to Noël's letter of introduction to the principal, Kenneth Barnes, Peter auditioned for RADA. He didn't, along with thousands of others, gain a place. RADA felt that Peter's accent and manner were very, very bad and that he was not the right material for them. This was a few years before the *angry young man era* would see an influx of working-class actors to RADA's esteemed, seemingly elitist, halls. Noël never gave up on his new godson, though, and had him stay on at Rutland Gate until he finally gained employment backstage in a theatre.

Peter must have indeed broken Noël's heart somewhat, for Noël to become his godfather, prevent his expulsion, allow him to live at Rutland Gate and gain him entrance into show business. Was Noël, in middle age, feeling a strong urge to be a father?

Peter wrote to Lorn and Noël a few years later, in 1959, asking for help, and it was not a problem. Peter, tired of backstage theatre work, was desperate to get into television. Noël connected him, via another letter of introduction, with the right people. Fast-forward to 1968 and there was Peter, having progressed rapidly through the industry, directing Noël in his final film appearance, as Mr Bridger in *The Italian Job*.

Peter insisted that Noël be called 'Master' by everyone on the set, and that 'Master' was to be treated with the utmost respect, which of course left Noël pleasantly bemused, and which he also thoroughly enjoyed. Peter was repaying his godfather's kindness and loyalty, and giving Noël a fabulous cinematic swansong.

It might be noted that Peter was known to be a slight bully as a director, just as he never did completely change his ways at the orphanage. But at least someone in his life had demonstratively cared about him. It must also be said that many of the actors on his sets generally adored him. He was rather wild, doing some of the most dangerous stunts in *The Italian Job* himself. During filming, Noël would reflect that it was heartening to think that the director was that same little boy that he'd saved from expulsion, by having a heart-to-heart with him on that garden wall at Silverlands all those years before.

SEVEN

Changes

1952-1956

There was no fear in her except for me. She was a great woman to whom I owe the whole of my life. I shall never be without her in my deep mind, but I shall never see her again. Goodbye, my darling.

– Noël Coward, on the death of his mother, *Diaries*, 1 July 1954

M r Waddington was the breath of fresh air needed. An eccentric man, he was very jolly, encouraging and funny. He'd recently appeared in a couple of West End flops, and when Noël Coward called him up for a meeting at Gerald Road, he was happy to go along. He knew it was regarding the Actors' Orphanage and not an acting role but, like everyone else in the profession, was rather in awe of Noël. Over dinner, Noël, along with Jill Esmond, persuaded Patrick to visit Silverlands to see if he felt up to the task of running the place after its recent troubles.

Patrick visited the very next day and was impressed by the house and the grounds. He sensed an apprehensive atmosphere and decided to rise to the challenge of reinfusing the place with some cheer. He wanted autonomy, though, which was not possible, and he was very suspicious of the famous committee, Noël included. He even cynically and naively suspected Noël was only the president in the hope of receiving honours. He did, however, take a strong shine to the Attenboroughs, Jill Esmond and Edith Evans.

Patrick Waddington was also in awe of the famous committee, and even a little jealous. They were, after all, show-business royalty. He wasn't, however, going to be a pushover. He was soon giving them grief over their refusal to let him have extended time off. He had had the odd film offer and hoped to revive his *'Old Colonel'* character. Noël had said, initially, that this would be perfectly fine, but in reality it proved impractical. Patrick had also, allegedly, been promised a car that had failed to materialise. These matters were discussed at committee meetings much to Patrick's embarrassment, so he took to leaving the room until they'd all finished discussing him and his needs.

In early 1953, Patrick sent an *eleven-page* letter to Lorn for Noël. It was, in truth, a protracted rant about how awful committees are, how they are not present on the ground yet interfere at the drop of a hat and are ready to pounce at the slightest thing. As if Noël didn't know this already. Patrick states that he is the secretary and thus ranked equivalent to the secretary of a large industrial or commercial company. Ranking as an executive director! He feels that the committee are 'ungracious, albeit distinguished', although he notes that only Dame Edith Evans actually outranks him in the theatrical profession and none of them do in academia. Indeed, not more than three have a particle of his qualifications!

Patrick is also keen to state that after six years of war service as an air marshal, he had never been spoken to as childishly as he had by the committee. He then thanks God that he had refused to sign a long-term contract. Next he recalls how he had told Lorn and Noël at the outset that he was 'honoured to work for you personally', but that 'I would die rather than place myself at the mercy of any committee'.

He goes on. He left Yorkshire twenty-eight years earlier and after two years in the Birmingham Rep, sat in on many committees and concluded that 'for some freak psychological reason', decent, kindly people become fickle, inconsistent, petty-minded and brutal when on a committee. They are also, 'notoriously', the worst employers in the world.

He signs it, 'Yours in extreme dejection'. It all seems to stem from the fact that the committee had decided that he could not play the wireless loudly to the children at breakfast, as it was a bit distracting. Also that he should not be making them recite prayers that he had written himself... and to stick to the classics.

Lorn replied by letter, 'Are you certain that you want me to forward it to Noël?' She also asked to see his prayers. The committee drafted a letter of response – half apology, half explanation – but never sent it. One suspects that Noël smoothed things over. For Noël certainly knew what a pain committees could be for he had written about that very problem in his diaries often enough, and occasionally even in his work. He had also warned Patrick about the committee before he accepted the post, and how they didn't always agree on things.

Although a slight headache for the committee, the children took a great shine to the eccentric Mr Waddington. On Saturdays, dressed in his tweeds, with his theatrical moustache and dogs in tow, he would lead the children on long walks, all singing *One Man Went to Mow* rather loudly. On Sunday mornings, Mr Waddington, now in his Sunday clothes of an Oxford gown and mortar board, noticed, as the children long had, that the local vicar at Lyne Holy Trinity Church was extremely dull and uninspiring. So they would now walk three miles instead of the usual one to Ottershaw's Christ Church, which was much livelier, and nicer all round.

Although the children missed singing their favourite song about the Trinity vicar's rather austere wife:

"Mrs Hodge is in the grass, with a flagpole up her arse!"

Noël knew church had to be on the agenda and was glad of the improvement, but he himself had always distrusted religion a bit; an agnostic all his life. His mother had been left partially deaf after a bad fever as a child, and often recalled to Noël how the nuns at school had been totally unsympathetic and cruel. Her deafness, incidentally, was why Noël had always enunciated with such precise and strong diction.

Noël, incidentally, had been twice approached by priests as a boy: 'The first gave me a random lecture on the almighty; the other gave me sixpence and pinched my knee. Of the two I preferred the latter'.

Patrick Waddington decided to remain as the general secretary, but now handed the headmastership over to the equally jolly and likable new staff member, the Scotsman Angus Fraser, and with his wife, Miss Fraser, also proving popular. Along with the much-loved matron, Miss Rennie, life at Silverlands had once again improved dramatically. Around this time too, the orphanage graduate Anthony Holmes worked as an under-housemaster. In a few years, he would be making a successful acting career for himself as Anthony Ainley.

Mr Fraser often held 'Chibby Nights' in the autumn months, roasting chestnuts for all on the open bonfire and having a sing-along. An avid farmer and gardener, he often had the children outside, helping. And unlike Mr Savage-Bailey, he could be stern when necessary. One evening, Judy and Liz were nowhere to be found, so he sat in their bedroom and waited. Eventually, the two girls climbed in through the window, having been to the Chertsey Picture House to watch *Rebel Without a Cause*. He calmly grounded them for a week.

More seriously, Liz was soon sent away to the vicarage for many months, after apparently upsetting the staff. To this day, she doesn't know exactly what she had done to warrant that. (It's possible that she caught two of the staff members canoodling.) Yet the balance between the happiness of the children and retaining the right level of discipline was generally achieving a far better result these days.

Post-Gordon there was also an increase in committee visits, and the children saw much more of the likes of Lorn, Edith Evans and Jill Esmond. They also saw a good deal of Richard Attenborough and Sheila Sim, currently starring in a long run of *The Mousetrap* in the West End. Little did anyone know that the production would still be running today! Richard and Sheila were very informal on their visits and always 'just popping in'. Their visits in particular are remembered as very natural, kindly affairs, as they chatted and had tea with the children. They were also much younger than the other committee members so perhaps more relatable.

The full executive committee at this time consisted of: Richard Attenborough, Sheila Sim, Adrianne Allen, Joyce Barbour, Clemence Dane, Douglas Byng, Joyce Carey, Angela Baddeley, Leslie Banks, Jill Esmond, Robert Flemyng, Nicholas Hannen, Lorn Loraine, Rodney Millington, Eva Moore, Cathleen Nesbit, Jessie Winter and Diana Wynyard.

Timetables from 1953, discovered in the archives, give us a real insight into the children's lives at the time. Once back from school, high tea was always at 5pm, followed by prayers. By 6pm, the infants were already being bathed for bed while the juniors and seniors did homework in the library. Then there would be a recreational activity, which could be reading, a film screening,

Road Code Games, photography or sewing. At 7pm, the juniors were cleaning their shoes and had to be in bed by 8pm. The seniors, meanwhile, had the privilege of a game of badminton, table tennis or continued reading, for they could stay up until the ludicrous hour of 9pm!

Saturdays saw a morning of chores, such as cleaning or tending to the livestock. Then pocket money was handed out before an afternoon of hockey or football. And 'lights out' would be slightly later. Sundays saw the long early morning walk to church, followed by an afternoon of letter-writing. The evenings would see more prayers and a discussion group for the older children. They were the last generation to experience life without television.

*

Through these years, of the early to mid-1950s, Noël was wishing to make plans for his future. His funds were still low after the War, and most of his plays and musicals were not nearly as successful as they had once been. He was looking for a way to put money aside for his future and release some of his many responsibilities. Noël saw in Richard Attenborough not only a close personal friend, but also a young, good man, very capable indeed of taking on the responsibility of the orphanage one day.

For now, though, things continued as they were, but with Richard assisting Noël wherever he needed it. Richard continued to check in at Silverlands on a regular basis, and to be a huge help producing and directing the Palladium fundraisers. In June 1953, the event was called 'Stars at Midnight', and Richard formed the sub-committee to organise it. He would liaise between Russell and Hamilton, the orphanage, the Palladium and the Jewish National Fund. And schedule in plenty of rehearsals. Thus, a lot of pressure was now taken off Noël and Lorn.

'Stars at Midnight' was the notorious occasion when David Niven was an usher, and Laurence Olivier, John Gielgud and John Mills, dressed as spivs, sang Noël's *Three Juvenile Delinquents*. Gilbert Harding hosted a live version of his popular show, *What's My Line?* Edith Evans and Hermione Gingold acted out a scene set on the Orient Express, and the irrepressible Robert Morley compared.

These were always joyous, celebratory, lavish evenings of sheer theatrical delight. The second half of this midnight matinee opened, as usual by now, with all of the stars dancing onto the stage one by one, past the band, as Vic Oliver announced them. They would then sit at tables upstage and sip champagne, creating a sort of nightclub atmosphere. Noël came on as the headline act, gave a speech, and sang his satirical version of Cole Porter's *Let's Do It*, which brought the house down. *The Sketch* magazine photographed the proceedings but sadly there is no film footage, or even sound recordings of these joyous shows.

1953's show had seen a split of profits with the Jewish National Fund, but as they raised over £19,000, this seemed to work. Yet the programme for the night's proceedings included a message from Noël admitting that the expenditure of recent years had 'something of the quality of a nightmare'. He talks of smaller incomes and higher prices and how they have strained every nerve to raise additional funds. Subscribers are even invited to visit Silverlands, by simply sending a written request to Patrick Waddington at Rutland Gate. Really it was the cost of running Silverlands *and* Rutland Gate that was still causing a problem.

Noël was as busy as ever, writing another new musical, *After the Ball*, and hoping to repeat the success of *Bitter Sweet* in 1929, and thus boost his post-war finances. His hugely popular cabaret continued apace and he had been performing the large, demanding lead role of King Magnus in George Bernard Shaw's

The Apple Cart at the Theatre Royal Haymarket, staged for the Coronation year (and with a charity gala performance for the orphanage, of course). It was during one matinee performance of *The Apple Cart* that one of the younger actors had had too much garlic at lunch. Noël apparently said, "Keep your mouth closed; you're burning the furniture polish. Get some bread and we'll all have a meal."

The Queen's Coronation had arrived on the 2nd of June and was magically projected onto a large screen in the assembly room at Silverlands, by a new wooden *television* projector, provided by Noël. (Afterwards, it was used to also project films.) The portrait over the main fireplace of King George VI was now replaced by one of Queen Elizabeth II. Noël was a staunch royalist, and good friends with the Queen Mother. He never saw the point in having a constitutional monarchy if you couldn't 'be a cosy royal snob'. Five of the children had been picked to go and stay with the Attenboroughs at Old Friars in Richmond, sleeping on the floor of the spare room, before heading to Westminster Abbey the next day.

Meanwhile, the orphanage was at least in better financial shape than it had been, and the generosity of those in the theatrical profession never ceased to help. In the April of 1953, the entire Easter week profits of the West End show *Love from Judy* at the Saville Theatre and starring Jean Carson, had been donated to the orphanage, gifted by the impresario and producer Emile Littler. Before the performance, various stars each night would sell programmes or sign and sell autographs in a gala atmosphere. 'At Every Performance Famous Stars Will Be Your Hosts', said a promotional poster. Noël attended twice and was absolutely mobbed.

The nine shows that week would make a tidy sum and in return Emile simply wanted Noël to ask the Queen and Prince Philip to attend the show. The prestige of their presence at his theatre was something he craved. Noël did indeed write to the royals (from Jamaica), but they were, of course, too busy for such a short-notice request. Emile Littler didn't really carry out his actions for favours. He did so much for the orphanage, even producing and selling a fundraiser board game called 'Show Business'. Very difficult to find these days, even on eBay.

All of the children got to see Love from Judy, and some of the older ones, including Susannah, sold the programmes at the matinees. Love from Judy is based on the novel Daddy-Long-Legs, by Jean Webster, and follows the story of a young orphan girl, Judy. So it was all rather appropriate and undoubtedly very moving for the children. The week ended up raising over £9,000 and everyone was ever so grateful to Emile.

Meanwhile, Susannah's little sister, Judy, was coming into her own and would be one of the very few Silverlands kids to sit and pass the fairly new eleven-plus exam. This meant acceptance at the Sir William Perkins's Grammar School in 1954. She would happily remain living at Silverlands while attending.

In 1954, the Actors' Orphanage Association was formed and one of its prime objectives was to organise more of the lucrative charity previews and matinees. And to keep the publicity ticking over. Noël had often arranged publicity quite off the cuff in the past. In 1953, he and Marlene Dietrich had visited Silverlands and asked one of the boys, Jon Morris, to put his pyjamas on over his clothes, in the middle of the day, and hop into bed while Noël and Marlene chatted with him for a naturalistic photograph. Jon remembered their burning cigarettes as well as their very similar-smelling colognes. This was all for the orphanage. Noël and Marlene hardly needed the publicity themselves, although Marlene couldn't resist handing out autographed publicity photographs. She then had all of the children and staff pose with them for a group photo, which was surely somewhat tongue-in-cheek.

Noël still, some nineteen years on, played the piano and made the children laugh. He took tea with the staff and examined the premises. He was still a sympathetic ear to those that needed it, including, on this occasion, one of the older boys coming to terms with his sexuality. He was also still encouraging and supporting Susannah Slater's career. I asked Susannah if they saw Noël in any way as a father figure, and she said that he was more like 'a benevolent angel'.

*

In regard to sexuality, specifically homosexuality, Noël, it seems, had accepted his early on. As a boy in the professional theatre from the age of eleven, he would have been aware of homosexuality and known homosexuals. At fourteen, he was befriended by a thirty-four-year-old upper-class artist, called Philip Streatfeild. Philip was a 'Uranian', an admirer and sometime painter of adolescent boys. The setting of these paintings was often by the lakes of Cornwall, rather like those of Henry Scott Tuke. Indeed, in one painting, it's believed that one of the boys is Noël. We must not judge events of the 1910s by the standards of the 2020s, and we simply don't know the truth of what was occurring here.

Pubescent Noël would often visit Philip's studio in Glebe Place, Chelsea, and watch as he painted models. One model, Doris, posed casually in the nude and then made tea afterwards. Noël soon became accustomed to these kinds of things and spoke of them at home in a worldly manner. No doubt there was some intoxication for Noël to be welcomed so into Philip's high milieu... but what did Mother think? Or know? Was she naïve? This was a prime opportunity to mix in upper-class circles. Was there a price of admission? We shall never know and can assume nothing.

Noël maintained that it was a very sweet and genuine friendship, and we can assume that Philip would have played some significant part in shaping Noël's attitude to and acceptance of homosexuality. That it was not evil, unnatural or a sin. That religion had it wrong. That it was a question of having an enlightened mind and of not taking sex so very seriously.

Noël was also often taken by Philip to Hambleton Hall, the country estate belonging to the great socialite Mrs Astley Cooper. However, slightly embarrassingly, Noël had to sleep in a separate building from the main house as he was of 'common stock'. He got a taste of *the high life*, though; however, one can't help but think of Noël's line: 'The cream of the aristocracy mingles with the clotted cream of the theatrical profession'.

Sadly, Philip was conscripted, contracted tuberculosis and died in 1915… on his deathbed at Hambleton Hall, he asked Mrs Astley Cooper to be good to Noël, to let him visit still, and to let him stay in the main hall. A deathbed request… and so, through chance, luck and tragedy, Noël was often to be a 'proper' guest at Hambleton. Introduced to all the right people, doors opened, introductions were made *and* he had a taste of the upper-class world that would inspire much of his future work. It was here too that he discovered a copy of Saki's short stories, *Beasts and Super-Beasts,* which hugely influenced his light, flippant comic style. Philip's death must have been a blow, though. Noël was in the midst of puberty and hormonal intensity… these experiences must have been profound.

How did Noël wed his, thanks in part to Philip, acceptance of his sexuality with the times he was living in? It's been said that Nicky Lancaster's drug-taking in 1924's *The Vortex* was a veiled reference to homosexuality, a rumour that Noël always denied. However, even his partner Graham Payn said that read that way, the play makes more dramatic sense. There's Nicky's intense relationship with his mother and his tortured, unhappy indifference to his relationship with his fiancée, Bunty. (There's also a supporting character called Pauncefort Quentin, an obvious homosexual to anyone with half a mind.)

It was 1924, however, and homosexuality would remain illegal for another forty-three years. No explicit reference would ever pass the theatre censor, and any gossip in the press could end a career overnight. Yet one's life inevitably creeps into one's work... but we must be careful. It's often been said that *Private Lives* should be played with an all-male cast, as that's *how Noël would have written it if he'd been able to*. Well, *Private Lives* was written for Gertrude Lawrence, who, by all accounts, was a woman.

There is, however, a recurring theme in much of Noël's work: that of the tension between who society expects us to be and who we really are. Which could certainly be argued as having come from a gay sensibility. 1933's *Design for Living* is more complicated as Noël ebbs closer to the truth. Otto and Leo both love Gilda, but one could easily see a love between Otto and Leo too. Broadway audiences of the time must have simply seen *jolly japes* and *not* rampant bisexuality. That would be unthinkable. Noël had been explicit once, in 1926's *Semi Monde*, as gay characters come and go in a Parisian hotel. It was never published or produced.

Then there were the songs, such as 1929's *Green Carnation* in *Bitter Sweet*; a biting satire of the aesthetes of the 1890s, such as Oscar Wilde. The classic 1932 song *Mad About the Boy* had a final verse about a man seeking therapy over his male infatuation. It was cut. In the mid-1950s, a bill had failed to pass in the House of Lords that would have decriminalised homosexuality. Noël, in his diary, expounded on the feelings that he had spent his life being so discreet about:

It is hard to believe in this scientific, psychiatric age when so many mysteries have been solved, even for the layman, that a group of bigoted old gentlemen should have the power to make the administration of British justice a laughing stock in the civilised world.

Emotional, uninformed prejudice can still send men to prison and ruin their lives for a crime that in the eyes of any intelligent human being isn't a crime at all.

The fact that two men, well over the age of consent, should be penalised for going to bed together in private is a devastating revelation that we have learned nothing from history, literature, biology, science or psychology. To regard homosexuality as a disease or a vice is, we know, archaic and ignorant. It has always existed and always will exist.

This seems profoundly progressive for 1955. He was never above a tasteful but *risqué* joke, either. On a troop concert tour during the War, one journalist asked:

"Are there any songs you'd like to perform that you've not?"

"I should love to perform Bea Lillie's *There Are Fairies in the Bottom of My Garden*, but I don't dare. It might come out as *There Are Fairies in the Garden of My Bottom*, which might be unfortunate."

Noël had peace and honesty in his private life. Once, giving a lecture on the birds and the bees to one of his many godchildren, the actor Daniel Massey, he said: "I have tried everything from soup to nuts and ended up with men and that's that." Though if there were ever any women, there's no evidence whatsoever. But then Noël was, if nothing else, a gentleman.

*

As the 1950s progressed, Noël was re-evaluating his life. He was now definitely middle-aged; his waist a little expanded, his jowls a little loose and his head growing steadily balder. More time would be spent in America and, in truth, he was ready to retire as president but, as he had written on the 29th of August 1952:

Long serious discussion about Actors' Orphanage. Decided to make drastic economies – sell Silverlands and get somewhere near London where the hostel and the orphanage can be under one roof. If we don't do something soon, we shall have exhausted our capital in a few years and have to close down. Much as I would like to resign, I cannot do so until the whole thing is properly solvent.

In the event, they would close Rutland Gate and remain at Silverlands, but Noël wasn't going to leave until things were in order. After 1951, the *midnight matinees* had begun to solve the financial problems, along with the theatre matinees and galas and cabarets. They also started to advertise for new subscribers in the actors' 'bible', the *Spotlight* directory. From time to time, other ideas came forward, such as the honourable Mrs Honor Earl's plan to sell some of her celebrity portraits in Mayfair to raise funds. (She also painted some of the children.)

1954 saw the necessary closure of Rutland Gate. A drop in numbers, propagated by the welfare state, was making it unnecessary to have two homes. Also, the £12,000 from the sale of Rutland Gate to the *Bahá'u'lláh* Spiritual Assembly, who are still there today, was a huge help. Not to mention the savings on the salaries of the second staff. (The *Bahá'u'lláh* incidentally are a peaceful and inclusive religious group.) 1954 also saw two Palladium fundraisers: 'Midnight Cavalcade' in March and 'Night of 100 Stars' in June. The fund office would now exist in a room at the more affordable 32 Shaftesbury Avenue, and any seventeen-year-olds needing housing while taking vocational training would still be helped out until they received their first pay cheque. As for Susannah Slater, she was already in Canada and acting in plays with her mother. And Peter Collinson was already working backstage at a theatre in Ireland.

That summer, Noël's ninety-one-year-old mother was in rapidly failing health, yet he headlined at *Night of 100 Stars*. A show of no small magnitude, the Palladium galas required long rehearsals, with Lance and Hamilton running around and Richard Attenborough cueing everyone on and off stage. And there were far too many stars for the dressing rooms available. On the day, Noël escorted the Duchess of Kent, Princess Alexandra and her party to his musical, *After the Ball*, at the Globe Theatre on Shaftesbury Avenue, and then had them to dine at Gerald Road, before escorting them to the Palladium and the royal box for midnight.

The show started and went wonderfully until Errol Flynn and Pat Wymore stayed on stage for twenty-five indulgent minutes instead of their allotted ten, and nearly derailed the whole show. Finally, Noël went on and later wrote in his diary of the 27th of June 1954:

> *I followed them and got the biggest ovation of my life; much of it, I suspect, was relief. Then Marlene came on and we finished up by singing a duet which neither of us knew. It was all good clean fun, however, and we made a clear profit of £10,000 for the orphanage.*

The show and Noël were a bigger hit than ever that night:

> *The whole business was gratifying in the extreme. News of my cosy personal triumph spread round theatrical London like feu sauvage.*

Underneath these events, however, Noël was preparing for the biggest sadness of his life. Four days later, Violet Coward died, and Noël was at her side. He had no regrets; he'd achieved his ambition of restoring family prosperity and of getting her out of the damned kitchen long ago. He'd had fifty-four years of love, devotion and fierce, honest loyalty. She also let him roam very free and he was never coddled.

Noël knew and said many times that he wouldn't have achieved a fraction of what he had in life without her. In terms of career but *also* in terms of personal happiness. Her only fear at the end was for him, but he surmised that he would always carry her with him in his deepest thoughts. This parental love and devotion highlighted to him, as ever, the sadness of the Silverlands children that lacked it.

*

In 1955, David and Kirsten Slater took charge at Silverlands, fresh from a boarding school in Welwyn Garden City and with their daughters, Becky and Lulu, in tow. They were to be the last and very beloved heads of Silverlands. They also formed a close bond and affiliation with Richard Attenborough and Sheila Sim, which was to prove vitally important.

Meanwhile, it was at this time that Noël was busy having one of the biggest and most unexpected successes of his career: his cabaret show at the Desert Inn, Las Vegas, followed by the best-selling live album. Because of this, he had missed headlining 1955's *Night of 100 Stars* at the Palladium, but was back in England and at a committee meeting in August to thank Russell, Hamilton, Richard and Lorn. These four, along with Emile Littler's brother, Prince Littler, were the main people responsible for the Actors' Orphanage Association. This was proving successful in the promotion of the orphanage, and for acquiring more subscribers and life members (for 2s.6d.).

With the charity *finally* out of financial danger, his mother

gone, and money being made in America that would get *himself*
out of financial trouble, Noël began to think seriously of leaving
the UK. As the press would put it, to be a 'tax exile'. Noël was
ready to take a drubbing in the press, accept the necessary sale
of his London and Kent homes... and could now comfortably
relinquish his presidency of the orphanage too.

The committee were very reluctant to accept his resignation
in 1956 and suggested he remain as an 'Honorary President'...
but he wanted a clean break and, besides, Laurence Olivier
could fulfil that role quite well. Lorn sought Richard's help in
persuading the committee to let Noël go and also to accept
Larry (who was no help as he wanted Noël to at least be a co-
president with him). Lorn knew of the financial sense in Noël's
plans, however, and how he would simply have to now resign
completely from the orphanage.

The committee had no idea that Noël had actually made a
firm decision to leave a full year before. In 1955, he had written a
piece called, *'The Importance of Happiness'*, for future fundraiser
programmes. It reads almost as his last word on the orphanage
and his long-held intentions.

THE IMPORTANCE OF HAPPINESS

*In this strange and difficult world there are, I fear,
more unhappy people than happy ones. Not unhappy
because of personal tragedy or loss or any specific
circumstances, but unhappy in themselves, twisted,
disgruntled, without confidence or hope or congenitally
at odds with life. It is fairly simple as a rule to trace
the first causes of this spiritual malaise directly back to
early environment, in fact to childhood: for it is when
we are very young children that we first learn to be*

afraid, and fear, of course, is the basis of much that is bad in human character.

I wonder, dear reader, how much you remember of your childhood? Possibly you seldom think of it, possibly it has become a very vague memory submerged by the activities and responsibilities of adult life; but if, for a moment, you shut out the present and let your mind travel back across the years you will probably find many incidents and emotional crises, trivial enough in themselves, that have had a lasting effect on your present conduct, behaviour and attitude of mind.

Personally, I believe strongly that people who are brave, confident and successful are, nearly always, those whose early years were graced with happiness, with a sense of security and, above all, the knowledge of being loved and wanted.

The small children we take into the Actors' Orphanage have none of this security. Some of them may have loving mothers who are too poor to keep them, or affectionate fathers without the means of looking after them; some have neither fathers nor mothers. None of them has a home in the accepted sense of the word and it is this that we try to give them. Somewhere safe and stable where birthdays and Christmases can be looked forward to with excitement and remembered with joy.

As President of the Actors' Orphanage I must, as part of the job, take an active interest in all sorts of things. Apart from the unending and vital task of raising money I am concerned with details of policy and of administration, with education, house repairs, estate development, the investment and re-investment of capital and many different problems.

But in my heart what I really mind about, what I

have minded about since I became President in 1934, is the happiness of the children who come into the care of this Charity.

It is my greatest hope that when these children have become men and women and look back into the past as I have asked my readers to do, they will be able to say: 'Whatever has happened since, those were good years that I spent at Silverlands; throughout that time I was a happy child.' That is my ideal, my dearest wish, and I am deeply grateful to anybody and everybody who helps to make it come true.

Noël Coward, 1955

EIGHT

The Future

1956 ONWARDS

Audience member: *"Could Mr Coward tell us why he prefers Swiss residency to British?"*

Mr Coward: *"A very simple answer in two words... Income tax!"*

– Interview at the NFT, London, December 1969

Joyce Carey and Gladys Calthrop were miffed that their great friend and the quintessential Englishman, Noël Coward, would even consider foreign citizenship. Lorn, however, fully supported *The Master's* decision. She knew the financial situation and it was time for Noël to think of his own future. His new plays and musicals were endlessly mauled by the British press, honours seemed to be withheld indefinitely and, at fifty-six, he was ripe for new horizons.

Noël knew that the committee would not accept his resignation easily, but he insisted not only that he would resign but that he would not stay on as an 'Honorary President' or patron of any kind. If he did, he would still feel the responsibility, and inevitably continue to fix problems and worry about funds.

No, he would go completely, and the young, much-admired, and highly capable Richard Attenborough would replace him. Sir Laurence Olivier was the most famous actor of the age, but Noël knew from his long experience that the orphanage needed a real leader, not a figurehead.

Richard Attenborough, still only thirty-three and boyish-looking, was officially asked to take on the responsibility. Lorn had written to him: 'I know you will say you are too young. Please realise that Noël became President when he was thirty-four' and 'Noël had no experience whatsoever of the organisation of this or any other charity.'

Yet Richard really didn't feel prestigious enough, so the role of *chairman* was created specifically for him, and Sir Laurence Olivier was promoted from vice president to president. Indeed, Olivier was to be, like those original presidents before Noël, just a name. As Susannah recalled, "We never bloody saw him!" (Although Olivier and Vivien Leigh did visit Silverlands that Christmas.)

It was to be Richard who, if anything, would be even more hands-on than Noël. He was shrewd and smart and incredibly capable and caring. (Richard only actually took the namesake 'president' when Sir Lawrence died in 1989.) For Richard, the chairmanship of the Actors' Orphanage was just the beginning of a lifelong commitment to charity and humanitarianism, along with the constant assistance and support of his beloved wife, Sheila.

Richard and Noël had a close bond (ever since Richard's career launch in *In Which We Serve*), and Richard sincerely promised Noël that he would stay with the Actors' Orphanage until he 'fell off his twig'. Richard's skill and care in taking the reins freed Noël, after his recent career failures and financial woes, to put his affairs in order, and to retire safe in the knowledge that the charity was in good hands. In Jamaica on the 29th of January

1956, Noël wrote in his diary that his resignation 'frankly is a great relief, it has cost me a lot of time, energy and money for twenty years'. It was time to pass the baton.

Emigration combined with new productions (*South Sea Bubble* and *Nude with Violin* in London), three American television specials for CBS (*Together with Music, Blithe Spirit* and *This Happy Breed*) and huge sales of the *Live at Las Vegas* album finally allowed Noël to put something aside for retirement. Though far from actually retiring, he could at least relax a little. Yet for his 'tax exile', the UK press, predictably and relentlessly, went in for the kill. Also, he could only be in England now for three months a year. Noël had weighed it up in his head many times... more press attacks... but more funds... not having to work until he dropped... England had withheld him honours... his mother was gone... he was increasingly out of fashion... he wanted to spend more time in Jamaica anyway... he wanted to build a new little house there, away from all interruptions... up on a hill... that second piece of land he owned... called *Firefly*.

Noël held one final committee meeting on the 22nd of February 1956 at Gerald Road before it was sold. One imagines that any *business arising* was solemnly gone through before a firm thank you was made by Noël to everyone for their support over the years. No doubt Noël received many a toast and word of praise in return. It must have all been rather bittersweet. A final meeting in the London home where, quite aside from writing, theatre business and parties, so much work concerning the orphanage had taken place.

Emergency meetings to expel Mr Austin in the 1930s. Lorn's endless letters and phone calls from her little office on the mews to arrange the garden parties. Evacuation plans being hurriedly made in 1940. The phone call coming in that Mr Gordon had to be dealt with as a matter of urgency. Letters from every star of the day either accepting or declining offers to appear at the Palladium fundraisers. And, on occasion, a letter of gratitude from a 'graduate' of the orphanage, telling them how they were progressing in life. Glasses were raised high to The Master and to Lornie.

Soon Noël would become a tax resident of Bermuda and would divide his time between a new house there, Spithead Lodge, and Blue Harbour and Firefly in Jamaica. Not to mention the high-end hotels of New York and London. As for Lorn, she would run a UK office from her house in central London, and remain on the executive committee of the orphanage.

*

1956 at Silverlands was extremely eventful. In February, a girl accused a staff member of sexual assault, but when the police arrived, she confessed that she'd made the entire episode up. Not long after, Patrick Waddington was riding his motorcycle from the London office to Silverlands when a woman stepped out in front of him at Notting Hill. He swerved to miss her but ended up flying over the handlebars and cracking his skull. He wasn't one for wearing a helmet.

After two weeks in hospital, he regained consciousness and Richard became a regular visitor to his bedside. Once recovered, he resigned as general secretary and went to America to resume, after almost four years with the orphanage, his acting career, although eventually he ended up back in England and appeared in the odd episode of *Dad's Army*.

The beloved matron, Miss Rennie, had gone too, due to health issues. Mr and Mrs Fraser had already departed, back to Scotland, then Norway. Times were drastically changing. It's almost as if without Noël's presence, others wanted to move on too... A Mrs Hollands became the new general secretary and, luckily, the new heads, David and Kirsten Slater, were utterly adored by the children.

The children were now, radically, put into 'family groups', with one staff member responsible for each group as a 'house parent'. Each group had a communal sitting room and dining room, and this simulation of family life proved successful. Mr Slater also purchased a minibus for more trips to town, and the older children could even attend Saturday night dances. They were also allowed to listen to much more pop music, as new-fangled *rock and roll* made it onto the gramophone at Silverlands.

The 1950s were sometimes called the decade that invented the Teenager. Times were changing and, on the whole, for the better. Judy certainly looked on these final Silverlands years as a blossoming time, with more freedom and more room for expression as an individual. In August, the Slaters went with all of the children on their two-week holiday to Margate. These last years were probably the most pleasant of all, but the writing was on the wall. There was a reason that there was now room for several communal sitting rooms, dining rooms and 'family groups'. The intake of children was drastically shrinking in size, and the need for the Actors' Orphanage lessening. The welfare state was having a huge impact on British life.

Numbers were dwindling so fast that the usual sixty to seventy children were down to little more than *thirty* by 1958. And what with Mr and Mrs Slater having their two daughters with them, Becky and Lulu, there was a strong, close-knit, relaxed family feel in these last years at Silverlands. Mr Slater had cubicles with front curtains placed around every single bed so that every child, for the first time ever, had a private space. Each cubicle also had its own dressing table, mirror and a new mattress. It was just luck whether you got a window or not. The older children also had a chair and desk. This was a far cry from the days of Langley Hall and dozens to a room.

Chairman Attenborough proved Noël right immediately by being totally responsible, hands-on and active in his leadership. Richard could see that the welfare state, improvements in Actors' Equity and improved theatrical employment were lowering the necessity for the orphanage. He also saw that the building by now desperately needed expensive repairs, especially on the roof.

Along with the committee, the decision would soon be made for the fund to offer subsidies to struggling actor-parents instead of a home for their child at the orphanage. Finally in a position of some financial stability (thanks largely to the Palladium fundraisers), this was a viable option. This had a profound effect on life at Silverlands for the *last orphans*. Some of the children, such as Caroline in 1958, were taken home quite suddenly. Dropped at Chertsey Station, Caroline, after *eleven years,* was *en route* to live with her actress mother. As for her Silverlands family? There would be no goodbyes; she was simply gone. One assumes that it was deemed easier and less emotional for all concerned if matters were handled in this way. It was undeniably a tricky situation. To leave your childhood home and created family to go and live with a mother that you barely knew, and that you might reasonably suspect might not really want you. How could it be handled? Emotional goodbyes and a possible refusal to leave? Or a quick, quiet and secret departure?

Judy, Liz and the others mourned Caroline's sudden disappearance dreadfully.

*

An AGM was held on the stage of the Saville Theatre in May 1958. Here, Richard led the way in discussing the issues at hand. There were only twenty-nine children now in residence, the roof repair would require a huge investment and there was the constant staffing difficulty due to the rural location. There was talk of moving to a smaller property closer to London, and on the 15th of May 1958, *The Stage* newspaper printed the headline:

ACTORS' ORPHANAGE MAY LEAVE SILVERLANDS

In truth, they had to phase out the orphanage, for it was suddenly becoming completely outmoded. In this era, many children's homes would close across the country. Richard said: "It is hoped that we may in the future be able to subsidise some needy children in their own homes and to save families from being split up. This is surely a better way of spending money than upon roof repairs!"

Of the remaining children, thirteen were either funded and placed back with a relative or given financial support to be put into a private school. The remaining children lived at two newly purchased suburban houses in Watford; six in Rookwood, and the remaining eight in Nascott Wood, under the care of staff members Mr and Mrs Piller. This included the girls Norma, Lally, Gaynor and the youngest child, three-year-old Sally. They were destined to be the last of the orphanage children.

Richard had given these last children a rare treat in 1958 when they came to watch him filming *Danger Within* on Chobham Common. They met the stars – Richard Todd and Michael Wilding – and had their photographs taken. This was no fundraiser; this was purely a gift to the children.

The last head, David Slater, would soon go on to study Theology at King's College, becoming a priest and eventual canon and vicar of the close at Salisbury Cathedral. Before this, however, David and Kirsten would have their third child. Simon Slater would actually be born at Silverlands in the June of 1958, with the remaining orphans keeping vigil and soon visiting Kirsten and the newborn baby in her bedroom. The close family feel of those last months evident.

In January 1959, the Actors' Orphanage not only left Silverlands but transformed into something quite different. The Actors' Charitable Trust, TACT, was born and donated subsidies to the families of struggling actors. Judy remembers the sadness she felt sat watching the removal men emptying Silverlands. Many of the furnishings going into storage for a long time before finally being redistributed to the actors' retirement home, Denville Hall, in 1965. The bust of Gerald du Maurier, the painting of William Terriss, the great wooden bookcases, the sports trophies from the Annual Actors' Cricket Matches, the grand piano…

Richard continued the Palladium fundraisers; indeed, they were such a success that they ran well into the 1960s. Proceeds now going to TACT, as well as combined theatrical charities. Lorn stayed active on the executive committee until ill health forced her resignation in 1966. Richard wrote to her to say that, Noël aside, she had done more than anyone for the orphanage.

Richard's acting career went from strength to strength with films like *Dunkirk, I'm All Right Jack* and *The Great Escape*. In time, he would become the Oscar-winning film director of classics such as *Gandhi* and *Shadowlands*; the president of RADA and BAFTA, as well as becoming Lord Attenborough, the baron of Richmond-upon-Thames. All the while never forgetting his responsibility to the actors' charity. In 1967, he wrote to Noël to say:

> *Noël dear, I am ever mindful that I owe so much to your help and guidance together with the inheritance of the orphanage which you entrusted to me. I shall always try to be worthy of that trust.*

After Richard's death in 2014, it was decided to leave the chairmanship empty, as he was irreplaceable. He had seen Noël as a mentor and after Noël's death he would often say, "When in doubt, do what Noël would have done." Noël had helped Richard come to terms with his fame by showing him how to put it to good use through the orphanage. Richard was even younger than Noël when he became famous. He remembered auditioning for Noël at Denham Studios in 1941 and having his nerves quickly quelled by Noël's thoughtfulness in saying: "You won't know me – I'm Noël Coward. You, of course, are Richard Attenborough."

We should also note that Richard's already strong grounding in social responsibility, social conscience and *giving back* came from his parents, who had taken in two Jewish-German girls during the War. They taught him early on that we are all our brothers' keeper.

*

TACT, since 2015, has become simply ACT: the Actors' Children's Trust. The retirement home for actors, Denville Hall, established in 1925, had sought TACT's help in 1965, because of Richard and Sheila Attenborough's experience in running the orphanage. This alliance continued through fifty years and two major refurbishments, although Denville Hall was always a separate charity.

Today, ACT supports actor-parents and their children in their own homes rather than through an orphanage. Ironically the need for childcare, welfare support and education is similar today to how it was under Noël Coward's stewardship. But from an average of sixty children then, ACT now funds more than 250 families.

Since its inauguration in 1896, the charity has changed with the times, supporting genuinely needy children for 124 years and counting.

*

Looking back, pre-war Silverlands seems idyllic; and post-war Silverlands as having had its ups and downs. What with its succession of variably inappropriate headmasters, from the too strict, to the too soft, to the abusive. With Patrick Waddington finally getting things on the right track. Yet overall it was a place of happiness and gave the children a sense of home.

After 1959, Silverlands became the Saint Peters' Hospital School of Nursing, for midwifes and nurses, much like it had been during the War. This lasted right to the end of the millennium, when everything was refurbished at a cost of 3.7 million pounds. Silverlands looked more glorious than ever. The plan was to reopen as a... clinic for paedophiles. The Ministry of Justice had implied that it would be a psychiatric hospital but without specifying that it would be geared towards child sex offenders. The local community were up in arms. They held protests, handed out flyers, contacted the press and held several candlelit vigils between 2001 and 2002. Seven thousand children lived within a 2.5 mile radius, and twenty-five schools were also within that radius. One school was virtually on the grounds.

It also seemed ironically inappropriate given the mansion's history as the Actors' Orphanage. The press covered the campaign and a minister admitted that things could have been handled better. The plans were called off. Sixteen years on, the Grade II listed mansion sat empty, boarded up, and like an orphan itself... abandoned. The voices of the children long gone...

In my research, I visited Chertsey, a small, friendly town in Surrey, just outside the M25. It's still fairly rural and I happened upon many a location. The Holy Trinity Church. The Sir William Perkins's School. The old Botleys Hospital. Although the Chertsey Picture House seems long gone. Walking along the Holloway Road to the Silverlands entrance, one comes across a high construction wall and huge gate. It is locked and decorated with razor wire, a camera and large warning signs. No one answers the buzzer and you can't see in. There's a sign that says: *Silverlands. European Institute of Health and Medical Sciences.*

I walk around the area and finally, from the nearby garden centre, can see part of the Silverlands roof in the distance. I ask locals for information, many unaware of the building's history but all quite curious. A friendly builder tells me that after numerous break-ins and damage by local teenagers, there is now industrial-strength security in place. Cameras and alarms surround the building, and even to walk across a field towards the property would, allegedly, set off an alarm and send a signal to the local police station. No one has any idea why there's a sign outside saying *Institute of Health and Medical Sciences.* The builder then tells me that Silverlands, like countless historical buildings before, and despite being Grade II listed, is being converted into flats.

Depressed that the building may soon be altered beyond recognition, I walk back to the gate to give the buzzer one last try. At the exact second I arrive, a security car pulls up. A man gets out and starts unlocking the gate. What perfect timing. Surely an innocent researcher and humble writer could pop up the path and have a quick look? No. Surely I can just take one picture? No. Surely I can stand quite far away from the building… and just look? No. Can they ask their boss? No. Can I ask their boss? No. Does the security guard know about the orphanage? No. Does he know who Noël Coward was? No. Richard Attenborough? No. John Hammond in *Jurassic Park*? Possibly.

I am then told not to follow him up the path because if I do... I chip in here, "An alarm will go off and the police will come." He is singularly unhelpful and I feel rather dejected. Silverlands will soon be carved up into flats and, realistically, it will be nothing like it was. History recedes from us evermore, but we should never forget it. There should, at the very least, be a plaque put up on the wall of these flats:

Silverlands. The Actors' Orphanage. 1938-1959

NINE

As for Noël?

Everybody worships me. It's nauseating.

– Garry Essendine, *Present Laughter*, 1942

As other twentieth-century playwrights and personalities have fallen by the wayside, Noël's work and influence remains. His *oeuvre* is a paradox of sentiment and cynicism, but if nothing else, his presidency of the Actors' Orphanage reveals that he very much had a heart. His popular comedies such as *Private Lives*, *Present Laughter* and *Relative Values* are flippant on the surface but with great depths of humanity playing out underneath. Perhaps they don't have the *heft* of an Anton Chekhov play, but then as Chekhov said himself, "Any fool can write a tragedy." Perennial light comedies are much rarer beasts. The plays contain meticulous construction and high-quality assurance. Noël's Victorian work ethic is never more exemplified - his commitment to the war effort and his presidency of the Actors' Orphanage aside – than in his writing.

In life, one of Noël's central philosophies, something he

repeats throughout his diaries, is the mantra, 'Rise above it'. A variation of this might be Laura's speech in *Brief Encounter*, as busybody Dolly witters on at her inanely in the train, quite oblivious to Laura's broken heart. We hear Laura's thoughts in voiceover:

> *This can't last. This misery can't last. I must remember that and try to control myself. Nothing lasts really. Neither happiness nor despair. Not even life lasts very long.*
> – *Brief Encounter*, 1945

Where did his strength of character come from? His mother and his success certainly played their part but we must remember too that he was homosexual when it was illegal to be so. He had to be strong. It would continue to be assumed by many that Churchill blocked his knighthood in 1942 due to homophobia. But I think we can now say that it was due to Noël having aggravated some influential Brits in America (to donate to the Actors' Orphanage to the point of their bitter resentment). Thus, the tax issue; thus, the blocked knighthood. The persistent assumption by many that it was homophobia speaks volumes. Noël certainly had to rise above certain things in his life, and charm, dignity, talent, intelligence and humour were his winning formula.

His personal philosophy and perspective certainly served him well in those difficult post-war years, as his style went increasingly out of fashion. He rose above this by reinventing himself as a wildly successful cabaret turn, another by-product of raising funds for the orphanage. He wrote so prolifically ('Work is much more fun than fun', being another of his mantras), that some hits did creep through, such as *Relative Values*. He also secured a loving private life with his created family of Graham, Lornie, Coley, Joyce and Gladys. Despite an intense and passionate, somewhat regretful, affair with a young actor in 1957 (during the New York run of *Nude with Violin*), Noël was more settled.

From 1957 until his 'rediscovery' from 1963 onwards (and thanks to a small revival of *Private Lives*, starring Edward de Souza and Rosemary Martin, at the New Theatre, Hampstead), Noël Coward was very out of fashion. At least with the critics, for he always had an appreciative fanbase that would guarantee his work some kind of a run, even for the most critically mauled of his plays or musicals. Meanwhile, producers who used to dream of a Coward contract now turned him down flat. It was the peak of the *angry young man* era and *kitchen sink realism*. Working-class drama of a gritty reality and angst had little in common with the warmth of Coward's occasional forays into the lower orders. *This Happy Breed* was a world away from John Osborne's *Look Back in Anger*. Class acceptance versus class resentment.

Noël did not endear himself to the new generation of Osborne, Harold Pinter and Arnold Wesker, either, by writing a series of articles for *The Sunday Times* in 1961. In them, he heavily criticised the modern theatre and its directors with their plays with *messages* and how they frequently bored the hell out of audiences. He mocked young actors too, for their jeans in the rehearsal room and for a lack of diction and audibility. Noël, constantly under criticism himself these days, was certainly fighting back.

His distaste for 'kitchen sink' dramas could be seen in some quarters as snobbism, yet Noël had made his name by satirising the upper classes. Not to mention his tongue-in-cheek philistinism when commenting on high culture. Mozart sounded: 'Like piddling on flannel'. On Richard Wagner: 'I do wish he'd get on with it'. Marcel Proust: 'What a tiresome, affected arse he must have been'. Even Oscar Wilde was a: 'Posing, artificial old queen'.

Noël was also not as grand as people imagined (or sometimes

hoped). Let's remember that he was born in a semi-detached house in Teddington. He did not attend a private school, Oxford or Cambridge, which only makes his journey and success all the more remarkable. And even as a star, his homes were modest and simply furnished. His eating habits too were simple. Eggs and bacon were a firm favourite, and he was no stranger to a pork pie.

His reputation and *image* as an elite Englishman was born out of his breakthrough success in the 1920s and the upper-class characters that he wrote and played. In reality he had known plenty of early struggle and uncertainty (realising later, post-fame, that one actually gets to know people much better in adversity than in success). Noël never forgot the months out of work, the overdue rent on his parents' lodging house and the rejection of his early plays.

Noël was patriotic, royalist and conservative, but then he had been born into Queen Victoria's Empire, within which society he had excelled and conquered. In the very early 1920s, Noël had been introduced to Ivor Novello on the street, while on tour, and was surprised at his scruffy, unshaven, unkempt appearance. Noël thought that if this wreck of a man could be thought of as the epitome of elegance and style then why not himself? From Teddington to the moon.

*

In 1960, Noël traded in Bermudian residency for Swiss and lived at *Chalet Coward* in Les Avants, where neighbours included David Niven and Charlie Chaplin. This worked well as a base in Europe and had stunning views of Lake Geneva. 'A room with a view over a ravishing tax advantage'. Noël did write some very fine work at this time too, such as the play *Waiting in the Wings*, that poignant study of a retirement home for elderly actresses (not unlike Denville Hall). The critics particularly mauled this play and Noël rather gave in. Deciding that Broadway could have his talent instead, he focussed on musicals, such as *Sail Away!*

Then, from 1963 onwards (and that Hampstead production of *Private Lives*), there was to be a constant reappraisal of his work. In 1964, Laurence Olivier's new National Theatre, at the Old Vic, staged a revival of *Hay Fever*. It ran for over a year. Noël directed Edith Evans, Maggie Smith and Derek Jacobi. A cast that could 'play the Albanian telephone directory'. His critical rediscovery led to his final play, which would also see him act on stage one last time. His swansong to the theatre, *A Song at Twilight*, was a timely and powerful study of the effect of being a closeted homosexual. It was produced, despite Noël's now declining health, in 1966, one year before the decriminalisation of homosexuality in England.

For Noël personally, there had been affairs and endless rumours of flings with everyone from Prince George to Michael Redgrave. Some true, some not. Noël certainly had no interest in ever *telling all*. When asked in later life about his private life, and after 1967's decriminalisation, he would simply give a variation of:

"I have no intention of coming out, there are still three little old ladies in Worthing who harbour secret desires for me, and I've no wish to shatter their illusions."

Noël had written (and published) openly gay characters in the 1950 short story *Me and the Girls*. A dying nightclub entertainer reflects on his life and the girls he looked after over the years. But it is *A Song at Twilight* that really addressed the issue. A loose take on an elderly Somerset Maugham (here called Sir Hugo Latymer), the play concerns a writer blackmailed over letters from an ancient homosexual love affair. There was no great controversy, just good reviews, sell-out box office and a sweet swansong for Noël. Finally, the subject could be raised on the London stage. It was only two months before the play's premiere that homosexuality had been set on the path to being decriminalised. Noël wrote in his diary on the 13th of February 1966:

> The Homosexual Bill has passed through the House of Commons. Some of the opposition speeches were so bigoted, ignorant and silly that one can hardly believe that adult minds, particularly those adult minds concerned with our government, should be so basically idiotic. However, now all will be well apparently. Nothing will convince the bigots, but the blackmailers will be discouraged and fewer haunted, terrified young men will commit suicide.

Noël's renaissance in the mid-1960s saw the newer playwrights and press remember that he had been the original angry young man with *The Vortex* back in 1924. That play saw themes of adultery, cocaine use and thinly veiled homosexuality play out. Noël had banked everything on getting it produced at the small Everyman Theatre in Hampstead; borrowed money, re-cast the female lead twice, fought the Lord Chamberlain's censorship and scored the colossal hit that bore the beginnings of his legend. The 1960s ended up revising Noël Coward's work not only as funny, but also as shocking, unique, full of subtext, satire and pathos.

The censor, incidentally, had tried to ban *The Vortex* on moral grounds regarding an intense bedroom scene between mother and son. Noël's winning argument was that if you banned *The Vortex* you'd have to ban *Hamlet* (not to mention the fact that murder had been perfectly acceptable on the stage for years).

*

Despite star turns in the films *Our Man in Havana* and *Surprise Package*, Noël now turned down several film offers. He didn't need the fame and no longer needed the money. Although out of offers such as *The King and I*, *My Fair Lady* and *Dr. No*, he did slightly regret turning down the Alec Guinness role in *The Bridge on the River Kwai*, his old friend picking up the Academy Award for Best Actor.

Even when ill health led Noël to stop acting and writing, with a smattering of unfinished projects in 1967, he continued to travel and socialise and simply *be* Noël Coward. Happily, he rested in Jamaica, where in 1956 he had built that second, smaller house high up on the hillside, called Firefly. It had one bedroom (but two pianos), and here he could read, paint, sleep and enjoy the wonderful climate and fabulous views undisturbed. After a lifetime of social engagement and the clamouring of people wanting to see him… there was peace. The guests could stay down at Blue Harbour and pop up *when invited.*

Apparently, when his doctor told him to change his lifestyle, otherwise he'd die, he replied, "I've had a perfectly lovely life and couldn't give a damn." Noël refused to stop drinking, smoking or to take exercise. A bad oyster in the Seychelles in 1965 had felled him for a while. And a facelift procedure had caused his heart to stop on the operating table, which can't be ideal. But it was really from 1967 onwards that he lost his vital energy and the writing (after the publication of his much-underrated poetry *Not Yet the Dodo*) stopped. Also, Lornie had died that same year and it felt like the end of an era. She was an irreplaceable part of his world. And he himself continued to deal with stomach troubles, a kidney stone 'the size of a Fabergé egg', and bad circulation… but could still be the wittiest and wisest conversationalist in any room.

In 1968, Noël made his last great travelling adventure with Graham and Coley. Even stopping to fire off the noonday guns in Hong Kong. And, of course, he acted in his final film, *The Italian Job*, for Peter Collinson. Graham played a small role and so was on hand to assist, for Noël was struggling to remember his lines these days and was a little delicate physically. This was mortifying to him, for he had been the consummate professional of the industry. Not to mention that he had banged on for years about actors being word-perfect before even the first rehearsal. He hadn't been up to a Broadway run of *A Song at Twilight* and its companion pieces, collectively called *Suite in Three Keys*. And he knew that this would be his last film too. He would never act again.

On set, Peter knew that he owed Noël so much. From his second chance at Rutland Gate, to his vital introductions into show business. And for the kudos of having Noël Coward as a godfather. As for Noël, he could look at the handsome young director and see that the graft, concern, effort and multifarious challenges of the orphanage for all those years had been worth it. There was a huge mutual respect between them, and how fitting that *The Master* should have his screen swansong in a film directed by a boy from the Actors' Orphanage.

*

Noël's humour never left him, even in poorly old age, once writing, 'Who can truly say that there is more truth in tears than in laughter?' He claimed that the only regret he had about death was that he wouldn't be around to read the utter balls that would be written about him. It's true that there are so many anecdotes and quotes that it's hard to know which are true or half true or total fabrications. It is also true, however, that Noël was pure show business and as such could be bawdy, rude and blasphemous, once saying of a picture of the aged, heavily lined face of WH Auden, "Imagine his scrotum."

Some other gems include seeing a production of *Titus Andronicus* with Vivien Leigh. As Lavinia, she came on at the end, with no hands and no tongue, so that she could not communicate her attacker's name, but with a stick between her arms to write his name in the sand. As she hobbled on in this emotional, climactic scene, she dropped the stick and it rolled off the edge of the raked stage. After the performance, Noël went backstage, opened the door to Vivien's dressing room and said, "Tut-tut, butter-stumps."

On seeing a film poster of *The Sea Shall Not Have Them*, starring Michael Redgrave and Dirk Bogarde, Noël said, "I don't see why not, everyone else has." On making the perfect martini, one should simply, "Fill a glass full of gin and wave it in the general direction of Italy."

Noël's seventieth birthday celebrations, in December 1969, went on for a week (he dubbed it 'Holy Week'). There were screenings at the National Film Theatre, where Richard interviewed Noël in front of such notables as Prince Charles. A *four-hour* midnight matinee at the Phoenix Theatre, which featured a hundred stars performing scenes, sketches, poems and songs by Noël *for Noël*. A reception at the Savoy and lunch at Clarence House where, finally, he was offered a knighthood by the Queen herself. It was awarded for his contribution to the theatre (*not* for his charity work), but Noël had also, for most of the century, contributed to national life in general. It's been said that he invented Englishness for the twentieth century, which is quite an achievement.

During Noël's last years, Michael Attenborough (another of Noël's godchildren) recalled the genuine affection between Noël and his father. Richard, now a highly respected film director, chairman of TACT and university chancellor, was sickened by the UK's lack of honours for *The Master*. He made sure that Noël received an Honorary Doctorate from the University of Sussex. (The investiture was, by glorious coincidence, the ceremony where Michael received his degree. An unforgettable day with Noël, apparently being very impish.) He also kept an eye on him, visited him in Jamaica, organised and hosted the deeply moving midnight matinee celebration for his seventieth birthday... and would forever defend him as a Man.

Whenever Noël was accused of being shallow, irrelevant or without substance, Richard knew first-hand that the opposite was true. Later on, Richard would cringe at his own brand of personal insult by the British press, that of being a 'Luvvie', when in truth he simply believed that 'The Arts' were vital and chose to wear his heart on his sleeve. Who else in society does this? Politicians?

Michael Attenborough recalls the elderly Sir Noël as naturally charming, conscientious and alert to everything... yet somehow relaxed. When Noël died at his beloved home, Firefly, Jamaica, in the early hours of the 26th of March 1973, his father, Richard, was very cut up about it. At least Noël had those last tranquil years, critical reappraisal, musical revues of his work in the West End and on Broadway, and plenty of honours, including the elusive knighthood.

Noël and Richard were in some ways total opposites. Noël was that conservative, nostalgic champion for Empire and royalty, resenting bitterly the decline in British power after the War. Richard was famously a 'leftie' and a passionate champion of Independence heroes, such as Mahatma Gandhi. (Noël had written of Gandhi's assassination in 1948: 'A bloody good thing but far too late.') Yet these two men loved and respected each other deeply. Beyond politics, which one doubts they ever really discussed, they were kind, caring, decent, hardworking, moral men. Richard thought Noël to be probably the kindest, most generous person he had ever encountered in his long life.

Interviewer:	"How would you sum up your life in one word?"
Sir Noël:	"Now comes the terrible decision as to whether to be corny or not. The real answer is one word, love. The real answer is to know that you are among people whom you love and who love you. And that has made all the successes wonderful, much more wonderful than there'd have been anyway. And I don't think there's anything more to be said after that. That's it."

– *Chalet Coward*, Les Avants, Switzerland, 1972

TEN

As for the Children?

We've come here to pay our respects to Great Aunt Nelly. She brought us up properly and taught us loyalty.

– Mr Bridger, *The Italian Job*, 1969

H ere's just a sample of what happened to some of the children that attended the orphanage over the years, but they are those predominantly mentioned in this book, and that I have been able to acquire most information about and permission from.

Dan Taylor was one of the few genuine orphans, having lost both his actor-father and his mother, arriving at Langley in 1931, aged five. (His father was Dan Rolyat, a music hall comic who had died following an accident on stage.) Dan was adopted while at the Gould Institute and graduated from the Hill School in Pennsylvania. He served in the US military, having become a US citizen in 1945, and eventually, via New York, ended up working for CBS Television in Los Angeles and raising a family.

Many ended up all over the globe: Jon Morris to America

too, Roy Williams to Canada, Norma Gumley to Australia, some to New Zealand, Mallorca and, of course, all across the UK.

Jimmy Burke's orphanage report of 1948 said that he ardently desired to join the Navy and go to sea. Despite Miss Rodda thinking that he should stay on at the orphanage, Commander Aggitter okayed his decision. Jimmy had a long, satisfying and successful Naval career. He sadly passed in 2020.

Granville Bantock returned to his mother in England in late 1942, where he had a meeting with Miss Rodda at the orphanage office. He gave feedback of his experiences in New York and an update on how the other children were doing. (A few of the parents contacted him for information too as their faraway children were failing to write any letters home.) He found a job in a factory before joining the Army and active service in the December of 1943. He would marry Brenda Lorden, also of the Actors' Orphanage (the first of only two orphanage marriages ever to occur). The marriage took place at the Holy Trinity Church, near Silverlands.

Hugo Bergström also served in the Army before marrying and living in Buckinghamshire. In 2000, he penned *An Orphan's War*, covering his years at Langley, Silverlands and the Gould Institute.

Peter Collinson left Rutland Gate in 1954, worked backstage in the theatre and then served two years of national service in Malaya. On returning to England, he spent some years in various roles at the BBC and at ATV. Eventually, he was asked to direct, and his best-remembered films of many are *Up the Junction* in 1968 and *The Italian Job* in 1969. He moved to Los Angeles with his beloved wife Hazel in the 1970s and sadly died, aged just forty-four, in 1980.

Brian Terriss, after playing no small part in saving the orphanage from the reign of Mr Gordon and Miss Berry, continued on at Silverlands and enjoyed a close bond with the

Slaters. He also became Mr Hazell's assistant but one day ran away to Guernsey, eventually married and became a talented and successful artist.

Gerry Norman had been the head boy at Silverlands. He later had a small role in Richard Attenborough's *Gandhi* and worked often as a much-loved film extra.

Susannah Slater had joined her mother, Joan White, in Canada in 1954 and continued her acting career. Indeed, she acted with her mother in *The Reluctant Debutante*. At twenty-one, she tracked down her and Judy's father, before he died two years later. In 1961, she returned to England and started a family before a career in PR and television in the 1980s and '90s. Susannah also ran the backstage bar at Wembley, spent time in Spain, worked for various theatre groups and performed in numerous murder mysteries. In 2000, Susannah was pivotal in organising an Actors' Orphanage reunion in Chertsey. Today, Susannah still acts and works with the charity *Talking Newspapers for the Blind*.

Judy Staber was one of the last to leave Silverlands in early 1959. She stayed with a family in Staines to complete her A levels and then visited her mother in the USA. She refused to leave and found work and an apartment in New York, studied acting, toured in *A Man for All Seasons* and eventually moved to Old Chatham in upstate New York to raise a family. Judy published an account of her childhood, *Silverlands*, in 2010, and appeared on a 2011 panel at the Lincoln Center to discuss the Actors' Orphanage. In researching her book, Judy discovered the missing pieces to her and Susannah's childhood. Their father, AP Moore, was the manager of the Duke of York's Theatre in London's West End and had married Joan White in 1935. During the War, he was court martialled for a minor money quibble, but in all likelihood it was for his homosexuality. After a small scandal, he was forbidden from seeing his children and emigrated. Judy today continues to write, volunteer in local theatre and curate an art gallery in upstate New York.

Liz Eastham left Silverlands in 1958, and briefly worked on Oxford Street before becoming a nanny in the United States, where she would marry and raise a family in Kingston, New York. Liz had a long career in medical administration, and with her half Yorkshire, half American accent, says that she's had a good life in America. (Liz had a brief second marriage to fellow orphan Jon Morris in 2004.) She now lives in the Hudson Valley, New York, and sees Judy often. She long ago accepted that her actress-mother had no choice but to leave them at the orphanage once their father had disappeared. Her mother felt guilty but Liz always told her not to.

Caroline Baldwin, Liz's younger sister, raised a family and lives in Lancashire, where she continues to work as a district nurse. Caroline hasn't talked about the orphanage very much in her life and when I quizzed her as to why, replied, "You move on. No one's ever asked me about it before."

Several months before she died, Ann Hollis spoke to me from Australia. She left Silverlands in 1954 and, though a timid child, recalled announcing visitors into the study to see Noël on one of his visits. Like so many of the children, she knew Noël Coward from overhearing grown-up conversation without ever having actually seen any of his plays, musicals or films. She remembered Miss Rennie as very motherly, as she taught her how to apply make-up. In 1954, the orphanage secured her a place in secretarial college, before her career as an army wife, and an eventual and happy move to Australia.

Norma Gumley, the girl on the step, waiting for the mother that never visited, was told one day that her mother was remarrying but still didn't want her. She was adopted finally by the Rieley family but couldn't connect with them. The fund acquired a job for her as an apprentice cook in London... but she was terribly unhappy. At twenty-one, she paid £10 and boarded a ship to Australia.

Norma chose to forget her past as she moved forward with her life. There was an unhappy, short-lived marriage but two wonderful daughters. Norma could never dream of sending them away anywhere, even as a struggling single mother in a foreign country. She would never give them up, no matter what. Happily, Norma found good employment and today owns twenty acres of land in the Australian Bush, near Bendigo in Victoria.

Lally Ingram (now Goodwin) worked as a medical secretary for many years at the Chelsea and Westminster Hospital in London. Then there's Lizzie Trigg, Michael Garood, Gay Oliver, Jon Morris and so many others. The youngest orphanage child, Sally Montegue Brooks, was only three when Silverlands closed its doors. They were all to live vastly differing lives in different countries… but all remained and remain linked by the unique connection of the Actors' Orphanage.

*

The 2000 reunion in Chertsey, two years in the planning and arranged by Susannah (with the help of Judy and Liz among others), reconnected many of the children. Canon David Slater and his wife Kirsten, the beloved last headmasters, were on hand to host the occasion. They couldn't get permission to hold the reunion in the newly and expensively renovated, but troubled, Silverlands, so held it at the Bridge Hotel, Chertsey instead. However, they were permitted to walk around Silverlands that afternoon, a television film crew in tow and a world of memories reignited.

The attendees were aged from their forties to their nineties, and the reception room at the Bridge Hotel was full of old friends and even a few old enemies, although the decades had healed many a rift. A sumptuous dinner was had and at the top table, Lord Attenborough was guest of honour (Sheila had sadly hurt her back and couldn't attend). After-dinner speeches were made, gifts presented and a, rather large, group photograph was taken. Lord Attenborough was by now, as well as the Oscar-winning director of *Gandhi,* and John Hammond in *Jurassic Park,* the head of dozens of charities. But it had all started with Noël and Lorn asking him to head the Actors' Orphanage back in 1956.

During the evening, it was clear that some present had forgiven their parents for the abandonment, some not. But there were many memories shared of the happy times. Going to the pantomime at the Theatre Royal, Windsor or getting on the coach to see *Where the Rainbow Ends* in the West End. Marlene Dietrich walking them down to the pigsty. Meeting Boris Karloff backstage in his Broadway dressing room. Being filmed for a BBC Christmas feature. Noël playing the piano. Performing gymnastics at the Theatrical Garden Party. Moving into the opulent Silverlands. Buying sweets from Mr Lazell on Saturdays. Singing naughty songs about the vicar's wife. All being together by the seaside in the summer holidays. Telling Lorn, or rather, Mrs Loraine, what they wanted to do when they grew up. Playing cricket against IAR Peebles. Performing on Broadway stages in *Gratefully Yours.* Or on the West End in *Robinson Crusoe* or *Cinderella.* Meeting Charlie Chaplin! Having Matey Irving look after you when you were ill. Living in a posh house in Knightsbridge while you trained for work. The fear but sheer excitement of crossing the Atlantic in 1940. American summer camps. Noël providing a television projector to watch the Queen's Coronation in 1953. Richard and Sheila taking them to Regent's Park Zoo, and then to their house in Richmond for tea and cake. Mr Fraser's Chibby Nights. Handing flowers to the Queen at a glamorous premiere. Selling the programmes at a star-studded charity matinee. Singing along with Mr Waddington on Sunday walks to church. All being together on Christmas Day.

In terms of any bad memories, they were mainly of Mr Austin or of Miss Berry and Mr Gordon. Perhaps too they were of the occasional vicious or abusive child. Then there were the six boys that had been killed in the War. At best, one can only quote Charles Dickens in *The Pickwick Papers*: 'There are dark shadows on the earth, but its lights are stronger in the contrast.'

As for Sir Noël Coward, it's clear that the children carried him in their hearts all through their lives. Judy Staber wrote that, 'It was abundantly clear that he took a genuine interest in us', and that, 'We all registered with him as individuals'. Liz Eastham said, "He was the sweetest man, and really seemed to love us all."

Lest we sugarcoat the history of Noël and the Actors' Orphanage, we must remember that many of the children never did forgive their parents for the, as they saw it, abandonment. Some parents chose to see the orphanage as a boarding school, but it wasn't. And whether their parents were alive or not, many of the children felt outcast, unwanted, unloved, insecure, lacking, alone, anxious about the future, confused and damaged.

Some of the parents could have possibly managed to keep their children at home, but many really couldn't. Shell shock, poverty, death and severe illness were very real reasons why many a child ended up at the orphanage. Some of the children could stand on their own two feet early on, but many struggled. At least until they were older. The feeling of being a 'charity brat' lingered for many, but also gave them a survival instinct. As they lived their various lives, many grew to see how lucky they had been that the Actors' Orphanage existed at all. They had a home, they had an education, they had many happy memories, and they had each other.

Conclusion

No one is useless in this world who lightens the burdens of another.

– *Doctor Marigold*, by Charles Dickens, 1865

Noël knew the importance of family, whether biological or constructed. He himself had his created family of Graham, Coley, Lornie, Joyce and Gladys supporting and sustaining him for years. These people kept him grounded and sane, when most others in the world struggled to see past his extreme fame, success and legend.

The children of the Actors' Orphanage found their family in each other and their shared experience of life at Langley, the Gould Institute, Silverlands or Rutland Gate. Those with no visitors or living parent must have wondered who they were. Where were they from? Had their parents been famous? Would they *ever* know? Where would they end up in life? Yet the fellow children, to all intents and purposes, were their brothers and sisters.

To varying extents, the experience defined their lives. As the years went by, they might catch sight of Noël or Richard or a committee member on television or film, whereupon they inevitably would smile. Noël had taken over from Sir Gerald du Maurier in 1934 when he was at his professional zenith. He had wondered, 'What now? What else was there to life?' The orphanage gave him an answer. And in some ways, the whole enterprise may have been a way for Noël to have children in his life, despite his, eventual, *fourteen* godchildren.

He had needed an antidote, a tonic, to balance out his life. Far from the egocentric actresses, cruel critics, judgemental tabloids, pressure to write masterpieces, pressure to be the great wit, and the fawning and clawing attention of, well, everyone… Noël could focus, for periods of time, on the welfare of a group of abandoned, needy, troublesome, but also lovable, children.

The experience enriched his life, and the time, effort and energy he committed was a true testament to altruism.

*

At the 2000 reunion in Chertsey, in front of the now middle-aged and old-aged former orphanage residents, Lord Attenborough spoke of what the Actors' Orphanage had meant to him and to Sheila and to Noël:

> "I believe passionately in family. I worshipped my own mother and father and they taught me from the word go that we are all of a species of people that live under particular circumstances. Some with great good fortune. Some with cruel misfortune. Some happy. Some sad. But we, none of us, live alone. We live with other people. My mother looked after sixty plus Basque refugee children during the Spanish Civil War. And just before the Second World War, we took in two little girls. Jewish girls from Germany, whose parents were in a concentration camp. And because war broke out while we were looking after

them, my mother and father adopted them. So for eight years, my brother Dave, my brother John and I had two little German Jewish sisters.

They were not, sensibly, to call my mother and father, Mother and Father, because they always hoped that their parents would come out of the concentration camp, which of course they never did. But they called my mother and father, Auntie and Uncle. They were treated with the same love that we were given by our family. In fact, I remember my mother saying, 'Boys, you will have to understand that no matter how much we love you three, we now have two daughters, you have two sisters, and we must give them even more love than we're able to give you. Because they have no love.'

Silverlands... Langley Hall... was an effort, not by Sheila and me, we merely inherited the attitude, to find a home where people who were denied the direct love that we all need and search for so desperately, could find somewhere, where those who looked after them, with varying degrees of success, but certainly in the main, attempted to give love that had been denied them.

So many of you over the years have kept in touch. So many, over the years, have told us what you were doing. When in 1959 we decided to end Silverlands, as such, and operate in a different way, we changed our name from the Actors' Orphanage to the Actors' Charitable Trust. And the Trust that we've inherited is also now a home for actors and actresses who can't any longer look after themselves. Either physically or financially. You, the orphanage, are the parents of Denville, in a way. Because the love that was gathered together with you has now been passed on to Denville Hall.

We owe our inspiration to Noël. Many of you will

remember Noël. Fabulous man. Glorious man. Gave Sheila her first job. Gave me my first job. Was our son's godfather. And there were many, many others at that time. Extraordinary people, who understood the joys of our profession, which is a loving profession.

And so, when you thank us, it is really we who should thank you. Love goes both ways, and the love that you have shown to us, and the affection that you have shown to us, and your awareness of what the Actors' Charitable Trust, the Actors' Orphanage, has done over the years, has brought us joy and reward beyond words.

It is not you who should be thanking Sheila and me, or Noël, or any of the other great people, who were our predecessors, for we should be thanking you, for the love and loyalty and affection you've granted us. We owe you the debt for the love that you've put into our lives."

Acknowledgements and Thanks

Alan Brodie, LJ Elliott, Carrie Kruitwagen, Mia Christou, Alison Lee, Sophie Dayman, Robert Hazle and Katie Butler at ABR (Alan Brodie Representation) and the Noël Coward Estate. Robert Ashby at ACT (Actors' Children's Trust), Michael Attenborough CBE, Susannah Slater, Judy Staber, Liz Eastham, Ann Hollis, Caroline Baldwin, Lally Goodwin, Jimmy Burke, Granville Bantock and Canon David Slater. Hazel Collinson. Jessica Clark at the Cadbury Research Library: Special Collections at the University of Birmingham. The University of York. Peter Behek at the V&A Theatre Archives. Belinda Haley at the Imperial War Museum. Michele, Leroy, Roy and Ernie at Blue Harbour, Jamaica. Robert Weinberg and the National Spiritual Assembly of the Bahá'u'lláh at 27 Rutland Gate. Lalla Ward at Denville Hall. John Knowles and Stephen Duckham at the Noël Coward Society. Stephen Garnett at This England Magazine. Neera Puttapipat at Getty Images. Shutterstock. Alamy. Vicky Mitchell and Yvette Pusey at the BBC. Laura Scougall at ITV. Fahmida Miah at the ESI Library. Rogan Dixon at the Evening Standard. Charlotte Coulthard at Samuel French Ltd. Louise Henderson at the Orion Publishing group. Claire Weatherhead at Bloomsbury. Niall Harman at Curtis Brown. Robert Gwyn Palmer. Geoffrey Johnson and Barry Day. Lauren Bailey, Hannah Dakin, Rosie Lowe, Sophie Morgan, Jonathan White and all at Troubador Publishing.

Source Notes

'Home is a name, a word...' Charles Dickens, *Martin Chuzzlewit*, 1844

'Cora: 'I know that they get a lot...' Noël Coward, *Waiting in the Wings*, 1960

INTRODUCTION

'I have been bitterly hurt inside...' Noël Coward, *Diaries*, 31 December 1956

'Impressionist exhibition...' Noël Coward, *Pomp and Circumstance*, 1960

'Due to start next Tuesday...' Noël Coward, letter to Lorn Loraine, dated 17 July 1956

'Little private menopause...' Noël Coward, *Diaries*, 31 December 1956

'He was wonderful, he really...' Susannah Slater, interview with the author at the Savoy, October 2016

'It was our home...' Brian Terriss, film footage of reunion in Chertsey, care of Susannah Slater, 2000

CHAPTER ONE: A NEW PRESIDENT

'I am the darned President...' The *Times of Ceylon*, 3 June 1935

'Dear Sappho, why ever didn't you...' The *Daily Dispatch*, 1920

'Played with a stubborn Mayfair...' review of *Knight of the Burning Pestle*, 1919

'Devoted thirty years to the good...' Noël Coward, *Past Conditional*, 1965

'I present the player to you exceptionally...' Charles Dickens, speech at the Adelphi Theatre, 11 May 1864

'It is a safe prophesy...' The *Birmingham Daily Post*, 1911

'Let me go, you're 'urtin me...' (and other extracts of dialogue), *Where the Rainbow Ends*, by Clifford Mills and John Ramsey, 1911

'The whole thing went with...' *The Sketch* magazine, 28 July 1915

'Had my formative years passed...' Noël Coward, *Diaries*, 21 December 1967

'If Mother had been able to send...' Noël Coward, *Diaries*, 21 December 1967

'I believe my colleague Will took...' Unverifiable Cowardism

'Sir Gerald... having enthusiastically...' Noël Coward, *A Reply to the Critics*, *Three Plays*, 1925

'Langley Hall, standing amidst cherry blossom...' Actors' Orphanage brochure, 1934

'They're white.' Hugo Bergström, *An Orphan's War*, 2000

CHAPTER TWO: LANGLEY HALL

'I have since often observed...' Daniel Dafoe, *Robinson Crusoe*, 1719

'Stormy', 'long', 'complicated', 'boring...' Noël Coward, *Diaries*, various dates

'How proud and honoured I am...' Noël Coward, *Star Chamber*, 1935

'Listen old girl – a committee's...' Noël Coward, *Waiting in the Wings*, 1960

'As President of the Actors'...' Noël Coward, *Past Conditional*, 1965

'Mr Austin is undoubtedly...' *Irregularities and Illegalities During the Secretarship of Mr. A.J. Austin*, 1936

'Traders in the avarice, indifference...' Charles Dickens, *Nicholas Nickleby*, 1839

'I remember at the time...' Noël Coward, *Waiting in the Wings*, 1960

'Everything possible has been done...' *The Stage*, June 1937

'I'd rather play a bad...' Noël Coward, NFT interview, 1969

'I am sure that the Actors'...' Hugo Bergström, *An Orphan's War*, 2000

'Everyday for four weeks...' Unknown local newspaper, 1937

'Exciting end to Annual...' *Windsor, Slough and Eton Express*, June 1938

'Charming performances...' *Windsor Observer*, 10 January 1936

'After all, they are amateurs...' *Windsor Observer*, 31 December 1937

CHAPTER THREE: SILVERLANDS

'This blessed land, this earth...' William Shakespeare, *Richard II*, 1597

'By destitute children....' Silverlands brochure, 1938

'We are going mad at the...' Noël Coward, letter to Alexander Woollcott, 31 May 1939

'Let fame, that all hunt after in...' William Shakespeare, *Love's Labours Lost*, 1597

'This morning, the British Ambassador...' Neville Chamberlain, 3 September 1939

'We've got the day off...' Hugo Bergström, *An Orphan's War*, 2000

'They're off to Hollywood.' *London Evening Standard*, 11 July 1940

'By the fact that all of us being actors...' Noël Coward, *Future Indefinite*, 1954

'Up in arms...' Noël Coward, letter to Lorn Loraine, 6 September, 1940

CHAPTER FOUR: EVACUEES IN AMERICA

'It's just Sherry, heavily...' Captain Kinross, *In Which We Serve*, 1942

'To think of all the new...' Princess Elizabeth, BBC radio broadcast, 13 October 1940

'My faith in my own...' Noël Coward, *Present Indicative*, 1937

'Did a lot of manly...' Noël Coward, *Present Indicative*, 1937

'For $500 I'd gladly...' Noël Coward, *Present Indicative*, 1937

'Abandoned the drawing room...' Noël Coward, *Present Indicative*, 1937

'Had a few drinks. Pretty...' Noël Coward, *Diaries*, 19 April 1941

'While the guns are...' Noël Coward, *Future Indefinite*, 1954

'Britain can take it...' Noël Coward, *Frost on Coward*, ITV, September 1968

'Now was the moment...' Noël Coward, *Future Indefinite*, 1954

'Wonderful to the children...' Noël Coward, letter to Lorn Loraine, 15 December 1943

'Where's the other half...' Granville Bantock, *Lucky Orphan*, 1996

'50 English Child Actors...' *New York Herald Tribune*, May 1942

'I will give you not...' Captain Kinross, *In Which We Serve*, 1942

'I could not advise...' Winston Churchill, letter to King George VI, 29 December 1942

'Paul Bantock, who was...' Noël Coward, Actors' Orphanage AGM, 1943

'When I get back from...' Noël Coward, letter to Lorn Loraine, 15 December 1943

'I explained at the outset...' Noël Coward, letter to Lorn Loraine, 30 December 1943

'In comparison with the War...' Noël Coward, *Post Mortem*, 1931

'First of all, my dear...' Noël Coward, *Cavalcade*, 1931

'27 Young British...' The *London Evening Standard*, May 1945

'The holiday I had with...' Hugo Bergström, *An Orphan's War*, 2000

'Last night? Very cold...' Winston Churchill, unverifiable quote.

Chapter Five: Return to Silverlands

'For not an orphan in the...' Charles Dickens, *Dombey and Sons*, 1848

'Jesus, where do I belong?' Hugo Bergström, *An Orphan's War*, 2000

'The age of the common...' Noël Coward, *Diaries*, 31 December 1956

'Terriss was an actor...' Henry Irving, *attributed* December 1897

'A lot of Hollywood....' Noël Coward, *Diaries*, 10 November 1947

'All I know was...' Judy Staber, *Silverlands*, 2010

'Debonair, nice-smelling...' Susannah Slater, interview with the author, October 2016

'He was like a daddy...' Caroline Baldwin, interview with the author, November 2016

'Stormy Actors' Orphanage...' Noël Coward, *Diaries*, 22 September 1949

'Too kind.' Susannah Slater, interview with the author, October 2016

Chapter Six: Troubles Anew

'There are bad times just...' Noël Coward song, The Globe Revue, 1952

'I was very privileged...' (and other quotes) Susannah Slater, interview with the author, October 2016

'Talented, attractive...' Noël Coward interview with Patrick Garland, *Omnibus (Noël Coward: Playwright)*, BBC Television, 1969

'Second day of the…' Noël Coward, *Diaries*, 3 June 1950
'Frankly non-existent…' Noël Coward, *Present Indicative*, 1937
'No child ever…' *Night of 100 Stars* brochure, 1951
'He is obviously a…' Noël Coward, *Diaries*, 20 October 1949
'Mother! I've lost my…' Noël Coward, *Present Indicative*, 1937
'All your life you've…' Noël Coward, *Easy Virtue*, 1926
'To me the whole…' Noël Coward, *Present Laughter*, 1942
'Expert but vulgar…' Noël Coward, *Diaries*, 9 October 1950
'Sounds to me as though…' Noël Coward, NFT interview, December 1969
'No one I've ever…' Noël Coward, obituary for Gertrude Lawrence, *The Sunday Times*, 7 September 1952
'Long Orphanage meeting…' Noël Coward, *Diaries*, 14 April 1950
'I have formed a very…' Noël Coward, *Diaries*, 23 January 1952
'Last one up to the…' Judy Staber, *Silverlands*, 2010
'Ah, there you…' Susannah Slater, interview with the author, October 2016
'Rise and shine…' Judy Staber, *Silverlands*, 2010
'I read and read, I…' Noël Coward interview with Patrick Garland, *Omnibus (Noël Coward: Playwright)*, BBC Television, 1969
'He is being torn…' Noël Coward, *Diaries*, 10 July 1950

CHAPTER SEVEN: CHANGES
'There was no fear in…' Noël Coward, *Diaries*, 1 July 1954
'Ungracious, albeit…' Patrick Waddington letter to Lorn Loraine, 1953
'Are you certain that…' Lorn Loraine letter to Patrick Waddington, 1953
'The first gave me a…' Noël Coward, *Present Indicative*, 1937
'Something of the quality…' Noël Coward, Actors' Orphanage brochure, 1953
'Keep your mouth closed, you're…' Unverifiable Cowardism during the run of *The Apple Cart*, 1953

'A benevolent angel...' Susannah Slater, interview with the
   author, October 2016

'The cream of the...' Noël Coward, *A Reply to the Critics, Three
   Plays,* 1925

'It is hard to believe...' Noël Coward, *Diaries,* 10 November 1955

'Are there any songs...' Unverifiable Cowardism

'I have tried everything...' Interview with Daniel Massey, 1982
   (re-used in *Omnibus: Noël Coward,* BBC, 1999)

'Long serious discussion...' Noël Coward, *Diaries,* 29 August
   1952

'Cosy royal snob...' Noël Coward, *Diaries,* 23 June 1957

'I followed them and yet...' Noël Coward, *Diaries,* 27 June 1954

'In this strange and difficult...' Noël Coward, Actors' Orphanage
   brochure, 1955

CHAPTER EIGHT: THE FUTURE

'Could Mister Coward...' Noël Coward, NFT interview,
   December 1969

'I know you will say...' Letter from Lorn Loraine to Richard
   Attenborough, 1956

'We never bloody saw...' Susannah Slater, interview with the
   author, October 2016

'Frankly is a great...' Noël Coward, *Diaries,* 29 January 1956

'ACTORS' ORPHANAGE...' *The Stage,* 15 May 1958

'It is hoped that we...' Richard Attenborough, Actors' Orphanage
   AGM, Saville Theatre, May 1958

'When in doubt, do what...' Robert Ashby, interview with the
   author at ACT office, Bloomsbury, October 2016

'Noël dear, I am ever mindful...' Letter from Richard
   Attenborough to Noël Coward, 11 July 1967

'You won't know me – I'm...' Interview with Michael
   Attenborough, November 2016

CHAPTER NINE: AS FOR NOËL?
'Everybody worships…' Noël Coward, *Present Laughter*, 1942
'This can't last. This misery…' Noël Coward, *Brief Encounter*, 1945
'Like piddling on flannel…' John Gielgud interview, *The South Bank Show*, ITV 1992
'Work is much more…' Noël Coward, interview with the *Observer*, 1963
'I do wish he'd get…' Unverifiable Cowardism
'What a tiresome, affected…' Noël Coward, *Diaries*, 25 July 1950
'Posing, artificial…' Noël Coward, *Diaries*, 2 July 1962
'A room with a view over…' Noël Coward, *The Sunday Times*, 1961
'I have no intention…' Unverifiable Cowardism
'Play the Albanian…' Unverifiable Cowardism
'I've had a perfectly…' Unverifiable Cowardism
'The homosexual…' Noël Coward, *Diaries*, 13 February 1966
'Who can truly say…' Unverifiable Cowardism
'Imagine his scrotum…' Unverifiable Cowardism
'Tut-tut, butter-stumps…' Unverifiable Cowardism
'I don't see why not…' Unverifiable Cowardism
'Fill a glass full of…' Unverifiable Cowardism
'A bloody good thing…' Noël Coward, *Diaries*, 30 January 1948
'How would you sum up…' Interview with Noël Coward at Chalet Coward, Les Avants, Switzerland, 1972

CHAPTER TEN: AS FOR THE CHILDREN?
'We've come here to pay…' Mr Bridger, *The Italian Job*, Paramount Pictures, 1969
'You move on. No one's…' Caroline Baldwin, interview with the author, November 2016
'There are dark shadows…' Charles Dickens, *The Pickwick Papers*, 1837

'It was abundantly...' Judy Staber, *Silverlands*, 2010
'He was the sweetest...' Liz Eastham, interview with the author, November 2016

CONCLUSION

'No one is useless...' Charles Dickens, *Doctor Marigold*, 1865
'I believe passionately...' Richard Attenborough, speech at the Actors' Orphanage reunion, Bridge Hotel, Chertsey, 2000

Permissions

Richard Attenborough's reunion speech (2000) with permission of Michael Attenborough.

The Sunday Times / News Licensing.

ESI Library on behalf of the *Evening Standard*.

Extract from Winston Churchill's letter reproduced with permission of Curtis Brown, London on behalf of the Estate of Winston S. Churchill ©

PHOTO PERMISSIONS

Cover Photo: Noël Coward at Silverlands, Christmas 1950 (Courtesy of Keystone / Hulton Archive / via Getty Images).

Kittie Carson, date unknown (Courtesy of ACT).

Moreland Road, Croydon, 1906 (Courtesy of ACT).

Paul and Granville Bantock at Langley, circa 1930 (Courtesy of ACT).

Noël Coward publicity photo, 1930 (Courtesy of Alamy Stock Photo).

Noël Coward at Langley, 1934 (Courtesy of ACT).

Theatrical Garden Party, featuring Noël Coward, Paul Bantock, and Prince George, The Duke of Kent, 1937 (Courtesy of ACT).

Cinderella Poster, 1938 (Courtesy of ACT).

Silverlands, 1938 (Courtesy of ACT).

They're off to Hollywood! The London Evening Standard, 11 July 1940 (Courtesy of SHUTTERSTOCK).

The Empress of Australia, 1940 (Courtesy of ACT).

Noël Coward as Captain Kinross, In Which We Serve, 1942 (Courtesy of Alamy Stock Photo).

Susannah Slater, 1946 (Courtesy of the Susannah Slater Collection).

Four girls at Silverlands (Judy Staber, Susannah Slater, Liz

Eastham, Caroline Baldwin), 1948 (Courtesy of the Judy Staber Collection).

Rutland Gate featuring Susannah Slater, Duncan and Yolande Rider, Peter Collinson and others, Christmas 1950 (Courtesy of ACT).

Mary Martin, Susannah Slater and Noël Coward at the Café de Paris, 1952 (Courtesy of Trinity Mirror / Mirrorpix / Alamy Stock Photo).

Noël Coward walking with children at Silverlands, 1953 (Courtesy of ACT).

Noël Coward, Jon Morris and Marlene Dietrich at Silverlands, 1953 (Courtesy of Pictorial Press Ltd / Alamy Stock Photo).

Noël Coward and Laurence Olivier at Night of 100 Stars, the London Palladium, 1954 (Courtesy of Alamy Stock Photo).

Richard Attenborough and Noël Coward, 1969 (Courtesy of ACT).

Noël Coward's grave, Firefly, Jamaica, 2017 (Author's private collection).

Every effort has been made by the author to seek all permissions. If any rights have been omitted, apologies will be given and permissions will be rectified for future editions.

Select Bibliography

The Diaries of Noël Coward edited by Sheridan Morley and Graham Payn, 1982

The Letters of Noël Coward by Barry Day, 2007

Present Indicative by Noël Coward, 1937

Future Indefinite by Noël Coward, 1954

Past Conditional by Noël Coward, 1965

A Talent to Amuse: A Biography of Noël Coward by Sheridan Morley, 1969

The Life of Noël Coward by Cole Lesley, 1976

My Life with Noël Coward by Graham Payn, 1994

Noël Coward: A Biography by Philip Hoare, 1995

Lucky Orphan by Granville Bantock, 1996

How Lucky Can You Get? (An account) by Dan Taylor, 1999

An Orphan's War by Hugo Bergström, 2000

Entirely Up to You, Darling by Richard Attenborough and Diana Hawkins, 2008

Silverlands: Growing Up at the Actors' Orphanage by Judy Staber, 2010

A Harvest of Friendships by Michael Henderson, 2017

Chronology of the Orphanage

1896 – The Actors' Orphanage Fund founded by Kittie Carson.
Sir Henry Irving as first president.

1899 – First fundraiser: the Actors' Cricket Match.

1901 – Royal patronage.

1906 – The Actors' Orphanage opens at 32 and 34 Moreland
Road, Croydon.
Actor-Manager Cyril Maude as new president.
First Theatrical Garden Party.

1914 – Move to Langley Place, Langley, Bucks. Sir Gerald du
Maurier elected president.

1934 – Noël Coward elected president.

1936 – Mr Austin is replaced by Mr Mowforth as head, who
is in turn replaced by Reverend Ruegg and a Miss King
as headmistress.

1937 – *Robinson Crusoe* performs three charity matinees in the
West End. (*Cinderella* does the same the following year.)

1938 – Move to Silverlands, Chertsey.
Theatrical Garden Parties move from Queen Mary
Gardens, Regent's Park to the Ranelagh Club, Barnes.

1940 – Evacuation to the Gould Institute, New York for the
duration of the War.

1942 – *Gratefully Yours,* a charity musical revue, performed at the Imperial Theatre and the Henry Street Resettlement Theatre, New York.

1945 – Return to Silverlands. Commander Aggitter as headmaster.

1947 – Richard Attenborough and Sheila Sim join the committee.

1949 – The Savage-Baileys as new heads.

1950 – Rutland Gate opens.
In Town Tonight feature for BBC Television News.

1951 – The Savage-Baileys replaced by Miss Berry.
Final Theatrical Garden Party.
First *midnight matinee* performed at the London Palladium.

1952 – First fundraiser cabaret by Noël and Mary Martin at the Café de Paris.
David Victor Gordon is employed as the new housemaster.

1953 – Patrick Waddington as headmaster, then Alistair Angus Fraser.

1954 – Rutland Gate closes.

1955 – David and Kirsten Slater as heads.

1956 – Noël Coward resigns as president, replaced by Sir Laurence Olivier. Richard Attenborough as chairman.

1959 – The Actors' Orphanage closes and becomes TACT: The Actors' Charitable Trust. Richard Attenborough as chairman and president for fifty-eight years.

2000 – Orphanage reunion at the Bridge Hotel, Chertsey.

2020 – The charity now exists as ACT (the Actors' Children's Trust) and is based in Bloomsbury.
www.actorschildren.org

Chronology of Noël Coward

1899 – Born on the 16th of December to Arthur and Violet Coward in Teddington, Middlesex. (A brother, Russell, had died in 1898, aged six.)

1904 – Brother, Eric, born.

1905 – They move to Sutton, Surrey.

1908 – They move to Battersea Park, London.

1910 – Noël attends Janet Thomas's Dancing Academy.

1911 – A schoolboy and Prince Mussel in *The Goldfish* at the Little Theatre.
Cannard the pageboy in *The Great Name* at the Prince of Wales Theatre.
William in *Where the Rainbow Ends* at the Savoy Theatre.

1912 – Move to Clapham Common, South London.
A mushroom in *An Autumn Idyll* at the Savoy Theatre.
William in *Where the Rainbow Ends* at the Garrick.

1913 – Schoolboy and angel in *Hannele*, Liverpool and Manchester, alongside Gertrude Lawrence.
Slightly in *Peter Pan* at the Duke of York's Theatre.

1914 – Tour of *Peter Pan* and second Christmas at the Duke of York's Theatre.

1915 – TB scare.

The Slacker in *Where the Rainbow Ends* at the Garrick.

1916 – Tour of *Charley's Aunt*.

1917 – *Ida Collaborates*, co-written with Esme Wynne, produced on tour.

Ripley Guildford in *The Saving Grace* at the Garrick.

Move to 111 Ebury Street, Pimlico. Mother runs it as a boarding house.

1918 – Military draft, several months in hospital.

Women and Whiskey, co-written with Esme Wynne, produced on tour.

1919 – Ralph in *The Knight of the Burning Pestle*, Birmingham Rep.

1920 – Bobbie Dermott in *I'll Leave It to You*, New Theatre.

1921 – Clay Collins in *Polly with a Past*, London.

Trip to New York.

1922 – *The Better Half*, produced at the Little Theatre.

1923 – Sholto Brent in *The Young Idea* at the Savoy.

Juvenile lead in *London Calling!*

1924 – Nicky Lancaster in *The Vortex* at the Everyman, Hampstead. (Then West End and Broadway).

1925 – *On with the Dance, Fallen Angels* and *Hay Fever*, London.

Hay Fever and *Easy Virtue*, New York.

1926 – Purchased Goldenhurst in Kent.

Easy Virtue and *The Queen Was in the Parlour*, produced in London.

Played Lewis Dodd in *The Constant Nymph*, London.

Nervous breakdown and an around-the-world trip.

1927 – Produced *The Marquise* and *Sirocco*, London.

The Marquise and *Fallen Angels*, New York.

1928 – Played Clark Storey in *The Second Man*, London.

Home Chat and *This Year of Grace*, produced in London.

1929 – *This Year of Grace* opens in New York.
        Bitter Sweet opens in London and New York.
1930 – Around-the-world travels. London home at Gerald Road, Belgravia.
        Private Lives opens at the Phoenix Theatre, London. (Later, New York.)
1931 – *Cavalcade* opens at the Theatre Royal, Drury Lane.
1932 – *Words and Music*, London. (Featuring *Mad Dogs and Englishmen*.)
1933 – *Design for Living*, New York.
1934 – *Conversation Piece*, London and New York.
        President of the Actors' Orphanage.
1935 – *Point Valaine*, New York.
        Acts in the film *The Scoundrel*.
1936 – *Tonight at Eight Thirty*, London and New York.
1937 – Autobiography, *Present Indicative*, published.
        Nervous breakdown.
1938 – *Operette*, London.
1939 – *Set to Music*, New York.
        Head of the Bureau of Propaganda in Paris.
        Short story collection, *To Step Aside*, published.
1940 – Propaganda tour of America, Australia and New Zealand.
1941 – *Blithe Spirit*, London. The song *London Pride* released.
1942 – *In Which We Serve* released.
        Acting in extensive UK tour of *Present Laughter, This Happy Breed* and *Blithe Spirit*. Factory concerts and hospital visits.
1943 – Acting in *Present Laughter* and *This Happy Breed*, London.
        Extensive tour of troop concerts in the Middle East.
        Song *Don't Let's Be Beastly to the Germans* released.

1944 – Troop concerts world-wide, including Burma, India, South Africa, Ceylon and France. *Middle East Diary* published.

1945 – *Sigh No More*, London.
Film *Brief Encounter* released.

1946 – *Pacific 1860*, Theatre Royal, Drury Lane, London.

1947 – Revives role in *Present Laughter*, Theatre Royal, Haymarket.
Point Valaine and *Peace in our Time*, London.

1948 – Appears in French adaptation of *Present Laughter*, Paris.
Builds a house, Blue Harbour, in Port Maria, Jamaica.

1949 – Christian Faber in the film *The Astonished Heart*.

1950 – *Ace of Clubs*, London.

1951 – First of several engagements performing cabaret at the Café de Paris.
Relative Values, London and *Island Fling*, New York.
Short story collection, *Star Quality*, released.

1952 – Café de Paris charity cabaret for the Actors' Orphanage.
Quadrille, London.

1953 – King Magnus in *The Apple Cart*, London.

1954 – *After the Ball*, London.
Autobiography, *Future Indefinite*, published.

1955 – Cabaret season at the Desert Inn, Las Vegas, resulting in the album *Noël Coward at Las Vegas*.
CBS television special, *Together With Music*.

1956 – CBS television productions of *Blithe Spirit* and *This Happy Breed*.
South Sea Bubble and *Nude with Violin*, London.
Resigns as President of the Actors' Orphanage.
Residency in Bermuda. Second house, Firefly, built in Port Maria, Jamaica.

1957 – Plays Sebastian in *Nude with Violin*, New York.

1958 – Plays *Nude with Violin* and *Present Laughter* in San Francisco and Los Angeles.

1959 – *Look After Lulu*, New York and London.

Plays Hawthorne in the film *Our Man in Havana*.

Switches residency to Switzerland, purchases Chalet Coward in Les Avants.

Produces the ballet *London Morning*, London.

1960 – Plays King of Anatolia in the film *Surprise Package*.

Waiting in the Wings, London.

Publishes the novel *Pomp and Circumstance*.

1961 – *Sail Away*, New York.

1962 – *Sail Away* at the Savoy, London.

1963 – *The Girl Who Came to Supper*, New York.

1964 – Short stories, *Pretty Polly Barlow*, published.

High Spirits, the Savoy, London.

Revives *Hay Fever* at Laurence Olivier's new National Theatre.

1965 – Health issues after a trip to the Seychelles.

Acts in the film *Bunny Lake is Missing*.

1966 – Stars in *Suite in Three Keys*, London.

1967 – Plays the *Witch of Capri* in the film *Boom*.

Lorn Loraine dies. Noël ceases to write.

Short stories, *Bon Voyage*, published.

Poetry, *Not Yet the Dodo*, published.

1968 – Plays Mr Bridger in *The Italian Job*, directed by Peter Collinson.

1969 – Seventieth birthday celebrations, including a reception at the Savoy, a midnight matinee at the Phoenix Theatre, lunch with the Queen, a season of films at the NFT and a television special.

1970 – Knighthood.

Tony Award for contribution to the theatre.

1972 – Honorary doctorate from the University of Sussex.

1973 –   Died on the 26th of March at Firefly, Jamaica. Buried on Firefly Hill.

Who's Who?

Ada Blanche (1862-1953) – A principal boy-player of burlesques and pantomimes of the 1890s. Her biggest success came in the musical comedy *The Arcadians*, from 1909-1911.

Adolf Hitler (1889-1945) – Not very nice.

Adrianne Allen (1907-1993) – Acted in *Easy Virtue* and *The Rat Trap* before originating the role of Sybil in *Private Lives*. Mother of Daniel and Anna Massey. A lovely long retirement in Switzerland.

Alan Ayckbourn (1939-) – A frightfully prolific playwright. In 1967, Noël sent a telegram congratulating him on his first West End success, *Relatively Speaking*. Ayckbourn thought it was a fake and threw the telegram away, before realising that it was genuine and hurriedly retrieving it.

Aldous Huxley (1894-1963) – Wrote a few books.

Alec Guinness (1914-2000) – An actor of vast stage and screen credits, including David Lean's *Oliver Twist*. He also accepted *The Bridge on the River Kwai* after Noël had turned it down, winning an Academy Award. In 1959, Coward and Guinness appeared together in *Our Man in Havana*. There were a few science-fiction movies later on.

Alexander Woollcott (1887-1943) – Drama critic for the *New Yorker* and member of the Algonquin Round Table. He dubbed Coward 'Destiny's Tot' and had a cameo appearance in *The Scoundrel*. Noël, along with Harpo Marx, was one of his best friends in show business.

Alfred Hitchcock (1899-1980) – British film director, he adapted Coward's wordy play *Easy Virtue* into a silent film in 1928.

Alfred Lunt (1892-1977) – Broadway star of plays by Shakespeare, Chekhov and Coward. He frequently starred opposite his wife, Lynn Fontanne, and they both acted with Noël in *Design for Living* in 1933. They also appeared in Coward's 1935 misfire, *Point Valaine,* and 1952's *Quadrille.* The Lunts kept a house in Alfred's home state of Wisconsin, where Noël occasionally popped in for tea.

André Charlot (1882-1956) – French-born impresario of London musical revues. Pivotal in launching Coward's career, he had, however, said upon their first meeting in 1917, "He plays the piano badly and sings worse."

Angela Baddeley (1904-1976) – An actress of Shakespeare and Shaw for decades, she is largely remembered now as Mrs Bridges, the cook from *Upstairs, Downstairs.*

Anthony Ainley (1932-2004) – Went from the orphanage to insurance clerk to RADA to playing *The Master* in *Doctor Who* throughout the 1980s. A private man, he never spoke of his childhood.

Antoinette Cellier (1913-1981) – Film and theatre actress, she attended RADA and was the granddaughter of Augustus Harris, actor-manager of the Theatre Royal, Drury Lane.

Arthur Wontner (1875-1960) – Played *Sherlock Holmes* in films of the 1930s, one of which, *The Missing Rembrandt,* is missing itself, an officially lost film. His son became Lord Mayor of London.

Baliol Holloway (1883-1967) – A splendidly named Shakespearean actor, he appeared in numerous plays at the

Old Vic. Forgotten now, he did appear on *This Is Your Life* in 1957.

Beatrice Lillie (1894-1989) – Canadian-born comedic actress and star, Lillie appeared in Coward's *This Year of Grace, Set to Music* and *High Spirits*. Once, when a pigeon landed on a table in her apartment, she said, "Any messages?"

Ben Webster (1864-1947) – Husband of Dame May Whitty, as an actor he appeared in a 1917 film called *The Gay Lord Quex*.

Benito Mussolini (1883-1945) – Former fascist ruler of Italy. It didn't end well when he was shot, and his corpse hung upside down from an Esso petrol station in Milan. He was once played by Bob Hoskins.

Benny Goodman (1909-1986) – Bandleader, liked to play the clarinet.

Bertrand Russell (1872-1970) – Philosopher, mathematician and activist. Author of *A History of Western Philosophy*. A taxi driver once remarked, "He was in the back of my cab and I said, 'What's it all about then, Bert?' And do you know, he couldn't tell me."

Binkie Beaumont (1908-1973) – Legendary West End producer and founder of HM Tennent Productions. He stopped producing Coward plays in the 1960s as he embraced the *Kitchen Sink* era. Noël rose above it.

Boris Karloff (1887-1969) – Born William Pratt in Camberwell, South London, and after years as a labourer in Canada, he became Frankenstein's monster in Hollywood movies of the 1930s. But he retained a bad back.

Bram Stoker (1847-1912) – Irish author. Assistant to Henry Irving (and manager of the Lyceum Theatre), they toured much of the world together. *Dracula* was published in 1897.

Brian Aherne (1902-1986) – An actor, he started early and appeared in the 1913 production of *Where the Rainbow*

Ends. On Broadway, he was *Mercutio* to Basil Rathbone's *Romeo.* In the War, he joined the Air Force in Arizona before resuming a successful movie career in Hollywood. A final role was *King Arthur* in *Lancelot and Guinevere.*

Brian Johnston (1912-1994) – An officer in the War, he received the Military Cross. At the BBC, he found fame as a cricket commentator but from the late 1940s to early '50s presented the light entertainment show *In Town Tonight.* A terrible giggler.

Burt Lancaster (1913-1994) – A young acrobat turned big beefy movie star, he appeared in everything from *The Birdman of Alcatraz* to *Field of Dreams.*

Carroll Gibbons (1903-1954) – American musician, he was an anglophile and left Hollywood and MGM to spend his life with *The Savoy Orpheans,* a dance band at a hotel.

Cary Grant (1904-1986) – Transatlantic movie star, appeared in such films as *The Philadelphia Story, An Affair to Remember* and *Notorious.* He was a fan of LSD and Eric Morecambe.

Cathleen Nesbit (1888-1982) – English actress and lover of the poet Rupert Brooke. She played Cary Grant's grandmother in *An Affair to Remember.* She was sixty-six and he was fifty-three.

Cecil Raleigh (1856-1914) – English actor and playwright, he was married to Effie Adelaide Henderson, an original orphanage committee member. His plays had titles such as *Hearts Are Trumps* and *Cheers Boys, Cheers!*

Cedric Hardwicke (1893-1964) – English actor and the youngest ever to be knighted, at forty-one. He originated several roles for George Bernard Shaw, who called him his 'fifth favourite actor after the four Marx Brothers'.

Celia Johnson (1908-1982) – Star of the Coward films *In Which We Serve, This Happy Breed, Brief Encounter* and *The Astonished Heart.* She once said, "I won't write my autobiography, because I haven't slept with Frank Sinatra, and if I had, I wouldn't tell anyone."

Cesar Romero (1907-1994) – American actor, he played *the Cisco Kid* in a series of western movies, but came to be known as *The Joker* in the 1960s *Batman* TV series. He also dated Sophia in an episode of *The Golden Girls*.

Charles Dickens (1812-1870) – A child factory worker turned greatest writer of the Victorian age. A theatre nut, he also wrote and acted in plays.

Charles Hawtrey (1858-1923) – The leading West End comedy actor of his age. He played Lord Goring for Oscar Wilde in 1895's *An Ideal Husband*. (He has nothing to do with *Carry On* films.)

Charles Kean (1811-1868) – The leading Shakespearean actor of his age. He *attempted* to make the plays historically accurate.

Charles Russell (1916-2009) – A costumier, impresario and, with his partner, **Lance Hamilton**, a theatrical producer. He worked for Coward as an assistant stage manager on his touring productions of the 1940s, then on costumes for *Sigh No More*, and then as producer of the Palladium fundraisers, and cabarets at the Café de Paris.

Charlie Chaplin (1889-1977) – Noël's neighbour in Switzerland.

Cicely Richards (1850-1933) – English actress, who appeared in one film, *Trilby*, in 1914. And then happily returned to the stage.

Clemence Dane (1888-1965) – aka Winifred Ashton, was a novelist and playwright. In 1921, her play *A Bill of Divorcement* was a huge success. Notably, she was the inspiration for Madame Arcati in *Blithe Spirit*. She was a fan of nude swimming and words such as 'randy' and 'erection'.

Clement Attlee (1883-1967) – A politician. Slightly on the left.

Clifford Mollison (1897-1986) – An English actor more

successful on stage than screen, although he did appear in 1974's *Frankenstein and the Monster from Hell.*

Cole Lesley (1904-1980) – Coward's personal assistant, secretary, advisor and close friend and confidant. He was utterly devoted to *The Master* and wrote the best biography of him, *The Life of Noël Coward.*

Constance Collier (1878-1955) – A leading English stage actress of her time, she eventually coached others and spent time attempting to teach diction in Hollywood.

Cyril Maude (1862-1951) – An actor-manager, he achieved success in the title role of *Grumpy*. He opened the Playhouse Theatre in London in 1907. A quietly humorous chap.

Danny Kaye (1911-1987) – American comedian, singer, dancer and actor. He starred in *The Secret Life of Walter Mitty* and was a huge success with the royal family when he performed at the London Palladium.

Daphne du Maurier (1907-1989) – Author of *Rebecca* and *Jamaica Inn.* Her hit play *September Tide* starred Gertrude Lawrence. Rumours of an affair between the two persist.

David Garrick (1717-1779) – The greatest actor-manager of the eighteenth century. He ran the Theatre Royal, Drury Lane and founded the influential Shakespeare Jubilee. In 1766, he launched the Theatrical Fund for the relief of actors in retirement or disability.

David Lean (1908-1991) – The co-director of *In Which We Serve* and director of *Brief Encounter, Blithe Spirit* and *This Happy Breed.* Some other films included *Lawrence of Arabia, Oliver Twist* and *A Passage to India.* He was a bit grumpy with actors and was awfully fond of getting married.

David Niven (1910-1983) – English actor. A graduate of Sandhurst, he ended up in Hollywood as a movie extra. Spotted by Sam Goldwyn, he was promoted to movie star. Yet also served in the War. When a journalist asked, "How's the front line treating you?" he replied, "I'd rather be tickling Ginger Rogers' tits." A neighbour of Noël's in Switzerland, they would always spend Christmas together.

Diana Wynyard (1906-1964) – English actress. She starred in the film of *Cavalcade* and on stage in *Design for Living*. The first British actress to be nominated for an Academy Award. She was married to the director Carol Reed.

Dirk Bogarde (1921-1999) – British actor and writer. He turned his back on Hollywood and made European films such as *Death in Venice* and *Victim*, a film which had some effect in the decriminalisation of homosexuality in England and Wales.

Dorothy Hyson (1914-1996) – American actress who worked primarily in England. Ivor Novello launched her career and she became synonymous with glamour. She also worked at Bletchley Park during the War.

Douglas Byng (1893-1987) – An English cabaret performer with a penchant for female impersonation. While performing in Coward's *On with the Dance,* he was also appearing in drag at his own London nightclub.

Douglas Fairbanks (1883-1939) – Hollywood's *Robin Hood* and *Zorro* of the silent era. He married Mary Pickford and was a co-founder of United Artists. His last words before a premature death were, "I've never felt better."

Duke and Duchess of Kent (Prince George: 1902-1942 and Princess Marina: 1906-1968) – Regular patrons of the Theatrical Garden Parties, and Prince George had been a good friend of Noël's since the early 1920s. He was bisexual and there have long been *rumours* of a one-time affair.

Dulcie Gray (1915-2011) – An actress and a writer of popular murder mysteries. She was married to Michael Denison. Her last appearance was on TV's *Doctors*.

Edith Evans (1888-1976) – A profoundly experienced stage actress, she had appeared with Coward in *Polly with a Past* in 1921. They were also neighbours in Pimlico. In the 1960s, she achieved three Academy Award nominations and starred in the National Theatre's revival of *Hay Fever*.

Edward de Souza (1932 -) – An actor whose career encapsulated everything from Shakespeare to Hammer Horror to *The Spy Who Loved Me* to *Coronation Street*. He was patron of the Academy Drama School for actors of limited means.

Ellen Terry (1847-1928) – Britain's leading Shakespearean actress, she worked with Henry Irving's company. Before that, she had worked with Charles Kean. She originated roles for Shaw, Ibsen and Barrie. Her great-nephew was John Gielgud.

Emile Littler (1903-1985) – Theatrical impresario. He started as a backstage assistant in Southend-on-Sea. By the 1930s, he was a West End producer.

Emlyn Williams (1905-1987) – Welsh actor and writer. Films include *Jamaica Inn* and *Major Barbara*. The John Goodman movie *King Ralph* was based on his novel *Headlong*.

Errol Flynn (1909-1959) – Hollywood's *Robin Hood* of the 1930s. Scandal, womanising and drink would slightly derail his later career. He once shared a house with David Niven, dubbed '*Cirrhosis by the Sea*'.

Esme Wynne (1898-1972) – Coward's best friend in childhood. They appeared together in *Where the Rainbow Ends* and collaborated on several short plays. As an adult, she became heavily involved in Christian Science and vegetarianism.

Eva Astley Cooper (1854-1944) – Inherited Hambleton Hall in Rutland and introduced Noël to upper-class country living in the 1910s. Hambleton is now a hotel and restaurant.

Eva Moore (1868-1955) – An actress and suffragist, she was the mother of Jill Esmond and thus Laurence Olivier's mother-in-law.

Evelyn Laye (1900-1996) – English actress married to Frank Lawton. She debuted on Broadway in Coward's *Bitter Sweet* in 1929. Her friends called her *Boo*.

Fanny Holtzmann (1902-1990) – A pioneering female lawyer from Brooklyn, New York, serving the show-business community.

Fay Compton (1894-1978) – She made her name in the plays of JM Barrie but also played Ophelia to Gielgud's *Hamlet* and appeared in the original production of *Blithe Spirit* in 1941, playing Ruth.

Francis Beaumont (1584-1616) – Playwright of the English Renaissance. A contemporary of Shakespeare, he once wrote a play with John Fletcher, called *Beggars' Bush*.

Frank Lawton (1904-1969) – A graduate of the Actors' Orphanage at Langley, his father had been a famous American vaudeville entertainer of the same name, and had died prematurely in 1914. The son became a film star, appearing in *Cavalcade* in 1933 and starring in *David Copperfield* in 1935. He was married to Evelyn Laye.

Frank Sinatra (1915-1998) – A singer who acted a bit.

Franklin Delano Roosevelt (1882-1945) – A four-term American President of the Democratic Party. He died on the job.

George Bernard Shaw (1856-1950) – Author of classic plays such as *Pygmalion, Man and Superman* and *Saint Joan*. Rather political and slightly verbose.

George Grossmith (1874-1935) – A Star of Edwardian musical comedies such as *A Gaiety Girl* and comedy plays such as *The Gay Lord Quex*. His father had originated roles for Gilbert and Sullivan.

George Hurst (1871-1954) – A professional cricketer from Yorkshire. He ended up coaching at Eton College.

Gerald du Maurier (1873-1934) – A pioneer in 'naturalistic' acting. He originated roles for JM Barrie's *Peter Pan, Admiral Crichton* and *Dear Brutus*. Du Maurier Cigarettes were named after him. He smoked a different brand.

Gertie Millar (1879-1952) – A musical comedy star of the Edwardian era. Coward saw her in *The Quaker Girl* in 1910 and she became his favourite performer.

Gertrude Lawrence (1898-1952) – A star of the West End and Broadway, she had been a child actress, touring *Hannele* with Coward in 1913. She went on to star in *London Calling, Private Lives* and *Tonight at 8:30*. The Coward-Lawrence chemistry went into legend. Daphne du Maurier wrote *September Tide* specifically for her and she died prematurely while performing in the original production of *The King and I* on Broadway (for which she had already won a Tony Award). A great lover of men and, possibly, women.

Gilbert Harding (1907-1960) – A British television and radio personality, he was a regular panellist on the extremely popular BBC show *What's My Line?*

Gladys Calthrop (1894-1980) – A rather stately set and costume designer, she worked on all of Coward's stage productions from *The Vortex* in 1924 until *Ace of Clubs* in 1950. And also several of his films, including *In Which We Serve* and *Brief Encounter*.

Gladys Cooper (1888-1971) – A prolific actress, she appeared in the films *My Fair Lady, Now Voyager* and *Rebecca*. She was also Robert Morley's mother-in-law. For Coward, she appeared in *Relative Values* in 1951.

Glenn Miller (1904-1944) – A very popular American trombonist. His plane disappeared over the English Channel in 1944.

Googie Withers (1917-2011) – A British film star of the 1930s, '40s and '50s. She then moved to Australia. Her name is Hindi and means 'pigeon'.

Graham Payn (1918-2005) – Boy soprano who grew up to be Coward's life partner, lead actor and inheritor of his estate. He died at Chalet Coward in Switzerland.

Granville Bantock (1868-1946) – A classical composer and uncle of his namesake at the orphanage. He was knighted in 1930.

Guy Middleton (1907-1973) – A British character actor of the moustached and rakish type. He once appeared in a film called *The Gay Adventure*.

Harley Granville Barker (1877-1946) – Actor, director, writer, theorist, manager and critic. A bit left wing, he declined a knighthood.

Harold Norman (unknown to 1947) – An unlucky actor; credits included *Macbeth*.

Harold Pinter (1930-2008) – A writer, director and actor from Hackney. One of the few young playwrights of the 1960s that Coward could bear. Though stylistically very different, theirs was a mutual love affair.

Helena Pickard (1900-1957) – Wife of Cedric Hardwicke, and mother of Edward. She appeared in prominent West End plays, such as *Flare Path*.

Henry Irving (1838-1905) – The great actor-manager of the Lyceum Theatre, a leading man to Ellen Terry, the first actor to ever be knighted and first president of the Actors' Orphanage. He never saw his wife again after she expressed that acting was silly.

Hermione Gingold (1897-1987) – An actress with a very deep voice, she started in London revue and ended up in New York. She once starred in a revival of *Fallen Angels* for which Coward found her a *few decades* too old. Her autobiography was called *How to Grow Old Disgracefully*.

HM Tennent (1879-1942) – Harry Tennent was a theatre producer whose company went to his *protégé* and partner, Binkie Beaumont, upon his death.

Honor Earl (1901-1996) – An artist and aristocrat, but not necessarily in that order.

Howard Lindsey (1889-1968) – An American actor, producer, writer and director, he would work on *The Sound of Music*.

Hugh Williams (1904-1969) – An actor who appeared in the film *Bitter Sweet* and with Frank Lawton in *David Copperfield*. His nickname was Tam and he is the father of actor Simon Williams.

IAR Peebles (1908-1980) – A professional cricketer for England. He wrote many books, all of them about cricket.

Irene Vanbrugh (1872-1949) – An actress who worked for Pinero, Barrie, Shaw, Maugham and Milne. RADA's Vanbrugh Theatre is named after her. For Coward, she appeared in *Operette* in 1938.

Italia Conti (1873-1946) – An actress employed by Sir Charles Hawtrey to train the child actors in 1911's *Where the Rainbow Ends*. She founded her own training academy in 1925. She liked to force Epsom Salts on the children to keep their bowels moving.

Ivor Novello (1893-1951) – An actor and composer, he had a huge hit with the song *Keep the Home Fires Burning* during the First World War. A huge musical star, productions included *The Dancing Years*, *King's Rhapsody* and *Gay's the Word*. For Coward, he acted in his biggest flop, *Sirocco*, in 1927. He lived in a flat above the Strand Theatre and after his premature death, John Gielgud said, "I'm sure there isn't an afterlife. If there was, Ivor Novello would have got a message to us."

Ivy St. Helier (1886-1971) – Actress and composer. She starred in *Words and Music* in 1932 and appeared in Olivier's film of *Henry V*.

Jack Buchanan (1891-1957) – An all-round performer, famous for his debonair, man-about-town persona. He worked in everything from music hall to movies, including the original *Brewster's Millions* in 1935.

Jack Hawkins (1910-1974) – The son of a North London builder, Hawkins got a start in the 1923 production of *Where the Rainbow Ends*. In the 1950s, he became a huge film star, appearing in such classics as *The Cruel Sea, The Malta Story, Ben Hur* and *Zulu*.

Jack Hulbert (1892-1978) – British film star of the 1930s, he was married to Cicely Courtneige. His autobiography was called *The Little Woman's Always Right*.

JB Priestly (1894-1984) – Author of *An Inspector Calls* and influential in the founding of the welfare state. He loved chamber music.

Jean Carson (1923-2005) – An American actress, she appeared in the film *I Married a Monster from Outer Space*.

Jean Forbes-Robertson (1905-1962) – An actress who played *Peter Pan* from 1927 to 1938. She was also a famous *Puck* and *Jim Hawkins*.

Jean Webster (1876-1916) – American author of *Daddy-Long-Legs*. She was a distant relative of Mark Twain.

Jessie Winter (1886-1971) – A long-forgotten, once prolific actress of the 1910s to '30s. She died in Denville Hall.

Jill Esmond (1908-1990) – A very popular committee member, she played Wendy in *Peter Pan,* and *Sybil* in the Broadway production of *Private Lives*. She married Laurence Olivier and they had a son called Tarquin.

JM Barrie (1860-1937) – He left the rights for *Peter Pan* to the Great Ormond Street Hospital. His brother died when they were boys and their mother thought of him ever after as the *boy who would never grow up*. Barrie lived by Kensington Gardens.

Joan Sims (1930-2001) – *Carry On* actress and star of *On the Up*. She turned down a wedding proposal from Kenneth Williams.

Joan White (1909-1999) – A successful West End actress of the 1930s and '40s, she was quite short and played children until she was forty. White appeared in the 1936 film *As You Like It* with Laurence Olivier. She married AP Moore, the manager of the Duke of York's Theatre and in 1954 moved to Canada, where she had a successful theatre career in Toronto. Eventually, she returned to England to teach at RADA and appear on television shows such as *Jeeves and Wooster* and *The Singing Detective.* She died at Denville Hall.

John C Wilson (1899-1961) – An American stockbroker turned theatre producer and director. Jack was Noël Coward's lover from 1925 until the early '30s, but remained his business manager for much longer. He married Natalia Paley, who liked the idea of a homosexual husband.

John Gielgud (1904-2000) – An actor who played all the great stage roles, knew everybody, won an Oscar for playing a butler, and worked until he was ninety-six. But it all started as an understudy to Noël Coward in *The Vortex* in 1924.

John Hartley Manners (1870-1928) – Playwright and husband of Laurette Taylor. His biggest hit was *Peg o' My Heart.*

John Mills (1908-2005) – An actor, he met Noël Coward while playing in a double bill of *Hamlet* and *Mr Cinders* in Singapore in 1930. Mills ended up in the stage productions of *Cavalcade* and *Words and Music.* And the films *In Which We Serve* and *This Happy Breed.* He went on to star in *many, many* war films. As well as *Cats.*

John Osborne (1929-1994) – The writer of the game-changing West End play *Look Back in Anger.* He played an *Aborian priest* in the 1980 film *Flash Gordon.*

Joyce Barbour (1901-1977) – A West End actress of the 1920s and '30s, she appeared in *Words and Music* at the Adelphi Theatre in 1932.

Joyce Carey (1898-1993) – An actress with seventy-one

years of stage experience. Her father was in Henry Irving's Shakespeare Company and her mother was Lilian Braithwaite, star of *The Vortex*. Carey met Coward during rehearsals and became a member of his private circle. She acted on stage in *Easy Virtue, Tonight at 8:30, This Happy Breed, Blithe Spirit* and *Present Laughter*. And on film in *Brief Encounter, Blithe Spirit* and *The Astonished Heart*, alongside a vast amount of non-Coward credits.

Judy Campbell (1916-2004) – An actress and singer, she originated the role of Joanna in *Present Laughter*, and had a hit with the song *A Nightingale Sang in Berkeley Square*.

Judy Garland (1922-1969) – The owner of red ruby slippers.

Kenneth Barnes (1878-1957) – The director of RADA for forty-six years. He was nicknamed '*Granny*' by some of the students.

Kenneth Tynan (1927-1980) – A theatre critic and writer. He upset a lot of people by saying 'fuck' on live television in 1965.

King Edward VIII (1894-1972) – King for a year in 1936, only to abdicate for the love of an American divorcee, Wallis Simpson. Slightly friendly with Hitler.

King George V (1865-1936) – King from 1910 to 1936. And the first to bear the name *Windsor*.

King George VI (1895-1952) – Unexpectedly King from 1936 to 1952. Known as Bertie to his friends, he oversaw the end of the British Empire. He has been played by Colin Firth *and* Rupert Everett.

Kirk Douglas (1916-2020) – A star from the Golden Age of Hollywood. Films include *Paths of Glory, Spartacus* and *Saturn 3*. As a child, his name was Izzy Demsky.

Kittie Carson (dates unknown) – An actress, she founded the Theatrical Ladies Guild in 1891 and the Actors' Orphanage Fund in 1896. She retired in 1906.

Lauren Bacall (1924-2014) – Starred with her husband Humphrey Bogart in Hollywood classics such as *The Big Sleep* and *Key Largo*. Her real name was Betty and she finally won an Oscar, aged seventy-two, for *The Mirror Has Two Faces*.

Laurence Olivier (1907-1989) – After Coward gave him his first break, playing Victor in *Private Lives,* he became the greatest actor of the twentieth century. He played everything from *Hamlet* to *Rudolf Hess*.

Laurette Taylor (1883-1946) – The wife of J. Hartley Manners, and praised for her naturalism in acting, she starred in the 1922 silent classic *Peg o' My Heart*. She was the inspiration for Judith Bliss in *Hay Fever*.

Leslie Banks (1890-1952) – Menacing character actor of the 1930s and '40s. Films included *The Man Who Knew Too Much* and *Jamaica Inn*.

Leslie Henson (1891-1957) – Music hall star who helped found ENSA during World War Two. He had a very raspy voice.

Lilian Braithwaite (1873-1948) – Debuted in *As You Like It* in 1900, but her finest hour was playing Florence Lancaster in *The Vortex* from 1924 to 1926.

Lilli Palmer (1914-1986) – A German-born actress, she found fame in Britain and then America. She starred alongside Coward in *Suite in Three Keys* at the Queen's Theatre in the spring of 1966.

Lorn Loraine (1899-1967) – Coward's secretary and personal assistant from 1925, and later on, his representative. It was a set-up that lasted for over forty years and they trusted each other implicitly. Loraine was immortalised as the character of Monica Reed in *Present Laughter*.

Lucinda Ballard (1906-1993) – Broadway costume designer. She won a Tony Award for a musical called *The Gay Life*.

Lynn Fontanne (1887-1983) – A Broadway star, she was born in Woodford, North London. Married to Alfred Lunt, they starred together in many productions, including *Design for Living, Point Valaine* and *Quadrille*. They relaxed often at their home, *Ten Chimneys,* in Wisconsin, which is now a museum and arts education institute.

Margaret Leighton (1922-1976) – From the Old Vic to Broadway, she won two Tony Awards, for *Separate Tables* and *The Night of the Iguana*. In 1969, she starred in a TV version of *The Vortex*. She also played the femme fatale, opposite Coward, in *The Astonished Heart* in 1950.

Margaret Rutherford (1892-1972) – A piano teacher, she only started acting in her thirties, and Madame Arcati in *Blithe Spirit* made her a star. She was also a famous Lady Bracknell and Miss Marple. (Agatha Christie dedicated *The Mirror Crack'd* to her.) A self-confessed eccentric, she has been portrayed by Timothy Spall.

Margaret Webster (1905-1972) – The daughter of May Whitty, she was a successful actress in her own right, often appearing in Shakespeare.

Marie Lohr (1890-1975) – A star of the London stage, she later moved into film, notably *Pygmalion,* in 1938.

Marie Tempest (1864-1942) – A megastar of Victorian opera, Edwardian music hall and then West End comedy plays. She turned down *Hay Fever,* until *The Vortex* was a huge hit... at which point she accepted *Hay Fever*.

Marlene Dietrich (1901-1992) – A silent movie actress from Germany, she conquered Hollywood, and later became a cabaret star. During the War, she turned down requests from the Nazis to return to Germany, and performed troop concerts for the allied forces.

Mary Ellis (1897-2003) – A star of Ivor Novello musicals, she also appeared in a 1947 production of Coward's *Point Valaine*.

Mary Martin (1913-1990) – Texas-born Broadway star of *South Pacific* and *The Sound of Music*. She played *Peter Pan* several times and was famous for the song *My Heart Belongs to Daddy*.

Mary Pickford (1892-1979) – Silent movie star and co-founder of United Artists. Known as *The Queen of the Movies*, she was the first actress ever to receive a close-up.

Maureen O'Sullivan (1911-1998) – Jane in the *Tarzan* movies of the 1930s and '40s, she also appeared in *Hannah and Her Sisters*.

Maurice Chevalier (1888-1972) – French singer and actor, he was a POW during the First World War. Films included *Gigi* and *Fanny*.

Max Bygraves (1922-2012) – British comedian and singer, who had a hit record with *Meet Me on the Corner*. He once had a near-death experience hanging off a cliff in Bournemouth.

May Whitty (1865-1948) – The first actress to become a Dame (in 1918). Actors' Equity was founded in her living room and she worked consistently for several actors' charities. Her husband was the actor-manager Ben Webster. Aged seventy-two, she moved to Beverly Hills, and films included *The Lady Vanishes*, *Mrs. Miniver* and *Gaslight*.

Michael Attenborough (1950-) – Theatre director and former artistic director of the Almeida and Hampstead Theatres. Noël Coward's godson.

Michael Denison (1915-1998) – An actor who worked often with his wife, Dulcie Gray. Films included the role of Algernon in 1952's *The Importance of Being Ernest*, and Richard Attenborough's *Shadowlands*.

Micheál Mac Liammóir (1899-1978) – Actor and co-founder of the Gate Theatre, Ireland. He toured for many years in his one-man show, *The Importance of Being Oscar*. He had hair but wore a toupée anyway.

Michael Redgrave (1908-1985) – An actor and director, whose career started with Tyrone Guthrie's company at the Old Vic in the 1930s. He was the father of the actors Vanessa, Corin and Lynn. His films included *The Lady Vanishes, The Importance of Being Ernest, The Dam Busters* and *Oh! What a Lovely War.*

Michael Wilding (1912-1979) – An actor, his first film was as an extra in 1933's *Bitter Sweet.* 1943's *Dear Octopus* made his name, and he was one of the most popular British stars of the 1940s to '50s. His third wife was Margaret Leighton.

Moira Lister (1923-2007) – An actress who appeared in *The Cruel Sea* and was a regular on *Hancock's Half Hour.* She starred in a television adaptation of *Hay Fever* in 1984, and for many of her later years toured a one-woman show, about Noël Coward.

Napoleon Bonaparte (1769-1821) – Former Emperor of France, he ended up exiled on Saint Helena in the middle of the Atlantic Ocean, where he wrote his memoirs. He was once played by Ian Holm.

Natalia Pavlovna Paley (1905-1981) – Russian aristocrat, she was a first cousin of Nicholas II. After the Revolution, she emigrated. She married Jack Wilson in Connecticut in 1937.

Nell Gwyn (1650-1687) – Comic actress of Restoration Theatre, and mistress of Charles II. He bought her a house next to Windsor Castle.

Nelson Keys (1886-1939) – Musical theatre actor, he appeared in the *Ziegfeld Follies* and a film called *Mumsie.*

Neville Chamberlain (1869-1940) – British prime minister. He slightly misjudged the ambitions of the Nazi Party.

Nicholas Hannen (1881-1972) – An actor of numerous stage credits, he also appeared in films such as *Henry V, Richard III* and *Dunkirk.*

Oscar Wilde (1864-1900) – An aesthete and playwright. His last words were, allegedly, "This wallpaper and I are fighting a duel to the death. Either it goes or I do." Got into a spot of bother with the law.

Owen Nares (1888-1943) – A leading stage actor of his day, he then moved into films. While visiting Sarah Siddons' birthplace in 1943... he died.

Pat Kirkwood (1921-2007) – A leading musical star, her career launched during the War and in the 1950s she starred in *The Pat Kirkwood Show* on the BBC.

Pat Wymore (1926-2014) – An American actress, she was married to Errol Flynn. Her credits included *King's Rhapsody* and *Ocean's Eleven*. She died in Jamaica.

Patrick Waddington (1901-1987) – An Oxford graduate turned actor, he toured in *My Fair Lady* and appeared in the film *A Night to Remember.*

Paul Robeson (1898-1976) – A Columbia graduate and lawyer, he gave it up due to intense racism, and tried acting instead. He became a cultural icon and political activist. Films included *Camille* and *Showboat.*

Pauline Chase (1885-1962) – She played *Peter Pan* at the Duke of York's Theatre from 1906 to 1913. She then retired.

Peggy Wood (1892-1978) – American actress, who starred in the Broadway productions of *Bitter Sweet* and *Blithe Spirit.* She also appeared in the film *The Sound of Music.*

Peter Ustinov (1921-2004) – A beloved polymath, who couldn't stop writing, acting, directing, presenting, award winning, talking, impersonating, designing, good-willing or intellectualising. He was *Poirot* in the 1970s.

Philip Streatfeild (1879-1915) – A bohemian painter.

Philip Tonge (1897-1959) – The greatest boy-actor of his age, he appeared in plays such as *Pinkie and the Faeries.* As an adult, he moved to New York and had smaller roles in Coward productions such as *Design for Living, Tonight at 8:30* and

Blithe Spirit. He then moved to Hollywood and did the odd film.

Raymond Massey (1896-1983) – A Canadian/American actor and graduate of Oxford. He made his name as the lead in the 1940 film *Abe Lincoln in Illinois.* He later appeared in *Dr. Kildare.*

Rebecca West (1892-1983) – Author and journalist. Rather political and intellectual. Her real name was Cicely Fairfield and she was friends with Frankie Howard.

Rex Harrison (1908-1990) – An actor famous for playing Henry Higgins in *My Fair Lady.* Unable to sing, he 'spoke sang'. And he *did* like to get married a lot.

Richard Attenborough (1923-2014) – Actor and director, he was also the president and patron of countless organisations, including BAFTA and RADA. In 1983, he won the Best Director Academy Award for *Gandhi.* He longed to make one more film, this time about Thomas Paine. He died at Denville Hall.

Richard Burbage (1567-1619) – The lead actor for Shakespeare at the Globe Theatre, he originated such roles as *Hamlet, Richard III* and *King Lear.* He was once played by Martin Clunes.

Richard Todd (1919-2009) – A major British film star, he appeared in *The Dam Busters* and *The Longest Day.* He was offered the role of *James Bond* in 1962 but was too busy.

Robert Douglas (1909-1999) – A jobbing actor and director, he once guest starred on *Columbo.*

Robert Flemyng (1912-1995) – A medical student turned actor, his films included *The Horrible Dr. Hitchcock, The Blood Beast Terrors* and *Shadowlands.*

Robert Morley (1908-1992) – A large actor, he made his name playing *Oscar Wilde* and *Louis XVI.* Films included *The African Queen, Murder at the Gallop, The Loved One* and

Theatre of Blood. An amazing character and raconteur, he once remarked, "I don't work, I merely inflict myself on the public."

Roger Livesey (1906-1976) – An actor at the Old Vic in the 1920s and '30s, he played the lead in the 1943 film *The Life and Death of Colonel Blimp*.

Rosemary Martin (1936-1998) – A jobbing actress, she appeared in everything from *Z Cars* to *Bergerac*.

Russell Crouse (1893-1966) – American writer and Broadway producer, he worked on the book for *Anything Goes*, as well as *The Sound of Music*.

Saki (1870-1916) – **HH Munro** wrote humorous short stories about the upper classes. Popular published collections included *Beasts and Super-Beasts* and *Reginald*. He was killed by a German sniper during the Great War.

Samuel Pepys (1633-1703) – A politician and enthusiastic diarist, he once buried cheese in his back garden, so as to save it from the *Great Fire of London*.

Sheila Sim (1922-2016) – An actress who appeared in films such as *The Magic Box*, as well as the original London production of *The Mousetrap*. Sheila stopped acting to raise a family and support the career of her husband, Richard Attenborough. She was extremely active in assisting with the orphanage and Denville Hall.

Sigmund Freud (1856-1939) – The founder of psychoanalysis. He experimented often with cocaine and read rather a lot into dreams.

Somerset Maugham (1874-1965) – A playwright of such classics as *Of Human Bondage* and *The Razor's Edge*. A slightly complicated love life.

Stanley Holloway (1890-1982) – A beloved comedy actor and singer, he appeared in *Brief Encounter*, *This Happy Breed* and *Passport to Pimlico*.

Sybil Thorndike (1882-1976) – A pianist and classical actress. George Bernard Shaw discovered her and wrote *Saint Joan* specifically for her. She has been portrayed by Judi Dench.

Tallulah Bankhead (1902-1968) – Risqué American actress, who once said, "There's less to this than meets the eye." And once described herself as 'ambisextrous'. She starred in the original London production of *Fallen Angels* in 1925 and a hugely successful Broadway revival of *Private Lives* in 1948.

The Crazy Gang (1931-1960) – Charlie Naughton, Teddy Know, Bud Flanagan, Jimmy Nervo, Jimmy Gold and Chesney Allen were a manic comedy troupe. Much beloved by King George VI, they performed at the London Palladium often.

Tommy Cooper (1921-1984) – Comedian and magician. He liked to slip a 'tip' into taxi drivers' pockets, say, "Have a drink on me," only for them to find a teabag in their pocket.

Tommy Dorsey (1905-1956) – American jazz composer. He played a trombone 'smoothly'.

Trevor Howard (1913-1988) – In 1945, *Brief Encounter* made him a star. Further films included *The Third Man, Mutiny on the Bounty, The Battle of Britain* and *Gandhi*. He declined a knighthood.

Tyrone Guthrie – (1900-1971) – A British theatre director for companies including the Shakespeare Repertory Company. He ended up as a founding member of the Stratford Festival of Canada. He also gave Joan White her career break in 1930 and was godfather to her daughter.

Vic Oliver (1898-1964) – Austrian-born actor and comedian. He also played the violin. He was married for a time to Winston Churchill's daughter, Sarah. But Daddy didn't approve of Vic from the music hall.

Vivien Leigh (1913-1967) – An English stage actress, she conquered Hollywood in *Gone with the Wind* and *A Streetcar Named Desire*. She was married to Lawrence Olivier for many years, and for Coward, she appeared in *South Sea Bubble* in the West End in 1956.

WC Fields (1880-1946) – American comedian. He often played a drunk misanthrope character. Some said in life as well as for audiences. Star of vaudeville, then movies of the silent era, and the early *talkies*.

WH Auden (1907-1973) – British poet famous for *Funeral Blues*. He lived in Berlin for a while and then New York. He once said, "We are all here on earth to help others; what on earth the others are here for I don't know."

William Makepeace Thackeray (1811-1863) – British novelist, famous for *Vanity Fair*. He popularised the word 'snob' and has been portrayed by Michael Palin.

Winifred Barnes (1892-1935) – Actress and singer. From a working-class background, she became a star of musical comedies such as *Betty,* only to die suddenly and tragically young.

Winston Churchill (1874-1965) – Two-time British prime minister, he was half American. A huge fan of animals, painting and alcohol. He penned the first known use of 'OMG' in a letter from 1917. Noël Coward narrated a television special for the occasion of his ninetieth birthday. He led the United Kingdom to victory during their darkest hour.